Pirates and Emperors, Old and New

Also by Noam Chomsky available from Between the Lines

The Culture of Terrorism

Fateful Triangle: The United States, Israel, and the Palestinians (Updated Edition)

Letters from Lexington: Reflections on Propaganda

After the Cataclysm: Postwar Indochina and the Reconstruction of Imperial Ideology

On Power and Ideology: The Managua Lectures

Year 501: The Conquest Continues

Powers and Prospects: Reflections on Human Nature and the Social Order

Rethinking Camelot: JFK, the Vietnam War, and U.S. Political Culture

Turning the Tide: U.S. Intervention in Central America and the Struggle for Peace

The Washington Connection and Third World Fascism

Pirates and Emperors, Old and New

International Terrorism in the Real World

New edition

Noam Chomsky

Between the Lines
TORONTO

Chapters 1–3 first published 1986 by Claremont Research & Publications
Chapter 4 first published 1991 by Black Rose Book
Chapter 5 first published 1991 by Polity/Blackwell
Chapter 7 first published 2001 by Verso

This edition first published in Canada in 2002 by
Between the Lines
720 Bathurst Street, Suite 404
Toronto, Ontario
M5S 2R4
www.btlbooks.com

Designed and produced by Chase Publishing Services, England
Typeset from disk by Stanford DTP Services, England
Printed in the United States of America

National Library of Canada Cataloguing in Publication Data
Chomsky, Noam
Pirates and emperors, old and new : international terrorism in the real world / Noam Chomsky. — New ed.
Includes index.
Previous ed. published under title: Pirates & emperors.
ISBN 1–896357–63–6
1. Terrorism. 2. Terrorism—Press coverage—United States. 3. Middle East—In mass media. 4. United States—Foreign relations—Arab countries. 5. Arab countries—Foreign relations—United States. 6. Arab-Israeli conflict. I. Title.

HV6431.C47 2003 327.1'6 C2002–903383–7

Contents

Preface to the First Edition (1986)

St. Augustine tells the story of a pirate captured by Alexander the Great, who asked him "how he dares molest the sea." "How dare you molest the whole world?" the pirate replied: "Because I do it with a little ship only, I am called a thief; you, doing it with a great navy, are called an Emperor."

The pirate's answer was "elegant and excellent," St. Augustine relates. It captures with some accuracy the current relations between the United States and various minor actors on the stage of international terrorism: Libya, factions of the PLO, and others. More generally, St. Augustine's tale illuminates the meaning of the concept of international terrorism in contemporary Western usage, and reaches to the heart of the frenzy over selected incidents of terrorism currently being orchestrated, with supreme cynicism, as a cover for Western violence.

The term "terrorism" came into use at the end of the eighteenth century, primarily to refer to violent acts of governments designed to ensure popular submission. That concept plainly is of little benefit to the practitioners of state terrorism, who, holding power, are in a position to control the system of thought and expression. The original sense has therefore been abandoned, and the term "terrorism" has come to be applied mainly to "retail terrorism" by individuals or groups.[1] Whereas the term was once applied to emperors who molest their own subjects and the world, now it is restricted to thieves who molest the powerful – though not entirely restricted: the term still applies to enemy emperors, a category that shifts with the needs of power and ideology.

Extricating ourselves from such practices, we use the term "terrorism" to refer to the threat or use of violence to intimidate or coerce (generally for political, religious, or other such ends), whether it is the terrorism of the emperor or of the thief.

The pirate's maxim explains the recently evolved concept of "international terrorism" only in part. It is necessary to add a second feature: an act of terrorism enters the canon only if it is committed by "their side," not ours. That was the guiding doctrine of the public relations campaign about "international terrorism" launched by the

Reagan Administration as it came to office. It relied on scholarship claiming to have established that the plague is a "Soviet-inspired" instrument, "aimed at the destabilization of Western democratic society," as shown by the alleged fact that terrorism is not "directed against the Soviet Union or any of its satellites or client states," but rather occurs "almost exclusively in democratic or relatively democratic countries."[2]

The thesis is true, in fact true by definition, given the way the term "terrorism" is employed by the emperor and his loyal coterie. Since only acts committed by "their side" count as terrorism, it follows that the thesis is necessarily correct, whatever the facts. In the real world, the story is quite different. The major victims of international terrorism[3] in the past several decades have been Cubans, Central Americans, and inhabitants of Lebanon, but none of this counts, by definition. When Israel bombs Palestinian refugee camps killing many civilians – often without even a pretense of "reprisal" – or sends its troops into Lebanese villages in "counterterror" operations where they murder and destroy, or hijacks ships and dispatches hundreds of hostages to prison camps under horrifying conditions, this is not "terrorism"; in fact, the rare voices of protest are thunderously condemned by loyal party liners for their "anti-Semitism" and "double standard," demonstrated by their failure to join the chorus of praise for "a country that cares for human life" (*Washington Post*), whose "high moral purpose" (*Time*) is the object of never-ending awe and acclaim, a country which, according to its admirers, "is held to a higher law, as interpreted for it by journalists" (Walter Goodman).[4]

Similarly, it is not terrorism when paramilitary forces operating from U.S. bases and trained by the CIA bombard Cuban hotels, sink fishing boats and attack Russian ships in Cuban harbors, poison crops and livestock, attempt to assassinate Castro, and so on, in missions that were running almost weekly at their peak.[5] These and many similar actions on the part of the emperor and his clients are not the subject of conferences and learned tomes, or of anguished commentary and diatribes in the media and journals of opinion.

Standards for the emperor and his court are unique in two closely related respects. First, their terrorist acts are excluded from the canon; second, while terrorist attacks against them are regarded with extreme seriousness, even requiring violence in "self-defense against future attack" as we will see, comparable or more serious terrorist attacks against others do not merit retaliation or preemptive action, and if undertaken would elicit fury and a fearsome response. The significance of such terrorist attacks is so slight that they need barely be reported, surely not remembered. Suppose, for example, that a seaborne Libyan force were to attack three American ships in the Israeli port of Haifa, sinking one of them and damaging the others, using East German-made missiles. There is no need to speculate on the reaction. Turning to the real world, on June 5, 1986, "a seaborne South African force attacked three Russian ships in the southern Angolan harbour of Namibe, sinking one of them," using "Israeli-made Scorpion [Gabriel] missiles."[6]

If the Soviet Union had responded to this terrorist attack against commercial shipping as the U.S. would have done under similar circumstances – perhaps by a firebombing that would have destroyed Johannesburg, to judge by the action-response scale of U.S. and Israeli "retaliation" – the U.S. might well have considered a nuclear strike as legitimate "retaliation" against the Communist devil. In the real world, the USSR did not respond, and the events were considered so insignificant that they were barely mentioned in the U.S. press.[7]

Suppose that Cuba were to have invaded Venezuela in late 1976 in self-defense against terrorist attack, with the intent of establishing a "New Order" there organized by elements under its control, killing 200 Americans manning an air defense system, heavily shelling the U.S. Embassy and finally occupying it for several days during its conquest of Caracas in violation of a cease-fire agreement.[8] Turning again to the real world, in 1982 Israel attacked Lebanon under the pretext of protecting the Galilee against terrorist attack (fabricated for the U.S. audience, as tacitly conceded internally), with the intent of establishing a "New Order" there organized by elements under its control, killing 200 Russians who were manning an air defense system, heavily shelling the Russian Embassy and finally occupying it for two days during its conquest of West Beirut in violation of a cease-fire agreement. The facts were casually reported in the U.S., with the context and crucial background ignored or denied. There was, fortunately, no Soviet response, or we would not be here today to discuss the matter.

In the real world, we assume as a matter of course that the Soviet Union and other official enemies, most of them defenseless, will calmly endure provocations and violence that would elicit a furious reaction, verbal and military, if the emperor and his court were the victims.

The stunning hypocrisy illustrated by these and innumerable other cases, some discussed below, is not restricted to the matter of international terrorism. To mention a different case, consider the World War II agreements that allocated control over parts of Europe and Asia to the several Allied powers and called for withdrawal at specified times. There was great outrage over (in fact, outrageous) Soviet actions in Eastern Europe modeled closely on what the U.S. had done in the areas assigned to Western control under wartime agreements (Italy, Greece, South Korea, etc.); and over the belated Soviet withdrawal from northern Iran, while the U.S. violated its wartime agreements to withdraw from Portugal, Iceland, Greenland, and elsewhere, on the grounds that "military considerations" make such withdrawal "inadvisable," the Joint Chiefs of Staff argued with State Department concurrence. There was – and to this day is – no outrage over the fact that West German espionage operations, directed against the USSR, were placed under the control of Reinhard Gehlen, who had conducted similar operations for the Nazis in Eastern Europe, or that the CIA was sending agents and supplies to aid armies encouraged by Hitler fighting in Eastern Europe and the Ukraine as late as the early 1950s as part of the "roll-back strategy" made official in NSC-68 (April 1950).[9] Soviet support for armies encouraged by Hitler fighting in the Rockies in 1952 might have elicited a different reaction.[10]

Examples are legion. One of the most notorious is the example regularly offered as the ultimate proof that Communists cannot be relied upon to live up to agreements: the 1973 Paris Peace treaty concerning Vietnam and its aftermath. The truth is that the U.S. announced at once that it would reject every term of the scrap of paper it had been compelled to sign, and proceeded to do so, while the media, in a display of servility that goes beyond the norm, accepted the U.S. version of the treaty (violating every essential element of it) as the actual text, so that U.S. violations were "in accord" with the treaty while the Communist reaction to these violations proved their innate treachery. This example is now regularly offered as justification for the U.S. rejection of a negotiated political settlement in Central America, demonstrating the usefulness of a well-run propaganda system.[11]

As noted, "international terrorism" (in the specific Western sense) was placed in the central focus of attention by the Reagan Administration as it came into office in 1981.[12] The reasons were not difficult to discern, though they were – and remain – inexpressible within the doctrinal system.

The Administration was committed to three related policies, all achieved with considerable success: 1) transfer of resources from the poor to the rich; 2) a large-scale increase in the state sector of the economy in the traditional way, through the Pentagon system, a device to compel the public to finance high technology industry by means of the state-guaranteed market for the production of high technology waste and thus to contribute to the program of public subsidy, private profit, called "free enterprise"; and 3) a substantial increase in U.S. intervention, subversion and international terrorism (in the literal sense). Such policies cannot be presented to the public in the terms in which they are intended. They can be implemented only if the general population is properly frightened by monsters against whom we must defend ourselves.

The standard device is an appeal to the threat of what the President called "the monolithic and ruthless conspiracy" bent on world conquest – President Kennedy, as he launched a rather similar program[13] – Reagan's "Evil Empire." But confrontation with the Empire itself would be a dangerous affair. It is far safer to do battle with defenseless enemies designated as the Evil Empire's proxies, a choice that conforms well to the third plank in the Reagan agenda, pursued for quite independent reasons: to ensure "stability" and "order" in Washington's global domains. The "terrorism" of properly chosen pirates, or of such enemies as Nicaragua or Salvadoran peasants who dare to defend themselves against international terrorist attack, is an easier target, and with an efficiently functioning propaganda system, it can be exploited to induce a proper sense of fear and mobilization among the domestic population.

It is in this context that "international terrorism" replaced human rights as "the Soul of our foreign policy" in the 1980s, human rights having achieved this status as part of the campaign to reverse the notable improvement in the moral and intellectual climate during the 1960s – termed the "Vietnam syndrome" – and to overcome the dread "crisis of democracy" that erupted in the same context as large elements of the general population became organized for political action, threatening the system of elite decision, public ratification, called "democracy" in Western parlance.[14]

In what follows, I will be concerned with international terrorism in the real world, focusing attention primarily on the Mediterranean region. "Mideast/Mediterranean terrorism" was selected as the top story of 1985 by editors and broadcasters – primarily American – polled by the Associated Press; the poll was taken before the terrorist attacks at the Rome and Vienna airports in December, which probably would have eliminated remaining doubts.[15] In the early months of 1986, concern over Mideast/Mediterranean terrorism reached a fever pitch, culminating in the U.S. bombing of Libya in April. The official story is that this courageous action aimed at the leading practitioner of international terrorism achieved its goal. Qaddafi and other major criminals are now cowering in their bunkers, tamed by the brave defender of human rights and dignity. But despite this grand victory over the forces of darkness, the issue of terrorism emanating from the Islamic world and the proper response for the democracies that defend civilized values remains a leading topic of concern and debate, as illustrated by numerous books, conferences, articles and editorials, television commentary, and so on. Insofar as any large or elite public can be reached, the discussion strictly observes the principles just enunciated: attention is restricted to the terrorism of the thief, not the emperor and his clients; to their crimes, not ours. I will, however, not observe these decencies.

Introduction (2002)

The impact of the terrorist atrocities of September 11, 2001 was so overwhelming that the identification just given is redundant: "9/11" suffices. It is widely agreed that the world has entered into a new age in which everything will be different: "the age of terror." Undoubtedly 9/11 will hold a prominent place in the annals of terrorism, though we should think carefully about just why this is the case. Anyone familiar with past and current history knows that the reason is not, regrettably, the scale of the crimes; rather, the choice of innocent victims. What the consequences will be depends substantially on how the rich and powerful interpret this dramatic demonstration that they are no longer immune from atrocities of the kind they routinely inflict on others, and how they choose to react.

In this connection, it is useful to consider several facts: 1) The "age of terror" was not unanticipated; 2) The "war on terror" declared on September 11 is no innovation, and the way it was conducted in the very recent past can hardly fail to be instructive today.

As for 1), though no one could have predicted the specific atrocities of 9/11, it had been understood for some time that with contemporary technology, the industrial world was likely to lose its virtual monopoly of violence. Well before 9/11, it was recognized that "a well-planned operation to smuggle [weapons of mass destruction] into the United States would have at least a 90 percent probability of success."[1] Among the contemplated threats are "small nukes," "dirty bombs," and a variety of biological weapons. Execution might not require unusual technical proficiency or organization. Furthermore, the source of terror might be hard to identify, hence to confront. Nine months after 9/11 and the anthrax scare that many analysts found even more terrifying,[2] the FBI reported that it still had only suspicions about the origins and planning of the 9/11 attacks – basically, those assumed at once, prior to what must be the most extraordinary international investigations in history, which yielded very little, they acknowledge; and the FBI reported no progress on identifying the perpetrators of the anthrax terror, though the source had been localized to Federal laboratories within the United States, and huge resources had been devoted to the investigation.

Turning to point 2), it is important to remember that the "war on terror" was not declared by George W. Bush on 9/11, but rather re-declared. It had been declared 20 years earlier by the Reagan–Bush (No. 1) Administration, with similar rhetoric and much the same personnel in leading positions. They pledged to excise the "cancers" that are bringing "a return to barbarism in the modern age." They identified two main centers of the "evil scourge of terrorism": Central America and the Middle East/Mediterranean region. Their campaigns to eradicate the plague in these two regions ranked high among the foreign policy issues of the decade. In the case of Central America, these campaigns quickly led to popular mobilization that was unprecedented in character. It had deep roots in mainstream American society, and broke new ground in the actions that were undertaken; during the U.S. wars in Indochina, as in earlier Western rampages in much of the world, few even thought of going to live in a village to help the victims and, by their presence, to provide some minimal protection from the foreign invaders and their local clients. There was also a large literature on the Reagan Administration's "war on terror." It found its place within the popular movements that sought to counter state-supported international terrorism, though it remained virtually unmentionable in the mainstream under the convention that only crimes of others are to command attention and elicit passionate denunciation. Much of what follows is drawn from writings of the 1980s on this topic,[3] which has considerable relevance for what lies ahead, I believe.

Washington's Central American base for countering the plague was Honduras. The official in charge during the most violent years was Ambassador John Negroponte, who was appointed by George Bush (No. 2) in 2001 to lead the diplomatic component of the re-declared "war on terror" at the United Nations. Reagan's special envoy to the Middle East through the period of the worst atrocities there was Defense Secretary Donald Rumsfeld, who directs the military component of the new phase of the campaign. Other leading planners in Washington also bring to the new "war on terror" the experience they gained from the first phase.

In both regions, the Reagan Administration carried out massive terrorist atrocities, vastly exceeding anything they claimed to be combating. In the Middle East, by a large margin the worst atrocities trace back to the U.S. and its local clients, who left a trail of bloodshed and devastation, particularly in the shattered societies of Lebanon and in the territories under Israeli military occupation.

Central America suffered even worse disasters at the hands of the terrorist commanders in Washington and their minions. One of the targets was a state, Nicaragua, which was therefore able to follow the course required by law and solemn treaties when a country is attacked: to appeal to international authorities. The World Court ruled in favor of Nicaragua, determining that the U.S. was guilty of "unlawful use of force" and violation of treaties, ordering Washington to terminate its international terrorist crimes and pay substantial reparations. The U.S. dismissed the Court ruling with contempt, on the official grounds that other nations do not agree with us so we must decide for ourselves what lies within our "domestic jurisdiction"; in this case, a terrorist war against Nicaragua. With bipartisan support, the Administration immediately escalated the crimes. Nicaragua appealed to the Security Council, where the U.S. vetoed a resolution supporting the Court decision and calling on all states to observe international law, also voting alone (with one or two client-states) against similar General Assembly resolutions. The U.S. escalated the attack further while undermining efforts of the Central American presidents to achieve a negotiated settlement. When the population finally succumbed, the national press, while acknowledging the terrorist methods employed, did not try to conceal its ecstasy, informing the world that Americans are "United in Joy" at this "Victory for U.S. Fair Play" (*New York Times*).

Elsewhere in Central America the population had no army to protect it. The atrocities carried out by the forces armed and trained by the U.S. and the states that joined its international terrorist network were therefore considerably more extreme than in Nicaragua, where they were horrifying enough. Conducted with unspeakable barbarism and brutality, the U.S. wars left some 200,000 corpses and millions of refugees and orphans in the shattered countries. One prime target of the "war on terror" was the Catholic Church, which had committed a grievous sin. Abandoning the traditional role of service to wealth and power, major segments of the Church adopted "the preferential option for the poor." Priests, nuns, and layworkers sought to organize people who lived in misery to take some control of their lives, thereby becoming "Communists" who must be exterminated. It was more than symbolic that the atrocious decade began with the assassination of a conservative Archbishop who had become "a voice for the voiceless," and ended with the brutal murder of six leading Jesuit intellectuals, in both cases by

Washington's favored clients. The events elicited little interest among those responsible. Few even know the names of the assassinated intellectuals, in dramatic contrast to dissidents in enemy states; one can imagine the reaction if they had not merely been jailed and exiled, but had their brains blown out by elite forces trained and armed by the Kremlin, capping a record of horrendous atrocities.

The basic facts are understood. The School of the Americas announces with pride that "liberation theology . . . was defeated with the assistance of the U.S. Army," thanks in no small measure to the training it provided to military officers of the client-states.

The "Victory for U.S. Fair Play" left more than a trail of mutilated corpses and ruined lives, in the midst of ecological disaster. After the U.S. took over again in 1990, Nicaragua declined to the rank of poorest country of the hemisphere after Haiti – which, by coincidence, has been the leading target of U.S. intervention and violence for a century, and now shares with Cuba the distinction of enduring a crushing U.S. embargo. Elsewhere in the region,

> neoliberal economic policies, such as ending price subsidies and increasing sales taxes, have worsened the situation for the poor, the UN believes. Annual social spending in the four drought-hit Central American countries is $100 a head, one sixth of the Latin American average [which is disgraceful enough]. Statistics compiled for the UN's Food and Agricultural Organization's annual meeting in Rome this week [June 11, 2002] show that the number of people with chronic hunger in Central America has risen by almost a third in the last decade, from 5 million to 6.4 million of the 28 million population.[4]

UN agencies are seeking remedies, "but without effective land reform these measures can have only limited impact." The popular organizations that might have led the way to land reform and other measures to benefit the poor majority were effectively destroyed by Washington's "war on terror." Formal democracy was instituted, but it impresses mostly ideologues. Polls throughout the hemisphere reveal that faith in democracy has steadily declined, in part because of the destruction of the social base for effective democracy, and in part, very likely, because the institution of formal democracy was accompanied by neoliberal policies that reduce the space for democratic participation.

Reviewing the program of "bringing democracy to Latin America," Thomas Carothers, who served in the "democracy enhancement" projects of the Reagan Administration, concludes that the policies were "sincere" but a "failure," of a peculiarly systematic kind. Where Washington's influence was least – in the southern cone – successes were greatest, despite the efforts of the Reagan Administration to impede them; where Washington's influence was greatest, successes were least. The reason, Carothers concludes, is that Washington sought to maintain "the basic order of . . . quite undemocratic societies" and to avoid "populist-based change . . . inevitably [seeking] only limited, top-down forms of democratic change that did not risk upsetting the traditional structures of power with which the United States has long been allied." He dismisses the "liberal critique" of this approach because of its "perennial weak spot": it offers no alternative. The option of allowing the population a meaningful voice in running their own affairs is not on the agenda.[5]

In the reigning culture of terrorism, the crimes of the "war on terror" and their aftermath arouse little articulate concern, apart from tactical considerations. The facts were amply reported by human rights organizations, church groups, and others, sometimes even the press, but were mostly dismissed with shameful apologetics. They are to teach us nothing about the "war on terror." Most of the story was excised from history, even hailed as "an inspiration for the triumph of democracy in our time" (*New Republic*). With the threat of meaningful democracy and desperately needed reform drowned in blood, the region drifted back to the obscurity of earlier years, when the vast majority suffered bitterly but in silence, while foreign investors and "the traditional structures of power with which the United States has long been allied" enriched themselves.

The reaction throughout makes good sense on the prevailing assumption that the victims are "mere things" whose lives have "no value," to borrow Hegel's elegant term for the lower orders. If they try to "raise their heads," they must be crushed by international terrorism, which will be honored as a noble cause. If they endure in silence, their misery can be ignored. History teaches few lessons with such crystal clarity.

Though Central America faded from view in the 1990s, terror elsewhere remained prominent on the policy agenda, and having defeated liberation theology, the U.S. military was directed to new tasks. In the Western hemisphere, Haiti and Colombia became the focus of concern. In Haiti, the U.S. had provided ample support for state violence through the 1980s (as before), but new problems arose in 1990, when to everyone's surprise, Haiti's first democratic election was won overwhelmingly by a populist priest, thanks to large-scale popular mobilization in the slums and rural areas that had been ignored. The democratic government was quickly overthrown by a military coup. The junta at once resorted to atrocious terror to destroy the popular organizations, with tacit support from Bush (No. 1) and Clinton. The elected president was finally restored, but on condition that he keep to the harsh neoliberal policies of the U.S.-backed candidate who had won 14 percent of the vote in the 1990 election. Haiti declined into further misery, while Washington again was hailed for its inspiring dedication to freedom, justice, and democracy.

Considerably more significant for U.S. policy is Colombia, where the terrible crimes of earlier years mounted sharply in the 1990s, and Colombia became the leading recipient of U.S. arms and training in the hemisphere, in conformity to a consistent pattern. By the decade's end political murders were running at about ten a day (since perhaps doubled according to Colombian human rights organizations), and the number of displaced people had risen to two million, with some 300,000 more each year, regularly increasing. The State Department and Rand Corporation concur with human rights organizations that some 75–80 percent of the atrocities are attributable to the military and paramilitaries. The latter are so closely linked to the military that Human Rights Watch refers to them as the army's "sixth division," alongside the five official divisions. The proportion of atrocities attributed to the six divisions has remained fairly constant through the decade, but with a shift from the military to the paramilitaries as terror has been privatized, a familiar device, employed in recent years by Serbia, Indonesia, and other terror states that seek "plausible deniability" for their crimes. The U.S. is employing a similar tactic, privatizing the training and direction of atrocities, as well as implementation, as in the chemical warfare operations ("fumigation") that have had a devastating impact on much of the peasant society under derisory drug war pretexts.[6] Increasingly, these operations are being transferred to private companies (MPRI, Dyncorps), which are funded by Washington and employ U.S. military officers, a useful device to escape the limited congressional scrutiny for direct involvement in state terror.

In 1999, as atrocities mounted, Colombia became the leading recipient of U.S. military aid worldwide (apart from the perennials, Israel–Egypt), replacing Turkey. A strategically placed ally, Turkey had received substantial U.S. military aid and training from the 1940s, but there was a sharp increase in the mid-1980s as Turkey launched a counterinsurgency campaign targeting its miserably repressed Kurdish population. State terror operations escalated in the 1990s, becoming some of the worst crimes of that gory decade. The operations, conducted with rampant torture and unspeakable barbarism, drove millions of people from the devastated countryside while killing tens of thousands. The remaining population is confined to a virtual dungeon, deprived of even the most elementary rights.[7] As state terror escalated, so did U.S. support for the crimes. Clinton provided Turkey with 80 percent of its arms; in 1997 alone arms flow exceeded the entire Cold War period combined up to the onset of the counterinsurgency campaign.[8]

It is instructive that in the deluge of commentary on the second phase of the "war on terror," the very recent and highly relevant history merits no attention. There is also no detectable concern over the fact that the second phase is led by the only state to have been condemned for international terrorism by the highest international authorities, and that the coalition of the just brings together a remarkable array of terrorist states: Russia, China, and others, eagerly joining so as to obtain authorization for their terrorist atrocities from the global leader who pledges to drive evil from the world. No eyebrows are raised when the defense of Kabul against terror passes from the hands of one terrorist state (Britain) to another, Turkey, which qualified for the post by its "positive experiences" in combating terror, according to the State Department and the press. Turkey has become a "pivotal ally in Washington's new war against terrorism," a Brookings Institution study explains. It has "struggled with terrorist violence" in recent years and "is thus uniquely positioned to help shape the new global effort to eliminate this threat."[9]

As the few examples cited illustrate – there are many more – Washington's role in state-directed international terrorism persisted without notable change in the interim between the two phases of the "war on terror," along with the reaction to it.

Just as had been true throughout the first phase of the "war on terror," ample information about more recent exploits of state-supported international terrorism has been available from the major human rights organizations and other highly reliable sources, which are eagerly sought when they have a story to tell that is ideologically serviceable. Here, that is most definitely not the case. The facts are therefore ignored, or if that is impossible, dismissed as a minor flaw or inadvertent deviation from our path of righteousness. The performance was particularly impressive in the 1990s, when it was necessary to suppress the role of the U.S. and its allies in Turkey, Colombia, East Timor, the Middle East, and elsewhere, while praising Washington for entering a "noble phase" in its foreign policy with a "saintly glow" as the leaders of the "idealistic New World bent on ending inhumanity," for the first time in history, dedicated themselves to "principles and values" in their zeal to uphold human rights and freedom. That the torrent could flow without embarrassment is remarkable enough; that it was unimpeded by the crucial participation of the same saintly figures in some of the worst crimes of the decade would have silenced even a Jonathan Swift.[10]

The successes of the first phase of the "war on terror" in Central America were mirrored in the second major area of concern, the Middle East/Mediterranean region. In Lebanon, Palestinian refugees were crushed by U.S.-backed terror operations, and Lebanese society suffered further trauma. Some 20,000 were killed during the 1982 Israeli invasion, many more in atrocities of the Israeli Army (IDF) and its mercenaries in occupied Lebanon in the years that followed, continuing through the 1990s with periodic Israeli invasions that drove hundreds of thousands from their homes, killing hundreds. The Lebanese government reports 25,000 killed after the 1982 invasion. There was rarely a credible pretext of self-defense, as Israeli authorities conceded (apart from propaganda directed to the U.S.). U.S. support was consistent and decisive throughout.

In the Israeli-occupied territories, terror and repression increased through the 1980s. Israel barred development in the occupied territories, taking over valuable lands and much of the resources, while organizing settlement projects in such a way as to leave the indigenous population isolated and helpless. The plans and programs relied crucially on U.S. military, economic, diplomatic, and ideological support.

In the early days of the 35-year military occupation, Moshe Dayan – one of the Israeli leaders most sympathetic to the plight of the Palestinians – advised his cabinet colleagues that Israel should tell Palestinians that they will "live like dogs, and whoever wishes, may leave."[11] Like many such exercises, the hallmark of the occupation has been humiliation and degradation of the "Araboushim" (the counterpart of "niggers," "kikes"), who must be taught not to "raise their heads," in the standard idiom. Twenty years ago, reviewing one of the earlier outbreaks of settler/IDF violence, political scientist Yoram Peri ruefully observed that three-quarters of a million young Israelis have learned from military service "that the task of the army is not only to defend the state in the battlefield against a foreign army, but to demolish the rights of innocent people just because they are Araboushim living in territories that God promised to us." The "two-legged beasts" (Prime Minister Menahem Begin) will then be able only "to scurry around like drugged roaches in a bottle" (Chief of Staff Rafael Eitan). Eitan's superior Ariel Sharon, fresh from his invasion of Lebanon and the Sabra-Shatila massacre, advised that the way to deal with demonstrators is to "cut off their testicles." The mainstream Hebrew press reported "detailed accounts of terrorist acts [by the IDF and settlers] in the conquered territories," which were presented to Prime Minister Begin by prominent political figures, including leading hawks. These included regular exercises of humiliation, such as forcing Araboushim to urinate and excrete on one another and crawl on the ground while they call out "Long Live the State of Israel" or lick the earth; or on Holocaust day, to write numbers on their own hands "in memory of Jews in the extermination camps." Such acts have scandalized much of the Israeli public since, again when they were repeated during Sharon's April 2002 invasion.

The respected human rights activist and legal specialist Raja Shehadah wrote 20 years ago that for Palestinians under occupation there are few choices: "Living like this, you must constantly resist the twin temptations of either acquiescing in the jailer's plan in numb despair, or becoming crazed by consuming hatred for your jailer and yourself, the prisoner." The only alternative is to be one of the "samidin," those who silently endure, controlling their fury.

One of Israel's most eminent writers, Boaz Evron, described the technique of the occupation succinctly: "to keep them on a short leash," to make sure that they recognize "that the whip is held over their heads." That makes more sense than slaughter, because then civilized folk can "accept it all peacefully," asking "What is so terrible? Is anyone being killed?"

Evron's acid critique is right on the mark. Its accuracy has repeatedly been demonstrated, very pointedly in April 2002, when the latest of Sharon's war crimes was neatly converted by the pro-Israel lobby to a demonstration that outside the U.S., the world is ruled by ineradicable anti-Semitism. The proof is that early fears of a huge slaughter proved unfounded, and all that happened was the destruction of the Jenin refugee camp, the old city of Nablus, and the cultural center and other civilian institutions in Ramallah, along with obscene humiliation of the normal variety, brutal collective punishment of hundreds of thousands of innocent people, and other trivialities of the kind that educated Americans and many Israelis can "accept peacefully." Surely no one but some hysterical anti-Iraqi racist would object if Saddam Hussein's forces were to carry out similar actions in Israel or the U.S.

Individual cases often reveal prevailing attitudes towards terror more graphically than the general picture. There is no more vivid and lasting symbol of "the evil scourge of terrorism" than the brutal murder of a crippled American in a wheelchair, Leon Klinghoffer, during the hijacking of the *Achille Lauro* in October 1985. The atrocity is in no way mitigated by the claim of the terrorists that the hijacking was in retaliation for the U.S.-backed Israeli bombing of Tunis a week earlier, which had killed 75 Tunisians and Palestinians with no credible pretext. Reactions were quite different when British reporters found "the flattened remains of a wheelchair" in the Jenin refugee camp after Sharon's onslaught. "It had been utterly crushed, ironed flat as if in a cartoon," they reported: "In the middle of the debris lay a broken white flag." A crippled Palestinian, Kemal Zughayer, "was shot dead as he tried to wheel himself up the road. The Israeli tanks must have driven over the body, because when [a friend] found it, one leg and both arms were missing, and the face, he said, had been ripped in two."[12] This apparently did not even merit report in the U.S., and if it were reported, it would be denied along with a flood of accusations of anti-Semitism that would probably lead to apology and retraction. If acknowledged, the crime would be dismissed as an inadvertent error in the course of justified retaliation, quite unlike the *Achille Lauro* atrocity. Kemal Zughayer will not enter the annals of terrorism along with Leon Klinghoffer.

It is all too easy to multiply such examples. U.S. allies must be distinguished from the Araboushim they grind under their boots, just as more generally over the centuries, human beings are not to be confused with "mere things."

Former Chief of Israeli intelligence Shlomo Gazit, a senior official of the military administration in its early years, described the occupation in 1985 as a "success story." The population was causing no problems. They were *samidin* who do not raise their heads. The primary goal had been achieved: "to prevent the inhabitants of the territories from participating in shaping the political future of the territory" or to "be seen as a partner for dealings with Israel." That entailed "the absolute prohibition of any political organization, for it was clearly understood by everyone that if political activism and organization were permitted, its leaders would become potential participants in political affairs." The same considerations require "the destruction of all initiative and every effort on the part of the inhabitants of the territories to serve as a pipeline for negotiations, to be a channel to the Palestinian Arab leadership outside of the territories." The guiding principle had been enunciated in 1972 by the distinguished Israeli diplomat Chaim Herzog, later President: "I do not deny the Palestinians a place or stand or opinion on every matter . . . But certainly I am not prepared to consider them as partners in any respect in a land that has been consecrated in the hands of our nation for thousands of years. For the Jews of this land there cannot be any partner."[13]

For the sponsors, problems arise only if the drugged roaches become so "crazed by consuming hatred" that they do raise their heads and even turn on their jailers. In that case punishment is severe, reaching extreme levels of brutality, always with impunity as long as the paymaster agrees. Until December 1987, when the first *Intifada* broke out, Palestinians within the territories were remarkably subdued. When they finally raised their heads within the occupied territories, the IDF, Border Patrol (who resemble paramilitaries), and settlers exploded in a paroxysm of terror and brutality.[14]

Reporting in the U.S. was scanty. The press and commentary also generally remained loyal, while Washington valiantly pretended "not to see" offers by the PLO and others for a political settlement. Finally, as it was becoming an object of international ridicule, Washington agreed to talk to the PLO, with the childish pretense, accepted without a qualm by the intellectual community and the media, that the PLO had succumbed and had now meekly agreed to accept the forthright U.S. stand. In the first meeting (reported in Israel and Egypt, but not in the U.S., within the mainstream), Washington demanded that the PLO call off the "riots" within the territories under military occupation, "which we view as terrorist acts against Israel," aiming to "undermine [its] security and stability." The "terrorism" is not that of the occupying army; their violence is legitimate, given U.S. government priorities, just as it was in Lebanon. It is those who dare to raise their heads who are culpable. Prime Minister Rabin informed Peace Now leaders that the purpose of the "low-level" U.S.–PLO negotiations was to provide Israel with ample time to crush the *Intifada* by "harsh military and economic pressure," and assured them that the Palestinians "will be broken."

As is commonly the case, violence worked. When they were "broken" and returned to the state of *samidin*, concerns in the U.S. abated, as in other cases, demonstrating again the accuracy of Evron's analysis, cited earlier.

So matters proceeded through the 1990s, now within the framework of the "Oslo peace process." In the Gaza Strip, a few thousand Jewish settlers live in luxury, with swimming pools, fishponds, and highly successful agriculture thanks to their appropriation of much of the region's meager water resources. A million Palestinians barely survive in misery, imprisoned behind a wall and barred access to the sea or to Egypt, often compelled to walk or swim around IDF barriers that serve little if any security function but do impose harsh and degrading punishment. Often they face live fire if they seek to travel within the dungeon. Gaza has become "the penal colony" of Israel, its "devils island, Alcatraz," the prominent columnist Nahum Barnea writes.

As in Central America, conditions deteriorated steadily through the 1990s.[15] The Clinton–Barak proposals of summer 2000 at Camp David were lavishly praised as "magnanimous" and "generous," and it is only fair to say that they did offer an improvement. At the time, Palestinians were confined to over 200 enclaves in the West Bank, most of them tiny. Clinton and Barak magnanimously offered to reduce the number to three cantons, effectively separated from one another and from the center of Palestinian life, culture, and communications in East Jerusalem. The Palestinian entity would then become a "neocolonial dependency" that will be "permanent," as Barak's Foreign Minister described the goal of the Oslo process, reiterating the observation of Moshe Dayan 30 years before that the occupation is "permanent." On the Gaza model, a wall was being constructed in summer 2002 to imprison the population, with internal barriers that will be passable, if at all, only after long periods of harassment and purposeful humiliation of people seeking to reach hospitals, visit relatives, go to school, find work, transfer produce, or otherwise survive within the dungeon. If such measures restore the monopoly of violence and terror previously enjoyed by Washington's client regime, the policy in the West Bank too will be deemed a success.

In mid-2002, the UN World Food Program requested donor support for a program to feed half a million Palestinians suffering from hunger and malnutrition, as "growing numbers of families in the Israeli-occupied territories are being forced to skip meals or reduce their food intake," the WFP warned, anticipating that the situation would deteriorate further as Israel prevents free movement of goods among the eight cantons it is establishing within the "penal colony."[16]

Like its Gaza model, the West Bank wall is to be "semi-permeable." The IDF, Jewish settlers, and foreign tourists can flow freely in either direction, but not the "mere things" whose lives have "no value" to the rulers.

As long as people whose lives have value are immune, the fate of their victims can be ignored. If they raise their heads, they must be taught lessons in obedience. Violence is typically the first choice, which is why state-directed international terrorism is such a rampant plague. If that fails, other means must be considered. During the first *Intifada* even extreme supporters of Israeli terror began to call for partial withdrawal because of the costs to Israel. In the early days of the second *Intifada*, the killing of hundreds of Palestinians and large-scale collective punishment did not even impede new shipments of helicopters and other terror weapons, but as the *Intifada* spun out of control, reaching to Israel itself, new steps were necessary. President Bush even proclaimed his "vision" of an eventual Palestinian state, to much acclaim, as he approached (from below) the stand of South African racists 40 years earlier, who not only had a "vision" of Black-run states, but actually implemented it.

Just what and where the eventual state should be remained an open question. House Majority Leader Dick Armey observed that "there are many Arab nations" that have plenty of "soil and property and opportunity to create a Palestinian state," so that Israel should "grab the entire West Bank" and "the Palestinians should leave." His counterparts point out that there are plenty of Jews in New York and Los Angeles and the richest country in the world would have no problem absorbing a few million more, solving the problem. At the opposite extreme of the spectrum, Anthony Lewis lauded "the unsentimental old soldier" Yitzhak Rabin, a man of "sheer intellectual honesty" who was willing to sign the Oslo agreements. But the Israeli right wing, unlike Rabin, "opposes any solution that would give the Palestinians a viable state – tiny, disarmed, poor, dominated by Israel, but their own." That is "the heart of the matter," and if Rabin's noble vision fails, the peace process will die.[17]

Meanwhile state terror remains the approved means of control. In the first days of the *Intifada*, Israel used U.S. helicopters to attack civilian targets, killing and wounding dozens of people. Clinton responded with the biggest shipment of military helicopters in a decade, and shipments continued as Israel began using them for political assassinations and other terrorist acts. The U.S. consistently refused to allow international monitors, whose presence is likely to reduce violence. In December 2001, along with vetoing another Security Council resolution calling for dispatch of monitors, the Bush Administration took a further step to "enhance terror" (Arafat's crime, according to the President) by undermining the international effort to terminate Israel's "grave breaches" of the Fourth Geneva Convention. The general attitude is well expressed by the President in his major political pronouncement on the Arab–Israel conflict (June 24, 2002): the guiding principle is that only "leaders not compromised by terror" will be admitted to the U.S.-run diplomatic process. Ariel Sharon automatically meets the condition, a fact that appears to have aroused no comment, though some winced when the President declared him to be "a man of peace" – as his 50-year record of terrorist atrocities fully demonstrates. No U.S. leader can be so compromised, by definition. It is the Palestinian leaders only who must satisfy the master's demand that their violence and repression be directed solely against other two-legged beasts, as in the past, when these practices won support and acclaim from the U.S.–Israel alliance through the Oslo years. If they depart from that mission or lose control, they must be eliminated and replaced by more reliable puppets, preferably by elections that will be termed "free" if the right person wins.

The basic principles concerning terror have been outlined with some candor by honest statesmen: Winston Churchill, for example. He informed Parliament before World War I that

> we are not a young people with an innocent record and a scanty inheritance. We have engrossed to ourselves . . . an altogether disproportionate share of the wealth and traffic of the world. We have got all we want in territory, and our claim to be left in the unmolested enjoyment of vast and splendid possessions, mainly acquired by violence, largely maintained by force, often seems less reasonable to others than to us.

As the U.S. and Britain emerged victorious in 1945, Churchill drew the appropriate conclusions from his realistic observations:

> the government of the world must be entrusted to satisfied nations, who wished nothing more for themselves than what they had. If the world-government were in the hands of hungry nations, there would always be danger. But none of us had any reason to seek for anything more. The peace would be kept by peoples who lived in their own way and were not ambitious. Our power placed us above the rest. We were like rich men dwelling at peace within their habitations.[18]

Others who have gained "vast and splendid possessions," also not very politely, understand the Churchillian principles well. The Kennedy and Reagan Administrations are considered to be at opposite poles of the U.S. political spectrum, but in this regard they were alike. Both recognized the need to resort to terror to ensure subordination to the rich men who wish to enjoy their possessions undisturbed. After only a few months in office, Kennedy ordered that the "terrors of the earth" must be visited upon Cuba until Fidel Castro is eliminated. Large-scale terror continued through Kennedy's years in office; he approved major new terror operations ten days before his assassination. The reasons were clear and explicit. Cubans had raised their heads; and worse, were providing an "example and general stimulus" that might "encourage agitation and radical change" in other parts of Latin America, where "social and economic conditions . . . invite opposition to ruling authority." It is not what Castro does that is important; rather, the Kennedy intellectuals recognized that "the very existence of his regime . . . represents a successful defiance of the U.S., a negation of our whole hemispheric policy of almost half a century," based on the principle of subordination to the will of the Colossus of the North. The threat posed by Castro, Kennedy's advisors warned the incoming President, is "the spread of the Castro idea of taking matters into one's own hands," a grave danger when "The distribution of land and other forms of national wealth greatly favors the propertied classes. . . [and] The poor and underprivileged, stimulated by the example of the Cuban revolution, are now demanding opportunities for a decent living."[19]

Even without the threat of a good example, "successful defiance of the U.S." cannot be tolerated. Quite generally, "maintaining credibility" is a leading principle of statecraft and a standard official justification for policy. If the world is suitably frightened, that is a net benefit. Reagan planners warned Europe that if they did not join Washington's "war on terror" with proper enthusiasm, "the crazy Americans" might "take matters into their own hands." The press lauded the success of this courageous stand in bringing European "wimps" into line. Clinton's Strategic Command (STRATCOM) advised that "part of the national persona we project" should be as an "irrational and vindictive" power, with some elements "potentially 'out of control'."

Prominent international affairs specialists have warned since the 1980s that the U.S. is perceived by many as a "rogue superpower" and a serious threat to their existence. But that is all to the good, if it induces fear and subordination.

Current policy-makers, many of them carry-overs from the Reagan years, are quite forthright in taking this stand. When Saudi Prince Abdullah visited the U.S. in April 2002 to urge Washington to pay some attention to the difficulties caused for its allies in the Arab world by its support for Israeli terror and repression, he was bluntly informed that his concerns did not matter: "The idea was, if he thought we were strong in Desert Storm, we're ten times as strong today," one official said. "This was to give him some idea what Afghanistan demonstrated about our capabilities."

The thinking at the top level of the Department of Defense was outlined by Jay Farrar, a former senior DOD official who directs special projects at the Center for Strategic and International Studies, a centrist Washington think tank: if the U.S. "was firm, tough, acted with resolve, especially in that area of the world, the rest of the world will come along and respect us for our toughness and won't mess with us."[20]

In short, get lost. You're either with us or against us, as the President said, and if you're not with us you'll be pulverized. That's why we bomb countries like Afghanistan: to give recalcitrants some idea of what we're capable of doing if someone gets in our way. The consequences for terrorism are of only secondary importance; in fact, U.S. intelligence concludes that bombing of Afghanistan probably increased the threat by scattering the al-Qaeda network and spawning others like it. Furthermore, as noted earlier, nine months after the 9/11 attacks U.S. intelligence knew little about their origin, still only "believing" that the idea may have been hatched in Afghanistan, though not the implementation and planning.[21] Under prevailing norms for the rich and powerful, that suffices to justify bombing innocent people and to elicit eloquent pronouncements about the respect of our leaders for the highest principles of morality and international law.

Indications are that the new "war on terror" will resemble its predecessor, and many other episodes of state terrorism that did not receive the official Orwellian designation. Nonetheless, there are crucial differences. In the present case, the war was re-declared in response to an actual and very serious terrorist atrocity, not concocted pretexts. But institutions remain stable, and the policies that flow from them tend to take similar forms, adapted to new circumstances. One stable feature is the Churchillian doctrine: the rich and powerful have every right to demand that they be left in peace to enjoy what they have gained, often by violence and terror; the rest can be ignored as long as they suffer in silence, but if they interfere with the lives of those who rule the world by right, the "terrors of the earth" will be visited upon them with righteous wrath, unless power is constrained from within.

The first five chapters below are concerned with the first phase of the "war on terror," during the Reagan–Bush (No. 1) Administrations. The preface and the first three chapters constitute the original publication: *Pirates and Emperors* (Claremont, 1986). Chapter 1 is devoted to the conceptual framework in which these and related issues are presented within the reigning doctrinal system. Chapter 2 provides a sample – only a sample – of Middle East terrorism in the real world, along with some discussion of the style of apologetics employed to ensure that it proceeds unhampered. Chapter 3 turns to the role played by Libya in the doctrinal system during those years. Chapter 4 appears in the 1987 edition of *Pirates and Emperors* (Black Rose, Montreal); it is a transcript of a keynote address at the Arab Association of University Graduates Convention, November 15, 1986. Chapter 5 (July 1989) appears in Alexander George, ed., *Western State Terrorism* (1991).

Chapter 6 turns to the second phase of the "war on terror," re-declared after 9/11. It is based on a talk at the Conference of the American Friends Service Committee and Tufts University's Peace and Justice Studies Program and Peace Coalition on "After September 11: Paths to Peace, Justice and Security," Tufts University, December 8, 2001. Chapter 7, like chapter 4, is concerned with U.S. policies in the Middle East. It is the introduction to Roane Carey, *The New Intifada* (2001).

Parts of chapter 1 appeared in the *Utne Reader*, February–March 1986, *Index on Censorship* (London, July 1986), and *Il Manifesto* (Rome, January 30, 1986). Excerpts from chapter 2 appear in *Race & Class* (London, Summer 1986), and another version in Michael Sprinker, ed., *Negations: Spurious Scholarship and the Palestinian Question* (Verso, 1987). The chapter also appears in Edward Said and Christopher Hitchens, eds., *Blaming the Victims* (Verso, 1988). Chapter 3 is a modified and expanded version of an article in *Covert Action Information Bulletin*, Summer 1986. Earlier versions of these articles appear in the *New Statesman* (London), *ENDpapers* (Nottingham), *El Pais* (Madrid), and in Italy, Mexico, Uruguay and elsewhere. Parts of chapters 2 and 3 are also included in my paper "International Terrorism: Image and Reality," delivered at the Frankfurt conference on International Terrorism, April 1986, published in *Crime and Social Justice* 27–28, 1987, an issue of the journal that reviews these topics broadly.

The chapters have been edited to eliminate matters no longer relevant, redundancies, etc. Throughout, the words "currently," "recently," etc. refer to the time of publication. I have not updated the notes to include the mass of highly relevant material after publication.

1 Thought Control: The Case of the Middle East (1986)

From a comparative perspective, the United States is unusual if not unique in its lack of restraints on freedom of expression. It is also unusual in the range and effectiveness of the methods employed to restrain freedom of thought. The two phenomena are related. Liberal democratic theorists have long observed that in a society where the voice of the people is heard, elite groups must ensure that that voice says the right things. The less the state is able to employ violence in defense of the interests of elite groups that effectively dominate it, the more it becomes necessary to devise techniques of "manufacture of consent," in the words of Walter Lippmann over 60 years ago, or "engineering of consent," the phrase preferred by Edward Bernays, one of the founding fathers of the American Public Relations industry.

In the entry on "propaganda" in the *Encyclopaedia of the Social Sciences* in 1933, Harold Lasswell explained that we must not succumb to "democratic dogmatisms about men being the best judges of their own interests." We must find ways to ensure that they endorse the decisions made by their far-sighted leaders – a lesson learned long before by dominant elites, the rise of the Public Relations industry being a notable illustration. Where obedience is guaranteed by violence, rulers may tend towards a "behaviorist" conception: it is enough that people obey; what they think does not matter too much. Where the state lacks adequate means of coercion, it is important to control what people think as well.[1]

The attitude is common among intellectuals across the political spectrum, and is regularly maintained when they shift across this spectrum as circumstances dictate. A version was expressed by the highly respected moralist and political commentator Reinhold Niebuhr when he wrote in 1932 – then from a Christian left perspective – that given "the stupidity of the average man," it is the responsibility of "cool observers" to provide the "necessary illusion" that provides the faith that must be instilled in the minds of the less endowed.[2] The doctrine is also familiar in its Leninist version, as in American social science and liberal commentary generally. Consider the bombing of Libya in April 1986. We read without surprise that it was a public relations success in the United States. It "is playing well in Peoria" and its "positive political impact" should "strengthen President Reagan's hand in dealing with Congress on issues like the military budget and aid to Nicaraguan 'Contras'." "This sort of public education campaign is the essence of statecraft," according to Dr Everett Ladd, a leading academic public opinion specialist, who added that a president "must be engaged in the engineering of democratic consent," the inspired Orwellism common in public relations and academic circles to refer to the methods for undermining meaningful democratic participation in shaping public policy.[3]

The problem of "engineering democratic consent" arises in a particularly sharp form when state policy is indefensible, and becomes serious to the extent that the issues are serious. There is no doubt about the seriousness of the issues arising in the Middle East, particularly the Arab–Israeli conflict, which is commonly – and plausibly – judged the most likely "tinderbox" that might set off a terminal nuclear war as regional conflict engages the superpowers, as has come too close for comfort in the past. Furthermore, U.S. policy has contributed materially to maintaining the state of military confrontation and is based on implicit racist assumptions that would not be tolerated if stated openly. There is also a marked divergence between popular attitudes, generally supportive of a Palestinian state when the question is raised in polls, and state policy, which explicitly bars this option,[4] though the divergence is of little moment as long as the politically active and articulate elements of the population maintain proper discipline. To assure this outcome, it is necessary to conduct what American historians called "historical engineering" when they lent their talents to the Wilson Administration during World War I in one of the early exercises of organized "manufacture of consent." There is a variety of ways in which this result is achieved.

One method is to devise an appropriate form of Newspeak in which crucial terms have a technical sense, divorced from their ordinary meanings. Consider, for example, the term "peace process." In its technical sense, as used in the mass media and scholarship generally in the United States, it refers to peace proposals advanced by the U.S. government. Right-thinking people hope that Jordan will join the peace process; that is, will accept U.S. dictates. The Big Question is whether the PLO will agree to join the peace process, or can be granted admission to this ceremony. The headline of a review of the "peace process" by Bernard Gwertzman in the *New York Times* reads: "Are the Palestinians Ready to Seek Peace?"[5] In the normal sense of the term "peace," the answer is of course "Yes." Everyone seeks peace, on their own terms; Hitler, for example, surely sought peace in 1939, on his terms. But in the system of thought control, the question means something else: Are the Palestinians ready to accept U.S. terms for peace? These terms happen to deny them the right of national self-determination, but unwillingness to accept this consequence demonstrates that the Palestinians do not seek peace, in the technical sense.

Note that it is unnecessary for Gwertzman to ask whether the United States or Israel is "ready to seek peace." For the U.S., this is true by definition, and the conventions of responsible journalism entail that the same must be true for a well-behaved client-state.

Gwertzman asserts further that the PLO has always rejected "any talk of negotiated peace with Israel." That is false, but it is true in the world of "necessary illusion" constructed by the Newspaper of Record, which, along with other responsible journals, has either suppressed the relevant facts or relegated them to Orwell's useful memory hole.

Of course, there are Arab peace proposals, including PLO proposals, but they are not part of the "peace process." Thus, in a review of "Two Decades of Seeking Peace in the Middle East," *Times* Jerusalem correspondent Thomas Friedman excludes the major Arab (including PLO) peace proposals; no Israeli proposals are listed, because no serious ones have been advanced, a fact not discussed.[6]

What is the character of the official "peace process" and the Arab proposals that are excluded from it? Before answering this question, we must clarify another technical term: "rejectionism." In its Orwellian usage, this term refers exclusively to the position of Arabs who deny the right of national self-determination to Israeli Jews, or who refuse to accept Israel's "right to exist," a novel and ingenious concept designed to bar Palestinians from the "peace process" by demonstrating the "extremism" of those who refuse to concede the justice of what they see as the robbery of their homeland, and who insist upon the traditional view – the view adopted by the reigning ideological system in the United States as well as prevailing international practice with regard to every state apart from Israel – that while states are recognized within the international order, their abstract "right to exist" is not.

There are elements in the Arab world to which the term "rejectionist" applies: Libya, the minority Rejection Front of the PLO, and others. But it should not escape notice that in official Newspeak, the term is used in a strictly racist sense. Abandoning such assumptions, we observe that there are two groups that claim the right of national self-determination in the former Palestine: the indigenous population and the Jewish settlers who largely displaced them, at times with considerable violence. Presumably, the indigenous population have rights comparable to those of the Jewish immigrants (some might argue that this does not go far enough, but I put that issue to the side). If so, then the term "rejectionism" should be used to refer to denial of the right of national self-determination to one or the other of the competing national groups. But the term cannot be used in its non-racist sense within the U.S. doctrinal system, or it will be seen at once that the U.S. and Israel lead the rejectionist camp.

With these clarifications, we can turn to the question: what is the "peace process"?

The official "peace process" is explicitly rejectionist, including the United States and both major political groupings in Israel. Their rejectionism is, in fact, so extreme that the Palestinians are not even to be permitted to select their own representatives in eventual negotiations about their fate – just as they are denied municipal elections or other democratic forms under the Israeli military occupation. Is there a non-rejectionist peace proposal on the agenda? In the U.S. doctrinal system, the answer is of course "No," by definition. In the real world, matters are different. The basic terms of this proposal are familiar, reflecting a broad international consensus: they include a Palestinian state in the West Bank and Gaza Strip alongside Israel and the principle that "it is essential to ensure the security and sovereignty of all states of the region including those of Israel."

The quoted words are those of Leonid Brezhnev in an address to the Soviet Communist Party Congress of February 1981, expressing the consistent Soviet position. Brezhnev's speech was excerpted in the *New York Times* with these crucial segments omitted; cuts in a Reagan post-summit statement in *Pravda* evoked much justified indignation. In April 1981, Brezhnev's statement was unanimously endorsed by the PLO, but the fact was not reported in the *Times*. Official doctrine holds that the Soviet Union, as always, is concerned only to cause trouble and block peace, and thus supports Arab rejectionism and extremism. The media dutifully fulfill their assigned role.

One might cite other examples. In October 1977, a joint Carter–Brezhnev statement called for the "termination of the state of war and establishment of normal peaceful relations" between Israel and its neighbors. This was endorsed by the PLO, and withdrawn by Carter after a furious reaction by Israel and its American lobby. In January 1976, Jordan, Syria and Egypt supported a proposal for a two-state settlement debated by the Security Council of the United Nations. The resolution incorporated the essential wording of UN 242, the core document of relevant diplomacy, guaranteeing the right of every state in the region "to live in peace within secure and recognized borders." The proposal was endorsed by the PLO; according to Israel's President Chaim Herzog (then UN Ambassador), it was "prepared" by the PLO. It was backed by virtually the entire world, and vetoed by the United States.[7]

Much of this has been eliminated from history, in journalism and scholarship. The 1976 international initiative is not even mentioned in the unusually careful review by Seth Tillman in his book *The United States and the Middle East* (Indiana, 1982). It is mentioned by Steven Spiegel in his *The Other Arab-Israeli Conflict* (Chicago, 1985, p. 306), a highly regarded work of scholarship, along with some interesting commentary. Spiegel writes that the U.S. "vetoed the pro-Palestinian resolution" so as "to demonstrate that the United States was willing to hear Palestinian aspirations but would not accede to demands that threatened Israel." The commitment to U.S.–Israeli rejectionism could hardly be clearer, and is accepted as quite proper in the United States, along with the principle that demands that threaten the Palestinians are entirely legitimate, indeed praiseworthy: the terms of the official "peace process," for example. In public discussion, it is a matter of doctrine that the Arab states and the PLO have never veered from their refusal to come to terms with Israel in any fashion, apart from Sadat, with his trip to Jerusalem in 1977. Facts need be no embarrassment, or even mild annoyance, to a well-functioning system of "historical engineering."

Israel's reaction to the 1976 peace proposal backed by the PLO and the Arab "confrontation states" was to bomb Lebanon (without a pretense of "retaliation," except against the UN Security Council), killing over 50 people, and to announce that Israel would enter into no dealings with any Palestinians on any political issue. This was the dovish Labor government headed by Yitzhak Rabin, who, in his memoirs, identifies two forms of "extremism": that of the Begin government, and the proposal of "the Palestinian extremists (basically the PLO)," namely, "to create a sovereign Palestinian state in the West Bank and the Gaza Strip." Only the Labor Party style of rejectionism departs from "extremism," a point of view shared by American commentators.[8]

We note another pair of Newspeak concepts: "extremist" and "moderate," the latter referring to those who accept the position of the United States, the former to those who do not. The American position is thus by definition moderate, as is that of the Israeli Labor coalition (generally), since its rhetoric tends to approximate that of the United States. Rabin thus conforms to approved practice in his use of the terms "moderate" and "extremist." Similarly, in an anguished review of "extremism" and its ascendance, *New York Times* Israel correspondent Thomas Friedman includes under this rubric those who advocate a non-racist settlement in accord with the international consensus, while the Western leaders of the rejectionist camp, who also hold a commanding lead in terrorist operations, are the "moderates"; by definition, one might add. Friedman writes that "Extremists have always been much better at exploiting the media." He is quite right; Israel and the U.S. have shown unparalleled mastery of this art, as his own articles and news reports indicate.[9] His convenient version of history and the conceptual framework of his reporting, as just illustrated, provide a few of the many examples of the success of extremists in "exploiting the media" – now using the term in its literal sense.

In adopting a conceptual framework designed to exclude comprehension of the facts and issues, the *Times* follows the practice of Israeli models such as Rabin, who achieve the status of "moderates" by virtue of their general conformity to U.S. government demands. It is, correspondingly, entirely natural that when Friedman reviews "Two Decades of Seeking Peace in the Mideast," major proposals rejected by the U.S. and Israel are omitted as inappropriate for the historical record. Meanwhile the Israeli leaders are praised by the *Times* editors for their "healthy pragmatism" while the PLO is denounced for standing in the way of peace.[10]

It is, incidentally, a staple of the ideological system that the media are highly critical of Israel and the U.S. and are far too forthcoming in their tolerance of Arab extremists. The fact that such statements can even be made without evoking ridicule is another sign of the extraordinary successes of the system of indoctrination.

Returning to the official "extremists," in April–May 1984, Yasser Arafat issued a series of statements calling for negotiations leading to mutual recognition. The national press refused to publish the facts; the *Times* even banned letters referring to them, while continuing to denounce the "extremist" Arafat for blocking a peaceful settlement.[11]

These and many other examples illustrate that there are non-rejectionist proposals that are widely supported; with some variations, by most of Europe, the USSR, the non-aligned states, the major Arab states and the mainstream of the PLO, and a majority of American public opinion (to judge by the few existing polls). But they are not part of the peace process because the U.S. government opposes them. The examples cited are thus excluded from the *Times* review of "Two Decades of Seeking Peace," and from the journalistic and even scholarly literature fairly generally.

There are other incidents that do not qualify as part of the peace process. Thus, the *Times* review does not mention Anwar Sadat's offer of a full peace treaty on the internationally recognized borders – in accord with official U.S. policy at the time – in February 1971, rejected by Israel with U.S. backing. Note that this proposal was rejectionist in that it offered nothing to the Palestinians. In his memoirs, Henry Kissinger explains his thinking at that time: "Until some Arab state showed a willingness to separate from the Soviets, or the Soviets were prepared to dissociate from the maximum Arab program, we had no reason to modify our policy" of "stalemate." The USSR was extremist, in the technical sense, supporting what happened to be official (though not operative) U.S. policy, which was remote from "the maximum Arab program." Kissinger was right to say that such Arab states as Saudi Arabia refused to "separate from the Soviets," though he did not observe, and appears to have been unaware, that this would have been a logical impossibility: Saudi Arabia did not even have diplomatic relations with the USSR and never had. The impressive discipline of the media and scholarship is revealed by the fact that these astonishing statements escape comment, just as no responsible commentator is likely to point out that Kissinger's blissful ignorance and insistence on military confrontation were primary factors that led to the 1973 war.[12]

Sadat's peace offer has been expunged from the historical record.[13] The standard story is that Sadat was a typical Arab thug, interested only in killing Jews, though he saw the error of his ways after his failed attempt to destroy Israel in 1973 and, under the kindly tutelage of Kissinger and Carter, became a man of peace. Thus in its two-page obituary after Sadat's assassination, the *Times* not only suppresses the actual facts but explicitly denies them, stating that until his 1977 trip to Jerusalem, Sadat was unwilling "to accept Israel's existence as a sovereign state."[14] *Newsweek* refused even to print a letter correcting outright falsehoods on this matter by their columnist George Will, though the research department privately conceded the facts. The practice is standard.

The terms "terrorism" and "retaliation" also have a special sense within the doctrinal system. "Terrorism" refers to terrorist acts by various pirates, particularly Arabs. Terrorist acts by the emperor and his clients are termed "retaliation" or perhaps "legitimate preemptive strikes to avert terrorism," quite independently of the facts, as will be discussed in the following chapters.

The term "hostage" – like "terrorism," "moderate," "democratic," and other terms of political discourse – also has a technical Orwellian sense within the reigning doctrinal system. In the dictionary sense of the words, the people of Nicaragua are now being held hostage in a major terrorist operation directed from the centers of international terrorism in Washington and Miami. The purpose of this campaign of international terrorism is to induce changes in the behavior of the Nicaraguan government: crucially, an end to programs that direct resources to the poor majority and a return to "moderate" and "democratic" policies that favor U.S. business interests and their local associates. A powerful case can be made that this is the central reason for the U.S.-run terrorist war against Nicaragua, a case that is not rejected but is rather not open for discussion.[15] This is a particularly sadistic exercise in terrorism, not only because of the scale and the purpose, but also because of the means employed, which go well beyond the usual practice of the retail terrorists whose exploits arouse such horror in civilized circles: Leon Klinghoffer and Natasha Simpson were murdered by terrorists, but not first subjected to brutal torture, mutilation, rape, and the other standard practices of the terrorists trained and supported by the U.S. and its clients, as the record, generally evaded, makes abundantly clear. U.S. policy is to ensure that the terrorist attacks continue until the government yields or is overthrown, while the emperor's minions utter soothing words about "democracy" and "human rights."

In the preferred technical usage, the terms "terrorism" and "hostage" are restricted to a certain class of terrorist acts: the terrorism of the pirate, directed against those who regard terrorism and the holding of hostages on a grand scale as their prerogative. In the Middle East, murderous bombing, piracy, hostage-taking, attacks on defenseless villages, etc., do not fall under the concept of terrorism, as properly construed within the doctrinal system, when conducted by Washington or its Israeli client.

The record of deceit concerning terrorism, to which I will turn in the chapters that follow, is highly instructive with regard to the nature of Western culture. The relevant point in the present context is that a proper history and appropriate form of discourse have been contrived in which terrorism is the province of Palestinians, while Israelis carry out "retaliation," or sometimes legitimate "preemption," occasionally reacting with regrettable harshness, as any state would do under such trying circumstances. The doctrinal system is designed to ensure that these conclusions are true by definition, regardless of the facts, which are either not reported, or reported in such a manner as to conform to doctrinal necessities, or – occasionally – reported honestly but then dispatched to the memory hole. Given that Israel is a loyal and very useful client-state, serving as a "strategic asset" in the Middle East and willing to undertake such tasks as support for near-genocide in Guatemala when the U.S. Administration is prevented by Congress from joining in this necessary exercise, it becomes true, irrespective of the facts, that Israel is dedicated to the highest moral values and "purity of arms" while the Palestinians are the very epitome of extremism, terrorism and barbarity. The suggestion that there might be a certain symmetry both in rights and in terrorist practice is dismissed with outrage in the mainstream – or would be, if the words could be heard – as barely disguised anti-Semitism. A rational assessment, giving an accurate portrayal and analysis of the scale and purposes of the terrorism of the emperor and the pirate, is excluded *a priori*, and would indeed be barely comprehensible, so remote would it be from received orthodoxies.

Israel's services to the U.S. as a "strategic asset" in the Middle East and elsewhere help explain the dedication of the United States, since Kissinger's takeover of Middle East policy-making in the early 1970s, to maintaining the military confrontation and Kissingerian "stalemate."[16] If the U.S. were to permit a peaceful settlement in accord with the international consensus, Israel would gradually be incorporated into the region and the U.S. would lose the services of a valuable mercenary state, militarily competent and technologically advanced, a pariah state, utterly dependent upon the U.S. for its economic and military survival and hence dependable, available for service where needed.

Elements of the so-called "Israeli lobby" also have a stake in maintaining the military confrontation, as the prominent Israeli journalist Danny Rubinstein learned on a visit to the United States in 1983.[17] In meetings with representatives of the major Jewish organizations (B'nai Brith, Anti-Defamation League, World Jewish Congress, Hadassah, Rabbis of all denominations, etc.), Rubinstein found that his presentations on the current situation in Israel aroused considerable hostility because he stressed the fact that Israel did not face military dangers so much as "political, social and moral destruction" resulting from its takeover of the occupied territories. "I am not interested," one functionary told him; "I can't do anything with such an argument." The point, Rubinstein discovered in many such interchanges, is that

> according to most of the people in the Jewish establishment the important thing is to stress again and again the external dangers that face Israel . . . the Jewish establishment in America needs Israel only as a victim of a cruel Arab attack. For such an Israel one can get support, donors and money. How can one raise money for fighting a demographic danger? Who will give even a single dollar to fight what I call 'the danger of annexation'?. . . Everybody knows the official tally of the contributions collected by the United Jewish Appeal in America, where the name of Israel is used and about half of the sum does not go to Israel but to the Jewish institutions in America. Is there a greater cynicism?

Rubinstein goes on to observe that the Appeal,

> which is managed as a tough and efficient business, has a common language with the hawkish positions in Israel. On the other hand, the attempt to communicate with Arabs, the striving for mutual recognition with the Palestinians, the moderate, dovish positions all work against the business of collecting contributions. They not only reduce the sum of money that is transferred to Israel. More to the point, they reduce the amount of money that is available for financing the activities of the Jewish communities.

Observers of the regular activities of the thought police of the Israeli lobby, keen to detect the slightest hint of a suggestion about reconciliation and a meaningful political settlement and to demolish this heresy with furious articles and letters to the press, circulation of fabricated defamatory material concerning the heretics, etc., will know just what Rubinstein was encountering.

Rubinstein's comments bring to our attention yet another Orwellism: the term "supporters of Israel," used conventionally to refer to those who are not troubled by "the political, social and moral destruction" of Israel (and in the longer term, very possibly its physical destruction as well), and indeed contribute to these consequences by the "blindly chauvinistic and narrow-minded" support they offer to Israel's "posture of calloused intransigence," as Israeli doves have often warned.[18]

A similar view was reiterated by Israeli military historian Col. (ret.) Meir Pail, who condemns the "idolatrous cult-worship of a Jewish fortress-state" on the part of the American Jewish community, warning that by their rejectionism they "have transformed the State of Israel into a war-god similar to Mars," a state that will be "a complex compound of the racist state structure of South Africa and the violent, terror-ridden social fabric of Northern Ireland," "an original contribution to the annals of 21st century political science: a unique kind of Jewish state that will be a cause for shame for every Jew wherever he may be, not only in the present, but in the future as well."[19]

In the same connection, we may observe the interesting way in which the term "Zionism" is tacitly defined by those who take on the role of guardians of doctrinal purity. My own views, for example, are regularly condemned as "militant anti-Zionism" by people who are well aware of these views, repeatedly and clearly expressed: that Israel within its internationally recognized borders should be accorded the rights of any state in the international system, no more, no less, and that in every state, including Israel, discriminatory structures that in law and in practice assign a special status to one category of citizens (Jews, Whites, Christians, etc.), granting them rights denied to others, should be dismantled. I will not enter here into the question of what should properly be called "Zionism," but merely note what follows from designation of these views as "militant anti-Zionism": Zionism is thereby conceived as the doctrine that Israel must be accorded rights beyond those of any other state; it must maintain control of occupied territories, thus barring any meaningful form of self-determination for Palestinians; and it must remain a state based on the principle of discrimination against non-Jewish citizens. It is perhaps of some interest that those who declare themselves "supporters of Israel" insist on the validity of the notorious UN resolution declaring Zionism to be racist.

These questions are not merely abstract and theoretical. The problem of discrimination is severe in Israel, where, for example, over 90 percent of the land is placed, by complex law and administrative practice, under the control of an organization devoted to the interests of "persons of Jewish religion, race or origin," so that non-Jewish citizens are effectively excluded. The commitment to discriminatory practice is so profound that the issue cannot even be addressed in Parliament, where new laws bar presentation of any bill that "negates the existence of the State of Israel as the state of the Jewish people." The legislation thus eliminates as illegal any parliamentary challenge to the discriminatory character of the state and effectively bars political parties committed to the democratic principle that a state is the state of its citizens.[20]

It is remarkable that the Israeli press and most of educated opinion appear to have perceived nothing strange about the fact that this new legislation was coupled with an "anti-racism" bill (the four opposing votes, in fact, were against this aspect of the measure). The *Jerusalem Post* headline reads: "Knesset forbids racist and anti-Zionist bills" – without irony, the term "Zionist" being interpreted as in the new legislation. Readers of the *Jerusalem Post* in the U.S. apparently also found nothing noteworthy in this conjunction, just as they have found no difficulty in reconciling the deeply anti-democratic character of their version of Zionism with enthusiastic acclaim for the democratic character of the state in which it is realized.

No less remarkable are the ingenious uses of the concept "anti-Semitism," for example, to refer to those who exhibit "the anti-imperialism of fools" (a variety of anti-Semitism) by objecting to Israel's role in the Third World in the service of U.S. power – in Guatemala, for example; or to Palestinians who refuse to understand that their problem can be overcome by "resettlement and some repatriation." If the remnants of the village of Doueimah, where perhaps hundreds were slaughtered by the Israeli Army in a land-clearing operation in 1948, or residents of the Soweto-like Gaza Strip object to resettlement and "repatriation," that proves that they are inspired by anti-Semitism.[21] One would have to descend to the annals of Stalinism to find something similar, but comparable examples in educated discourse in the United States with regard to Israel are not rare, and pass unnoticed in the U.S., though Israeli doves have not failed to perceive, and to condemn, the shameful performances.

The central device of the system of "brainwashing under freedom," developed in a most impressive fashion in the country that is perhaps the most free, is to encourage debate over policy issues but within a framework of presuppositions that incorporate the basic doctrines of the party line. The more vigorous the debate, the more effectively these presuppositions are instilled, while participants and onlookers are overcome with awe and self-adulation for their courage. Thus in the case of the Vietnam war, the ideological institutions permitted a debate between "hawks" and "doves"; in fact, the debate was not only permitted, but even encouraged by 1968, when substantial sectors of American business had turned against the war as too costly and harmful to their interests. The hawks held that with firmness and dedication the United States could succeed in its "defense of South Vietnam against Communist aggression." The doves countered by questioning the feasibility of this noble effort, or deplored the excessive use of force and violence in pursuing it. Or they bewailed the "errors" and "misunderstandings" that misled us in our "excess of righteousness and disinterested benevolence" (Harvard historian John King Fairbank, the dean of U.S. Asian studies and a noted academic dove) and "blundering efforts to do good" (Anthony Lewis, probably the leading media dove). Or sometimes, at the outer reaches of the doctrinal system, they asked whether indeed North Vietnam and the Viet Cong were guilty of aggression; perhaps, they suggest, the charge is exaggerated.

The central fact about the war, plainly enough, is that the U.S. was not defending the country that "was essentially the creation of the United States."[22] Rather, it was attacking the country, surely from 1962, when the U.S. air force began to participate in bombing South Vietnam, and chemical warfare (defoliation and crop destruction) was initiated as part of the effort to drive millions of people into camps where they could be "protected" from the South Vietnamese guerrillas they were willingly supporting (as the U.S. government privately conceded), after the U.S. had undermined any possibility of political settlement and had installed a client regime that had already killed tens of thousands of South Vietnamese. Throughout the war, the major U.S. assault was against South Vietnam, and it succeeded, by the late 1960s, in destroying the South Vietnamese resistance while spreading the war to the rest of Indochina. When the USSR attacks Afghanistan, we can perceive that this is aggression; when the U.S. attacks South Vietnam, it is "defense" – defense against "internal aggression," as Adlai Stevenson proclaimed at the

United Nations in 1964; against the "assault from the inside," in President Kennedy's words.

That the U.S. was engaged in an attack against South Vietnam is not denied; rather, the thought cannot be expressed or even imagined. One will find no hint of such an event as "the U.S. attack against South Vietnam" in mainstream media or scholarship, or even in most of the publications of the peace movement.[23]

There are few more striking illustrations of the power of the system of thought control under freedom than the debate that took place over North Vietnamese aggression and whether the U.S. had the right under international law to combat it in "collective self-defense against armed attack." Learned tomes were written advocating the opposing positions, and in less exalted terms, the debate was pursued in the public arena opened by the peace movement. The achievement is impressive: as long as debate is focused on the question of whether the Vietnamese are guilty of aggression in Vietnam, there can be no discussion of whether the U.S. aggression against South Vietnam was indeed what it plainly was. As one who took part in this debate, with complete awareness of what was happening, I can only report that opponents of state violence are trapped, enmeshed in a propaganda system of awesome effectiveness. It was necessary for critics of the U.S. war in Vietnam to become experts in the intricacies of Indochinese affairs; largely an irrelevance, since the issue, always avoided, was U.S. affairs, just as we need not become specialists in Afghanistan to oppose Soviet aggression there. It was necessary, throughout, to enter the arena of debate on the terms set by the state and the elite opinion that serves it, however one might understand that by doing so, one is making a further contribution to the system of indoctrination. The alternative is to tell the simple truth, which would be equivalent to speaking in some foreign tongue.

Much the same is true of the current debate over Central America. The U.S. terrorist war in El Salvador is not a topic for discussion among respectable people; it does not exist. The U.S. effort to "contain" Nicaragua is a permissible subject of debate, but within narrow limits. We may ask whether it is right to use force to "cut out the cancer" (Secretary of State George Shultz) and prevent the Sandinistas from exporting their "revolution without borders," a fanciful construction of the state propaganda system, known to be a fabrication by journalists and other commentators who adopt the rhetoric. But we may not discuss the idea that "the cancer" that must be excised is "the threat of a good example," which might spread "contagion" through the region and beyond – a fact sometimes obliquely conceded, as when Administration officials explain that the U.S. proxy army has succeeded in "forcing [the Sandinistas] to divert scarce resources to the war and away from social programs."[24]

In the first three months of 1986, when debate was intensifying over the impending Congressional votes on aid to the U.S. proxy army (as its most enthusiastic supporters privately describe it) attacking Nicaragua from its Honduran and Costa Rican bases, the national press (*New York Times* and *Washington Post*) ran 85 opinion pieces by columnists and invited contributors on U.S. policy toward Nicaragua. All were critical of the Sandinistas, ranging from bitterly critical (the vast majority) to moderately so. That is what is called "public debate." The unquestioned fact that the Sandinista government had carried out successful social reforms during the early years, before the U.S. war aborted these efforts, was close to unmentionable; in 85 columns, there were two phrases referring to the fact that there had been such social reforms, and the idea that this is the basic reason for the U.S. attack – hardly a great secret – was unmentionable.

Alleged "apologists" for the Sandinistas were harshly denounced (anonymously, to ensure that they would have no opportunity to respond, minimal as that possibility would be in any event), but none of these criminals were permitted to express their views. There was no reference to the conclusion of Oxfam that Nicaragua was "exceptional" among the 76 developing countries in which it worked in the commitment of the political leadership "to improving the condition of the people and encouraging their active participation in the development process," and that among the four Central American countries where Oxfam worked, "only in Nicaragua has a substantial effort been made to address inequities in landownership and to extend health, educational, and agricultural services to poor peasant families," though the Contra war terminated these threats and caused Oxfam to shift its efforts from development projects to war relief. It is scarcely conceivable that the national press would permit discussion of the suggestion that the dedicated U.S. effort to excise this "cancer" falls strictly within its historical vocation. Debate may proceed over the proper method for combating this vicious outpost of the Evil Empire, but may not pass beyond these permitted bounds in a national forum.[25]

In a dictatorship or military-run "democracy," the party line is clear, overt and explicit, either announced by the Ministry of Truth or made apparent in other ways. And it must be publicly obeyed; the cost of disobedience may range from prison and exile under terrible conditions, as in the USSR and its East European satellites, to hideous torture, rape, mutilation and mass slaughter, as in a typical U.S. dependency such as El Salvador. In a free society, these devices are not available and more subtle means are used. The party line is not enunciated, but is rather presupposed. Those who do not accept it are not imprisoned or deposited in ditches after torture and mutilation, but the population is protected from their heresies. Within the mainstream, it is barely possible even to understand their words on the rare occasions when such exotic discourse can be heard. In the medieval period, it was considered necessary to take heresy seriously, to understand it and combat it by rational argument. Today, it suffices to point to it. A whole battery of concepts have been concocted – "moral equivalence," "Marxist," "radical,". . . – to identify heresy, and thus to dismiss it without further argument or comment. These dangerous and virtually inexpressible doctrines even become "new orthodoxies"[26] to be combated (more accurately, identified and dismissed with horror) by the embattled minority who dominate public expression to something close to totality. But for the most part heresy is simply ignored, while debate rages over narrow and generally marginal issues among those who accept the doctrines of the faith.

Very much the same is true when we turn to our present topic, the Middle East. We may debate whether the Palestinians should be permitted to enter "the peace process," but we must not be permitted to understand that the U.S. and Israel lead the rejectionist camp and have consistently blocked any authentic "peace process," often with substantial violence. With regard to terrorism, a critical scholar warns that we should refrain from "oversimplification" and should "examine the social and ideological roots of current Middle Eastern and Islamic radicalism," which raises "intractable but nevertheless real problems"; we should seek to understand what leads the terrorists to pursue their evil ways.[27] The debate over terrorism, then, is neatly demarcated: at one extreme, we have those who see it as simply a conspiracy by the Evil Empire and its agents; and at the other extreme, we find more balanced thinkers who avoid this "oversimplification" and go on to investigate the domestic roots of Arab and Islamic terror. The idea that there may be other sources of terrorism in the Middle East – that the emperor and his clients may also have a hand in the drama – is excluded *a priori*; it is not denied, but is unthinkable, a considerable achievement.

Throughout, the moderates, the liberal doves, play a prominent role in ensuring the proper functioning of the indoctrination system, by setting firmly the bounds of thinkable thought.

In his *Journal*, Henry David Thoreau, who explained elsewhere that he wastes no time reading newspapers, wrote:

> There is no need of a law to check the license of the press. It is law enough, and more than enough, to itself. Virtually, the community have come together and agreed what things shall be uttered, have agreed on a platform and to excommunicate him who departs from it, and not one in a thousand dares utter anything else.

His statement is not quite accurate. Philosopher John Dolan observes: it "is not that people will lack the courage to express thoughts outside the permitted range: it is, rather, that they will be deprived of the capacity to think such thoughts."[28] That is the essential point, the driving motive of the "engineers of democratic consent."

In the *New York Times*, Walter Reich of the Woodrow Wilson International Center, referring to the *Achille Lauro* hijacking, demands that strict standards of justice be applied to people who have "committed terrorist murder," both the agents and planners of these acts:

> To mete out lesser punishment on the grounds that a terrorist believes himself to be a deprived, aggrieved freedom fighter undermines the ground on which justice stands by accepting terrorists' argument that only their concepts of justice and rights, and their sufferings, are valid . . . The Palestinians – and any of the many groups using terrorism to satisfy grievances – should scuttle terror and find other ways, inevitably involving compromise, to achieve their goals. And the Western democracies must reject the argument that any excuse – even one involving a background of deprivation – can 'attenuate' responsibility for terrorism against innocents.

Noble words, which could be taken seriously if the stern injunction to carry out harsh punitive action were applied to oneself, to the emperor and his clients; if not, these strictures have all the merit of no less high-minded phrases produced by the World Peace Council and other Communist front organizations with regard to atrocities of the Afghan resistance.

Mark Heller, deputy director of the Jaffee Center for Strategic Studies at Tel Aviv University, explains that "State-sponsored terrorism is low-intensity warfare, and its victims, including the United States, are therefore entitled to fight back with every means at their disposal." It follows, then, that other victims of "low-intensity warfare" and "state-sponsored terrorism" are "entitled to fight back with every means at their disposal": Salvadorans, Nicaraguans, Palestinians, Lebanese, and innumerable other victims of the emperor and his clients throughout a good part of the world.[29]

It is true that these consequences follow only if we accept an elementary moral principle: that we apply to ourselves the same standards we apply to others (and if serious, even stricter ones). But that principle, and what follows from adopting it, is scarcely comprehensible in the prevailing intellectual culture, and would hardly be expressible in the journals that demand stern punishment of others for their crimes. In fact, were anyone to draw the logical consequences of these dicta and express them clearly, they might well be subject to prosecution for inciting terrorist violence against political leaders of the United States and its allies.

The most skeptical voices in the U.S. agree that "Colonel Qaddafi's open support of terrorism is a blatant evil," and "There is no reason to let murderers go unpunished if you know their author [*sic*]. Nor can it be a decisive factor that retaliation will kill some innocent civilians, or murderous states would never fear retribution" (Anthony Lewis).[30] The principle entitles large numbers of people around the world to assassinate President Reagan and to bomb Washington even if this "retaliation will kill some innocent civilians." As long as such simple truths are inexpressible and beyond comprehension, in the cases illustrated here and many others, we delude ourselves if we believe that we participate in a democratic polity.

There is agonized debate in the media over whether it is proper to permit the pirates and thieves to express their demands and perceptions. NBC, for example, was bitterly condemned for running an interview with the man accused of planning the *Achille Lauro* hijacking, thus serving the interests of terrorists by allowing them free expression without rebuttal, a shameful departure from the uniformity demanded in a properly functioning free society. Should the media permit Ronald Reagan, George Shultz, Menachem Begin, Shimon Peres, and other voices of the emperor and his court to speak without rebuttal, advocating "low-intensity warfare" and "retaliation" or "preemption"? Are they thereby permitting terrorist commanders free expression, thus serving as agents of wholesale terrorism? The question cannot be asked, and if raised, could only be dismissed with distaste or horror.

Literal censorship barely exists in the United States, but thought control is a flourishing industry, indeed an indispensable one in a free society based on the principle of elite decision, public endorsement or passivity.

2 Middle East Terrorism and the American Ideological System (1986)

On October 17, 1985, President Reagan met in Washington with Israeli Prime Minister Shimon Peres, who told him that Israel was prepared to take "bold steps" in the Middle East and extend "the hand of peace" to Jordan. "Mr. Peres's visit comes at a moment of unusual American–Israeli harmony," David Shipler commented in the *Times*, quoting a State Department official who described U.S. relations with Israel as "extraordinarily close and strong." Peres was warmly welcomed as a man of peace, and commended for his forthright commitment to "bear the cost of peace in preference to the price of war," in his words. The President said that he and Mr Peres discussed "the evil scourge of terrorism, which has claimed so many Israeli, American and Arab victims and brought tragedy to many others," adding that "We agreed that terrorism must not blunt our efforts to achieve peace in the Middle East."[1]

It would require the talents of a Jonathan Swift to do justice to this exchange between two of the world's leading terrorist commanders, whose shared conception of "peace," furthermore, excludes entirely one of the two groups that claim the right of national self-determination in the former Palestine: the indigenous population. The Jordan Valley is "an inseparable part of the State of Israel," Peres declared while touring Israeli settlements there in 1985, consistent with his unwavering stand that "The past is immutable and the Bible is the decisive document in determining the fate of our land" and that a Palestinian state would "threaten Israel's very existence."[2] His conception of a Jewish state, much lauded in the U.S. for its moderation, does not *threaten*, but rather *eliminates* the existence of the Palestinian people. But this consequence is considered of little moment, at worst a minor defect in an imperfect world.

Neither Peres nor any other Israeli leader has yet moved an inch from the position of current President Chaim Herzog in 1972 that the Palestinians can never be "partners in any way in a land that has been holy to our people for thousands of years," though the doves prefer to exclude West Bank areas of heavy Arab population from the Jewish State to avoid what they euphemistically term "the demographic problem." All continue to accept the judgment of Shlomo Gazit (see p. 10) that the policies of "destruction of all initiative": for political action, democracy, or negotiations have been a "success story" and should be continued. Israel's position, with U.S. support, remains that of Prime Minister (now Defense Minister) Yitzhak Rabin, when the PLO and the Arab states supported a UN Security Council resolution calling for a peaceful two-state settlement in January 1976: Israel will reject any negotiations with the PLO even if it recognizes Israel and renounces terrorism, and will not enter into "political negotiations with Palestinians," PLO or not. Neither Peres nor Reagan has been willing even to consider the explicit proposals by the PLO – which both know has overwhelming support among the Palestinians and has as much legitimacy as did the Zionist organization in 1947 – for negotiations leading to mutual recognition in a two-state settlement in accord with the broad international consensus that has been blocked at every turn by the U.S. and Israel for many years.[3]

These crucial political realities provide the necessary framework for any discussion of "the evil scourge of terrorism," which, in the racist terms of American discourse, refers to terrorist acts by Arabs, but not by Jews, just as "peace" means a settlement that honors the right of national self-determination of Jews, but not of Palestinians.

Peres arrived in Washington to discourse on peace and terrorism with his partner in crime directly after having sent his bombers to attack Tunis, where they killed 20 Tunisians and 55 Palestinians, Israeli journalist Amnon Kapeliouk reported from the scene. The target was undefended, "a vacation resort with several dozen homes, vacation cottages and PLO offices side by side and intermingled in such a way that even from close by it is difficult to distinguish" among them. The weapons were more sophisticated than those used in Beirut, "smart bombs" apparently, which crushed their targets to dust.

> The people who were in the bombed buildings were torn to shreds beyond recognition. They showed me a series of pictures of the dead. 'You may take them,' I was told. I left the pictures in the office. No newspaper in the world would publish terror photos such as these. I was told that a Tunisian boy who sold sandwiches near the headquarters was torn to pieces. His father identified the body by a scar on his ankle. 'Some of the wounded were brought

> out from under the rubble, apparently healthy and unhurt,' my guide told me. 'Half an hour later they collapsed in contortions and died. Apparently their internal organs had been destroyed from the power of the blast.'[4]

Tunisia had accepted the Palestinians at Reagan's behest after they had been expelled from Beirut in a U.S.-supported invasion that left some 20,000 killed and much of the country destroyed. "You used a hammer against a fly," Israeli military correspondent Ze'ev Schiff was informed by "a leading Pentagon figure, a general who is familiar with the Israeli military (IDF) and several other armies of the region." "You struck many civilians without need. We were astounded by your attitude to the Lebanese civilians," a feeling shared by Israeli soldiers and senior officers, who were appalled at the savagery of the attack and the treatment of civilians and prisoners[5] – though support in Israel for the aggression and for the Begin–Sharon team increased in parallel to the atrocities, reaching its very high peak after the terror bombing of Beirut in August.[6] Shimon Peres, the man of peace and respected figure in the Socialist International, kept his silence until the costs to Israel began to mount with the postwar Sabra-Shatila massacres; and later, the toll taken by the Lebanese resistance, which undermined Israel's plan of establishing a "New Order" in Lebanon with Israel in control of large areas of the south and the remnants ruled by Israel's Phalangist allies and selected Muslim elites (see note 55, below).

There can be no doubt, Kapeliouk concludes, that Arafat was the target of the Tunis attack. In the PLO office to which he was taken, a picture of Arafat stands amidst the ruins with the caption: "They wanted to kill me instead of negotiating with me." "The PLO wishes negotiations," Kapeliouk was told, "but Israel rejects any discussion" – a simple statement of fact, effectively concealed in the U.S., or worse, dismissed as irrelevant given the guiding racist premises.

There can also be no serious doubt of U.S. complicity in the Tunis attack. The U.S. did not even warn the victims – American allies – that the killers were on the way. One who credits the pretense that the Sixth Fleet and the extensive surveillance system in the region were incapable of detecting the Israeli planes refueled en route over the Mediterranean should be calling for a Congressional investigation into the utter incompetence of the American military, which surely leaves us and our allies wide open to enemy attack. "News reports now quote government sources as saying the U.S. Sixth fleet was undoubtedly aware of the coming raid but decided not to inform Tunisian officials," the *Los Angeles Times* reported. But "that very significant statement was not reported in the two major east coast papers, *The New York Times* and *The Washington Post*, nor in the other U.S. papers, nor was it used in the overseas service" of Associated Press and UPI, London *Economist* Mideast correspondent Godfrey Jansen reported, adding that "U.S. passive collusion was absolutely certain."[7]

One of the victims of the Tunis bombing was Mahmoud el-Mughrabi, born in Jerusalem in 1960, under detention twelve times by the age of 16, one of the informants for the London *Sunday Times* investigation of torture in Israel (June 19, 1977), who "managed to escape to Jordan after years of increasingly marginal existence under steadily deteriorating conditions of the military occupation," according to a memorial notice by Israeli Jewish friends that was repeatedly denied publication in Arab newspapers in East Jerusalem by Israeli military censorship.[8] These facts would, of course, be meaningless in the United States, if only because the unusually careful *Sunday Times* study was largely excluded from the press, though it was noted in the liberal *New Republic*, along with an explicit defense of torture of Arabs that elicited no public reaction.[9]

The United States approved the Israeli bombing of Tunis as "a legitimate response" to "terrorist attacks." Secretary of State Shultz confirmed this judgment in a telephone call to Israeli Foreign Minister Yitzhak Shamir, informing him that the President and others "had considerable sympathy for the Israeli action."[10] Washington drew back from such open support after an adverse global reaction, but it abstained from the UN Security Council condemnation of this "act of armed aggression" in "flagrant violation of the Charter of the United Nations, international law and norms of conduct" – alone as usual. The intellectual and cultural climate in the U.S. is reflected by the fact that the abstention was bitterly condemned as yet another instance of a "pro-PLO" and "anti-Israel" stance, and a refusal to strike hard at – carefully selected – terrorists.

One might argue that the Israeli bombing does not fall under the rubric of international terrorism but rather the far more serious crime of aggression, as the UN Security Council maintained. Or one might hold that it is unfair to apply to Israel the definition of "international terrorism" designed by others. To counter the latter complaint, we may consider its own doctrine, as formulated by Ambassador Benjamin Netanyahu at an International Conference on Terrorism. The distinguishing factor in terrorism, he explained, is "deliberate and systematic murder and maiming [of civilians] designed to inspire fear."[11] Clearly the Tunis attack and other Israeli atrocities over the years fall under this concept, though most acts of international terrorism do not, including the most outrageous terrorist attacks against Israelis (Ma'alot, the Munich massacre, the coastal road atrocity of 1978 that provided the pretext for invading Lebanon, etc.), or even airplane hijacking or taking of hostages quite generally, the very topic of the conference he was attending.

The attack on Arafat's PLO headquarters was allegedly in retaliation for the murder of three Israelis in Larnaca, Cyprus, by assailants who were captured and face trial for their crime. "Western diplomatic experts on the P.L.O." doubt that Arafat was aware of the planned mission. "The Israelis, too, have dropped their original contention that Mr. Arafat had been involved."[12] Apologists for Israeli terrorism in the U.S., who assure us that "Israel's Tunisian raid precisely targeted people responsible for terrorist activities," are unimpressed, explaining that whatever the facts, "the larger moral responsibility for atrocities . . . is *all* Yasir Arafat's" because "he was, and remains, the founding father of contemporary Palestinian violence." In an address to the Israeli lobbying group AIPAC, Attorney-General Edwin Meese stated that the U.S. will hold Arafat "accountable for acts of international terrorism" quite generally, facts apparently being irrelevant.[13] Therefore any act "against the PLO" – a very broad category, as the historical record demonstrates – is legitimate.

The Tunis attack was consistent with Israeli practice since the earliest days of the state: retaliation is directed against those who are vulnerable, not the perpetrators of atrocities. A standard condemnation of the PLO is that "Instead of directly attacking security-minded foes like Israel, for example, Palestinians have attacked softer Israeli targets in Italy, Austria and elsewhere,"[14] another sign of their vile and cowardly nature. The similar Israeli practice, initiated long before and vastly greater in scale, escapes notice in the midst of the general praise for the heroism, military efficiency, and "purity of arms" of a favored U.S. ally. The concept of "retaliation" also raises more than a few questions, a matter to which we turn directly.

As 1985 came to an end, the press reviewed the record of "a year of bloody international terrorism," including the murders in Larnaca on September 25 and the Achille Lauro hijacking and brutal murder of a crippled American tourist, Leon Klinghoffer, on October 7.

Israel's October 1 attack on Tunis was not included in the list. In its lengthy year-end review of terrorism, the *Times* briefly notes the Tunis bombing, but as an example of retaliation, not terrorism, describing it as "an act of desperation that had little effect on Palestinian violence and provoked an outcry by other nations." Harvard Law Professor Alan Dershowitz, condemning Italy for complicity in international terrorism by releasing the man "who allegedly masterminded the [*Achille Lauro*] hijacking," observed that the U.S. "would certainly extradite any Israeli terrorist who had done violence to citizens of another country" – Ariel Sharon, Yitzhak Shamir or Menachem Begin, for example. This statement appeared on the very day that Peres was being feted in Washington shortly after the Tunis bombing and lauded for his commitment to peace, and is considered entirely natural in the prevailing cultural climate.[15]

Reagan's pronouncements on terrorism are reported and discussed with apparent seriousness in the mainstream, but occasional critics have remarked upon the hypocrisy of those who fulminate about international terrorism while sending their client armies to murder, mutilate, torture and destroy in Nicaragua and – less commonly noted, since these acts are considered a grand success – to massacre tens of thousands in El Salvador in a determined effort to avert the dread threat of meaningful democracy there. Shortly after the Reagan–Peres discourse on peace and terror, a group of 120 doctors, nurses and other health professionals returned from an investigation in Nicaragua endorsed by the American Public Health Association and the World Health Organization, reporting the destruction of clinics and hospitals, murder of health professionals, looting of rural pharmacies leading to critical shortage of medicines, and successful disruption of a polio vaccination program, one small part of a campaign of violence organized in the centers of international terrorism in Washington and Miami;[16] *Times* reporters in Nicaragua often match their *Pravda* counterparts in Afghanistan in their zeal to unearth or check the massive evidence of Contra atrocities, and this report, like many others, was ignored in the Newspaper of Record.

The raid near Tunis yields a measure of the hypocrisy, which is not always easy to grasp. Suppose that Nicaragua were to carry out bombings in Washington aimed at Reagan, Shultz and other international terrorists, killing some 100,000 people "by accident." This would be entirely justified retaliation by American standards, if indeed a ratio of 25 to one is acceptable, as in the Larnaca–Tunis exchange, though we might add for accuracy that in this case at least the perpetrators would be targeted and there is no question about who initiated the terror, and perhaps the appropriate number of deaths should be multiplied by some factor in consideration of the relative population sizes. "Terrorists, and those who support them, must, and will, be held to account," President Reagan declared,[17] thus providing the moral basis for any such act of retaliation, with his harshest critics in the mainstream press in full accord, as we have seen.

Peres had already distinguished himself as a man of peace in Lebanon.[18] After he became Prime Minister, Israel's "counterterror" programs against civilians in occupied southern Lebanon intensified, reaching their peak of savagery with the Iron Fist operations of early 1985, which had "the earmarks of Latin American death squads," Curtis Wilkie commented, affirming reports of other journalists on the scene. In the village of Zrariya, for example, the IDF carried out an operation well to the north of its then current frontline. After several hours of heavy shelling of Zrariya and three nearby villages, the IDF carted off the entire male population, killing 35–40 villagers, some in cars crushed by Israeli tanks; other villagers were beaten or murdered, a tank shell was fired at Red Cross workers who were warned to stay away, and Israeli troops miraculously escaped without casualties from what was officially described as a gun battle with heavily armed guerrillas. The day before, twelve Israeli soldiers had been killed in a suicide attack near the border, but Israel denied that the attack on Zrariya was retaliation. The Israeli denial is dutifully presented as fact by commentators in the U.S., who explain that "intelligence had established that the town had become a base for terrorists . . . No less than 34 Shi'ite guerrillas were killed in the gun battle and more than 100 men were taken away for questioning – from one small village" (Eric Breindel), which indicates the scale of the Shi'ite terror network. Unaware of the party line, Israeli soldiers painted the slogan "Revenge of the Israeli Defense Forces" in Arabic on walls of the town, reporters on the scene observed.[19]

Elsewhere, Israeli gunners shot at hospitals and schools and took "suspects," including patients in hospital beds and operating rooms, for "interrogation" or to Israeli concentration camps, among numerous other atrocities that a Western diplomat who often travels in the area described as reaching new depths of "calculated brutality and arbitrary murder."[20]

The head of the IDF liaison unit in Lebanon, General Shlomo Ilya, "said the only weapon against terrorism is terrorism and that Israel has options beyond those already used for 'speaking the language the terrorists understand'." The concept is not a novel one. Gestapo operations in occupied Europe also "were justified in the name of combating 'terrorism'," and one of Klaus Barbie's victims was found murdered with a note pinned to his chest reading "Terror against Terror" – incidentally, the name adopted by an Israeli terrorist group, and the heading of the cover story in *Der Spiegel* on the U.S. terror bombing of Libya in April 1986. A UN Security Council resolution calling for condemnation of "Israeli practices and measures against the civilian population in southern Lebanon" was vetoed by the United States on the grounds that it "applies double standards"; "We don't believe an unbalanced resolution will end the agony of Lebanon," Jeane Kirkpatrick explained.[21]

Israel's terror operations continued as its forces were compelled to withdraw by the resistance. Israeli troops and their South Lebanon Army (SLA) mercenaries brought the "year of bloody international terrorism" to an end on December 31, 1985 as they "stormed a Shi'ite Moslem village [Kunin] in southern Lebanon and forced its entire population of about 2,000 to leave," blowing up houses and setting others on fire and rounding up 32 young men; old men, women and children from the village were reported to be streaming into a town outside the Israeli "security zone," where the UN force had a command post.[22]

This report, based on witnesses quoted by the Lebanese police, a journalist from the conservative Beirut journal *An Nahar*, and the Shi'ite Amal movement, is filed from Beirut. From Jerusalem, Joel Greenberg provides a different version, not on the basis of any identified sources, but as simple fact: "villagers fearful of an SLA reprisal fled the Shi'ite village of Kunin after two SLA soldiers were slain in the village."[23]

The comparison, which is standard, is instructive. Israeli propaganda benefits greatly from the fact that the media rely overwhelmingly on Israel-based correspondents. This yields two crucial advantages: first, the "news" is presented to the American audience through official Israeli eyes; second, on the rare occasions when U.S. correspondents carry out independent inquiry instead of simply relying on their cooperative hosts, the Israeli propaganda system and its numerous U.S. affiliates can complain bitterly that Arab crimes are ignored while Israel is subjected to detailed scrutiny for any minor imperfection, given the density of reporting.

Inability to manage the news in the usual fashion sometimes creates problems, for example, during the 1982 Lebanon war, when Israel had no way to control the eyewitness reports by Lebanon-based journalists. This evoked an impressive outcry of protest over alleged atrocity-mongering and fabrication in a "broad-scale mass psychological war" waged against pitiful little Israel, another sign of the inveterate anti-Semitism of world opinion; Israel became the victim, not the aggressor. It is easily demonstrated that the charges are false, often merely comical, and that the media predictably bent over backwards to see things from the Israeli point of view, not an easy matter for journalists attempting to survive Israeli terror bombing. Testimony from Israeli sources was often far harsher than what was reported in the U.S. press, and what appeared in U.S. journals was often a considerably watered-down version of what journalists actually perceived.[24] But the charges are taken very seriously despite their manifest absurdity, while accurate critique of the media for its subordination to the U.S.–Israeli perspective and suppression of unacceptable facts is ignored. Typically, a study of "Published Analyses of Media Coverage of the 1982 War in Lebanon" includes numerous denunciations of the press for an alleged anti-Israel stance and a few defenses of the media against these charges, but not even a reference to the fact that there were extensive, and quite accurate, critical analyses of exactly the opposite phenomenon.[25] Within the narrow constraints of the highly ideological U.S. intellectual climate, only the former criticism can even be heard. This is quite a typical phenomenon, easily demonstrated in connection with the Indochina wars, the Central America wars, etc., and serving as yet another device of thought control.

The Iron Fist operations, which the Israeli command is happy to describe as "terrorism" (see General Ilya's remarks, cited above), had two main purposes. The first, John Kifner observes (from Lebanon), was "to turn the population against the guerrillas by making the cost of supporting them too high"; in short, to hold the population hostage to terrorist attack, unless they accept the arrangements Israel intends to impose by force. The second purpose was to exacerbate internal conflicts in Lebanon and to implement a general population exchange after intercommunal strife, much of which appears to have been incited by the occupier since 1982, in the classic manner. "There is a great deal of evidence," Lebanon-based correspondent Jim

Muir observes, "that the Israelis helped fuel and encourage the Christian–Druze conflict" in the Chouf region. In the south, a senior international aid official said: "Their dirty tricks department did everything it could to stir up trouble, but it just didn't work." "Their behaviour was wicked," a view "shared by the international relief community as a whole." "Local eyewitnesses reported that Israeli soldiers frequently shot into the Palestinian camps from nearby Christian areas in an effort to incite the Palestinians against the Christians," and residents in the Christian villages reported that Israeli patrols forced Christians and Muslims at gunpoint to punch one another among other forms of "bizarre humiliation." The techniques finally worked. Israel's Christian allies attacked Muslims near Sidon in a manner guaranteed to elicit a response from considerably more powerful forces, initiating a bloody cycle of violence that ultimately led to the flight of tens of thousands of Christians, many to the Israeli-dominated regions in the south, while tens of thousands of Shi'ites were driven north by Peres's Iron Fist operations.[26]

The pretense in the United States was that Israel was always planning to withdraw so that the Shi'ite terrorists were simply indulging in the usual Arab pleasure in violence for its own sake, delaying the planned withdrawal. But as Jim Muir correctly observes, "it is a historical fact beyond serious dispute that the Israelis would not be withdrawing now were it not for the attacks and the casualties they have caused," and the extent of the withdrawal would be determined by the intensity of the resistance.[27]

The Israeli high command explained that the victims of the Iron Fist operations were "terrorist villagers"; it was thus understandable that 13 villagers were massacred by SLA militiamen in the incident that elicited this observation. Yossi Olmert of the Shiloah Institute, Israel's Institute of Strategic Studies, observed that "these terrorists operate with the support of most of the local population." An Israeli commander complained that "the terrorist . . . has many eyes here, because he lives here," while the military correspondent of the *Jerusalem Post* described the problems faced in combating the "terrorist mercenary," "fanatics, all of whom are sufficiently dedicated to their causes to go on running the risk of being killed while operating against the IDF," which must "maintain order and security" in occupied southern Lebanon despite "the price the inhabitants will have to pay." He expressed his "admiration for the way in which they were doing their job."

Leon Wieseltier explained the difference between "Shi'ite terrorism" against the occupying army and Palestinian terrorism, each a manifestation of the evil Arab nature: "The Palestinians had murderers who wished to kill. The Shi'ites have murderers who wish to die," conducting actions "inspired by a chiliastic demand of the world for which there can be no merely political or diplomatic satisfaction," nothing so simple as removing the occupying army from their land. Rather, their "secret army" Amal has been "consecrated" to "the destruction of Israel" since its founding in 1975 – a discovery that goes well beyond the tales concocted in Israel's Hasbara system.[28]

The same concept of terrorism is widely used by U.S. officials and commentators. Thus the press reports, without comment, that Secretary of State Shultz's concern over "international terrorism" became "his passion" after the suicide bombing of U.S. Marines in Lebanon in October 1983, troops that much of the population saw, not too surprisingly, as a foreign military force sent to impose the "New Order" established by the Israeli aggression. Barry Rubin writes that "The most important use of Syrian-sponsored terrorism within Lebanon was to force the withdrawal of Israeli troops and U.S. Marines," while both Iran and Syria have supported "terrorist activity" by "Shi'ite extremist groups" in southern Lebanon, such as attacks on "the Israeli-backed South Lebanese Army." For the advocate of state terror, resistance to an occupying army or its local mercenaries is terrorism, meriting harsh reprisal. *Times* Israel correspondent Thomas Friedman routinely describes attacks in southern Lebanon directed against Israeli forces as "terrorist bombings" or "suicide terrorism," which, he assures us, is the product of "psychological weaknesses or religious fervor." He reports further that residents of Israel's "security zone" who violate the rules established by the occupiers are "shot on the spot, with questions asked later. Some of those shot have been innocent bystanders." But this practice is not state terrorism. He also notes that Israel "has taken great pains to limit the flow of news out of the area": "No reporters have been allowed to cover the aftermath of suicide attacks, and virtually no information is released about them." This fact does not prevent him from reporting with much confidence about the background and psychological states and disorders of those designated "terrorists" by the occupiers.[29]

As Reagan and Peres were congratulating one another on their principled stand against "the evil scourge of terrorism" before their admiring audience, the press reported yet another terrorist act in southern Lebanon: "Terrorists Kill 6, Demolish U.S.-Owned Christian Radio Station in S. Lebanon," the headlines read on the same day.[30] Why should Lebanese terrorists destroy "the Voice of Hope," run by American Christian missionaries? The question was barely raised, but let us look into it, in the interest of clarifying the concepts of terrorism and retaliation.

One reason is that the station "speaks for the South Lebanon Army,"[31] the mercenary force established by Israel in southern Lebanon to terrorize the population in its "security zone." The location of the station, near the village of Khiam, is also worthy of note. Khiam has a history, well known in Lebanon and Israel, if not in the U.S. Ze'ev Schiff alluded to this history in the midst of Peres's Iron Fist operations. He observed that when Israel invaded Lebanon in 1982, the village of Khiam was "empty of inhabitants," though now it has 10,000, and that the Lebanese town of Nabatiya had only 5,000 inhabitants, today 50,000. "These and others will once again be forced to abandon their homes if they permit extremists in their community or Palestinians to attack Israeli settlements," Schiff explained.[32] That will be their fate if they mimic the IDF, which was then attacking Lebanese villages, randomly murdering civilians and destroying in defense against the "terrorism [that] has not disappeared" as "Israeli soldiers are harassed daily in southern Lebanon."[33]

For the Lebanese to whom the warning was addressed, and for at least some better-informed elements of his Israeli audience, Schiff did not have to explain why the population of Nabatiya had been reduced to 5,000 and Khiam emptied by 1982. The population of Khiam had been driven out, with hundreds killed, by Israeli terror bombardment from the early 1970s, and the handful who remained in Khiam were slaughtered during the 1978 invasion of Lebanon, under the eyes of the elite Golani brigade, by Israel's Haddad militia, which "succeeded in establishing relative peace in the region and preventing the return of P.L.O. terrorists," the man of peace explained.[34]

Khiam is also the site of a "secret jail" maintained by "Israel and its local militia allies in south Lebanon . . . where detainees are held in appalling conditions and subjected to beatings and electric-shock torture, according to former inmates and international relief officials in the area." The Red Cross reported that "Israelis were running the center" and that it had been refused entry by the IDF.[35] Confirming these reports, Horowitz adds that Israel has learned "the lesson of Ansar," the concentration camp run by the IDF. It has therefore arranged for its SLA mercenaries to run the Khiam torture chamber so as to deflect criticism. Extensive reports of torture by former prisoners have been ignored in the U.S., but not elsewhere. Citing this evidence, Paul Kessler (of the Collège de France, co-founder of the French Physicians Committee on Soviet Jewry) observes that most of the prisoners "were picked up as suspects during search operations or were villagers arrested for refusing to cooperate with the occupying power, and in particular, for refusing to join the Israeli-led 'South Lebanese Army militia'"; none has been indicted or tried, though some had then been detained for over a year. Khiam is the principal, but not the only center. Kessler reports systematic torture by SLA guards, who operate the prisons "under the direction of Israeli officers."[36]

There might have been more to say, then, about the terrorist attack by "fanatics" at Khiam on October 17, 1985, were matters such as these considered fit to become part of historical memory alongside of other acts of terror of greater ideological serviceability.

Nabatiya too has further stories to tell. The flight of 50,000 of its 60,000 population "mostly because of fear of the [Israeli] shelling" was reported by two *Jerusalem Post* correspondents who were touring southern Lebanon in an effort to unearth evidence of PLO terror and atrocities, finding little, though there was ample evidence of Israeli terror and its effects.[37] One such bombardment was on November 4, 1977, when Nabatiya "came under heavy artillery fire from [Israeli-supported] Lebanese Maronite positions and also from Israeli batteries on both sides of the frontier – including some of the six Israeli strongpoints inside Lebanon." The attacks continued the next day, with three women killed among other casualties. On November 6, two rockets fired by Fatah guerrillas killed two Israelis in Nahariya, setting off an artillery battle and a second rocket attack that killed one Israeli. "Then came the Israeli air raids in which some 70 people, nearly all Lebanese, were killed."[38]

This Israeli-initiated exchange, which threatened to lead to a major war, was cited by Egyptian President Sadat as a reason for his offer to visit Jerusalem a few days later.[39]

These events have entered historical memory in a different form, however, not only in journalism but in scholarship: "In an effort to disrupt the movement towards a peace conference," Edward Haley writes (citing no evidence), "the PLO fired Katyusha rockets into the northern Israeli village of Nahariya, on November 6 and 8, killing three," and eliciting "the inevitable Israeli reprisal" on November 9, with over 100 killed in attacks "in and around Tyre and two small towns to the south."[40] As is the rule, in sanitized history Palestinians carry out terrorism, Israelis then retaliate, perhaps too harshly. In the real world, the truth is often rather different, a matter of no small significance for the study of terrorism in the Middle East.

The torment of Nabatiya was rarely noted by the Western press, though there are a few exceptions. One of the Israeli attacks was on December 2, 1975, when the Israeli air force bombed the town killing dozens of Lebanese and Palestinian civilians, using antipersonnel weapons, bombs and rockets.[41] This raid, unusual in that it was reported, aroused no interest or concern, perhaps because it was apparently a "retaliation": namely, retaliation against the UN Security Council, which had just agreed to devote a session to the peace proposals backed by Syria, Jordan, Egypt and the PLO, discussed in chapter 1.

The story continues with little change. In early 1986, while the eyes of the world were focused in horror on the lunatic terrorists in the Arab world, the press reported that Israeli tank cannon poured fire into the village of Sreifa in southern Lebanon, aiming at 30 houses from which the IDF claimed they had been fired upon by "armed terrorists" resisting their military actions in the course of what they described as a search for two Israeli soldiers who had been "kidnapped" in the Israeli "security zone" in Lebanon. Largely kept from the American press was the report by the UN peace-keeping forces that Israeli troops "went really crazy" in these operations, locking up entire villages, preventing the UN troops from sending in water, milk and oranges to the villagers subjected to "interrogation" – meaning brutal torture of men and women by Israeli forces, and by their local mercenaries with IDF troops standing by. The IDF then departed, taking away many villagers including pregnant women, some brought to Israel in further violation of international law, destroying houses and looting and wrecking others, while Shimon Peres said that Israel's search for its kidnapped soldiers "expresses our attitude towards the value of human life and dignity."[42]

A month later, on March 24, Lebanese radio reported that Israeli forces, either IDF or SLA mercenaries, shelled Nabatiya killing three civilians and wounding 22 as "shells slammed into the marketplace in the center of town at daybreak as crowds gathered for trading." The attack was allegedly in retaliation for an attack on Israel's mercenary forces in southern Lebanon. A leader of the Shi'ite Amal vowed that "Israeli settlements and installations will not be beyond the blows of the resistance." On March 27, a Katyusha rocket struck a schoolyard in northern Israel, injuring five people, and eliciting an Israeli attack on Palestinian refugee camps near Sidon, killing ten people and wounding 22, while Israel's northern commander stated over Israeli Army radio that the IDF had not determined whether the rocket had been fired by Shi'ite or Palestinian guerrillas. On April 7, Israeli planes bombed the same camps and a neighboring village, killing two and wounding 20, claiming that terrorists had set out from there with the intent of killing Israeli citizens.[43]

Of all these events, only the rocket attack on northern Israel merited anguished TV coverage and general outrage at "the evil scourge of terrorism," though this was somewhat muted because of the mass hysteria then being orchestrated over a Nicaraguan "invasion" of Honduras, as the Nicaraguan Army exercised its legal right of hot pursuit in driving out of its territory terrorist gangs dispatched by their U.S. directors in a show of force just prior to the Senate vote on Contra aid; recall that the only serious issue under debate in the terrorist state is whether the proxy army can accomplish the goals assigned them by their master.[44] Israel, in contrast, was not exercising a legal right of hot pursuit in shelling and bombing towns and refugee camps, nor have its acts of wholesale terrorism and outright aggression in Lebanon ever fallen under this concept. But as a client-state, Israel inherits from the emperor the right of terrorism, torture and aggression. And Nicaragua, as an enemy, plainly lacks the right to defend its territory from U.S. international terrorism. Consequently, it is natural that Israel's actions should be ignored, or dismissed as legitimate retaliation, while Congress, across the narrow spectrum, denounced the "Nicaraguan Marxist-Leninists" for this renewed demonstration of the threat they pose to regional peace and stability.

The Israeli invasion of Lebanon in June 1982 too is regularly presented in properly sanitized form. Shimon Peres writes that the "Peace for Galilee" operation was fought "in order to insure that the Galilee will no longer be shelled by Katyusha rockets." Eric Breindel explains that "of course, the principal aim of the Israeli invasion in 1982" was "to protect the Galilee region . . . from Katyusha-rocket attacks and other shelling from Lebanon." The news pages of the *Times* inform us that the invasion began "after attacks by Palestine Liberation Organization guerrillas on Israel's northern settlements," and (without comment) that Israeli leaders "said they wanted to end the rocket and shelling attacks on Israel's northern border," which "has been accomplished for the three years the Israeli Army has spent in Lebanon." Henry Kamm adds that "For nearly three years, the people of Qiryat Shemona have not slept in their bomb shelters, and parents have not worried when their children went out to school or to play. The Soviet-made Katyusha rockets, which for many years struck this town near the Lebanese border at random intervals, have not fallen since Israel invaded Lebanon in June 1982." And Thomas Friedman observes that "If rockets again rain down on Israel's northern border after all that has been expended on Lebanon, the Israeli public will be outraged"; ". . . right now there are no rockets landing in northern Israel . . . and if large-scale attacks begin afresh on Israel's northern border that minority [that favors keeping the army in Lebanon] could grow into a majority again." "Operation Peace for Galilee – the Israeli invasion of Lebanon – was originally undertaken" to protect the civilian population from Palestinian gunners, Friedman reports in one of the numerous human interest stories on the travail of the suffering Israelis. Political figures regularly expound the same doctrine. Zbigniew Brzezinski writes that "the increased Syrian military presence and the use of Lebanon by the Palestine Liberation Organization for incursions against Israel precipitated the Israeli invasion [of 1982]," and Ronald Reagan, in a yet another display of moral cowardice, asks us to "remember that when [the invasion] all started, Israel, because of the violations of its own northern border by the Palestinians, the P.L.O., had gone all the way to Beirut," where it was "10,000 Palestinians [!] who had been bringing ruin down on Beirut," not the bombers whom he was supporting.[45]

These and innumerable other accounts, many with vivid descriptions of the torment of the people of the Galilee subjected to random Katyusha bombardment, help create the approved picture of Soviet-armed Palestinian fanatics, a central component of the Russian-based international terror network, who compel Israel to invade and strike Palestinian refugee camps and other targets, as any state would do, to defend its people from merciless terrorist attack.

The real world, once again, is rather different. David Shipler writes that "In the four years between the previous Israeli invasion of southern Lebanon in 1978 and the invasion of June 6, 1982, a total of 29 people were killed in northern Israel in all forms of attacks from Lebanon, including shelling and border crossings by terrorists," but that for a year before the 1982 invasion, "the border was quiet."[46] This report is unusual in at least approaching half-truth. While the PLO refrained from cross-border actions for a year prior to the Israeli invasion, the border was far from quiet, since Israeli terror continued, killing many civilians; the border was "quiet" only in the racist terms of U.S. discourse, once again. Furthermore, neither Shipler nor his associates recall that while 29 people were killed in northern Israel from 1978, thousands were killed by Israeli bombardments in Lebanon, barely noted in the U.S., and rarely "retaliatory."

The bombardments from 1978 were a central element of the Camp David "peace process," which, predictably, freed Israel to extend its takeover and repression in the occupied territories while attacking its northern neighbor, with the main Arab deterrent (Egypt) now removed from the conflict and U.S. military support rapidly increasing. William Quandt notes further that "the Israeli operational planning for the invasion of Lebanon against the PLO [in 1981–2] seems to coincide with the consolidation of the Egyptian–Israeli peace treaty." It should be noted that the obvious significance of the Camp David agreements, though virtually inexpressible in the U.S. at the time and since, is understood by competent American journalists. Thus in an interview in Israel, David Shipler says that "On the Israeli side, it seems to me that the peace treaty set up the situation for the war in Lebanon. With Egypt no longer a confrontation state, Israel felt free to initiate a war in Lebanon, something it probably would not have dared to do before the peace treaty . . . It is an irony that the war in Lebanon could not have taken place without the peace treaty"; hardly an irony, but an intrinsic part of the process.[47] To my knowledge, he did not write that in the *Times* during his five years as its correspondent in Israel, ending in June 1984, or since.

Shipler adds, "I think there would not have been such tremendous opposition to the war among Israelis without this same peace treaty." Having been in Israel at the time, he can hardly fail to know that the "tremendous opposition to the war" is a *post hoc* propaganda fabrication designed to restore the image of "the beautiful Israel." Opposition was in fact slight until the postwar Sabra-Shatila massacres (when supporters of the war in the U.S. too deserted the sinking ship, constructing a fraudulent history of "earlier opposition," much as in the case of the Indochina war), and later the mounting costs of the occupation.[48]

Turning to the real world, consider first the immediate background of the "Peace for Galilee" operation. The PLO observed the U.S.-arranged cease-fire of July 1981 despite repeated Israeli efforts to evoke some action that could be used as a pretext for the planned invasion, including bombardment in late April 1982 killing two dozen people, sinking of fishing boats, etc. The only exceptions were a light retaliation in May after Israeli bombardment, and a response to heavy Israeli bombing and ground attacks in Lebanon in June that had caused many civilian casualties. These Israeli attacks were in "retaliation" for the attempted assassination of the Israeli Ambassador in London by Abu Nidal, a sworn enemy of the PLO, who did not even have an office in Lebanon – again, the familiar story of "retaliation." It was this assassination attempt that was used as the pretext for the long-planned invasion.

The *New Republic* informs us that the successes of UN negotiator Brian Urquhart "have been minor, somehow forgettable: his negotiation of a PLO cease-fire [*sic*] in southern Lebanon in 1981, for instance."[49] That strict party line journals should prefer to "forget" the facts is not surprising, but the prevalence of such convenient lapses of memory is noteworthy.

The events of July 1981 follow pretty much the same pattern. On May 28, Ze'ev Schiff and Ehud Ya'ari write, Prime Minister Menachem Begin and Chief-of-Staff Rafael Eitan "took another step that would bring their country appreciably closer to a war in Lebanon with an action that was essentially calculated towards that end"; namely, they broke the cease-fire with bombing of "PLO concentrations" (a term commonly used to refer to Israeli targets, whatever they are) in southern Lebanon. The attacks continued from air and sea until June 3, Schiff and Ya'ari continue, while "the Palestinians responded gingerly for fear that a vigorous reaction would only provoke a crushing Israeli ground operation." A cease-fire was again established, broken again by Israel on July 10, with renewed bombardments. This time there was a Palestinian reaction, with rocket attacks that caused panic in the northern Galilee followed by heavy Israeli bombing of Beirut and other civilian targets. By the time a cease-fire was declared on July 24, some 450 Arabs – nearly all Lebanese civilians – and six Israelis were killed.[50]

Of this story, all that is remembered is the torment of the northern Galilee, subjected to random Katyusha bombing by PLO terrorists that finally provoked Israel to retaliate in its June 1982 invasion of Lebanon. This is sometimes true even of serious journalists who do not simply provide a pipeline for official propaganda. Edward Walsh writes that "the repeated rocket attacks in 1981 had put [Qiryat Shemona] once again under siege," describing the "distraught parents" and the terror caused by "the pounding of artillery and rocket barrages from the nearby Palestinian bases" in 1981, with no further word on what was happening. Curtis Wilkie, one of the more skeptical and perceptive of American journalists in the Middle East, writes that Qiryat Shemona "came under withering fire from Palestinian Liberation Organization forces in 1981; the rain of Soviet-made Katyusha rockets was so intense at one point that those residents who had not fled were forced to spend eight consecutive days and nights in bomb shelters"; again, with no further word on the reasons for this "withering fire" or on the mood in Beirut and other civilian areas where hundreds were killed in the murderous Israeli bombardment.[51]

The example gives some further insight into the concepts of "terrorism" and "retaliation," as interpreted within the U.S. ideological system, and into the assumptions which, as a matter of course, exclude the suffering of the primary victims, for the usual reasons.

The official story that "the rocket and shelling attacks on Israel's northern border" were ended thanks to the "Peace for Galilee" operation (*NYT*; see above) is doubly false. First, the border was "quiet" for a year prior to the invasion apart from Israeli terror attacks and provocations; and the major rocket attacks, in July 1981, were a response to Israeli terror which in this incident alone exacted a toll almost 100 times greater than the PLO response. Second, in sharp contrast to the preceding period, rocket attacks against Israel began shortly after the invasion ended, from early 1983, and continued. A group of dissident Israeli journalists report that in two weeks of September 1985, 14 Katyusha rockets were fired at the Galilee. Furthermore, "terrorist attacks" increased by 50 percent in the West Bank in the months following the war, and by the end of 1983 had increased by 70 percent since the war in Lebanon, becoming a severe threat by 1985, not a surprising consequence of savage atrocities and the destruction of the civil society and political system of the Palestinians.[52]

The real reason for the 1982 invasion was not the threat to the northern Galilee, as sanitized history would have it, but rather the opposite, as was plausibly explained shortly after the invasion was launched by Israel's leading specialist on the Palestinians, Hebrew University Professor Yehoshua Porath (a "moderate" in Israeli parlance, who supports the Labor Party's "Jordanian solution" for the Palestinians). The decision to invade, he suggests, "flowed from the very fact that the cease-fire had been observed." This was a "veritable catastrophe" for the Israeli government, because it threatened the policy of evading a political settlement. "The government's hope," he continued, "is that the stricken PLO, lacking a logistic and territorial base, will return to its earlier terrorism; it will carry out bombings throughout the world, hijack airplanes, and murder many Israelis," and thus "will lose part of the political legitimacy it has gained" and "undercut the danger" of negotiations with representative Palestinians, which would threaten the policy – shared by both major political groupings – of keeping effective control over the occupied territories.[53]

The plausible assumption of the Israeli leadership was that those who shape public opinion in the United States – the only country that counts, now that Israel has chosen to become a mercenary state serving the interests of its provider – could be counted on to obliterate the actual history and portray the terrorist acts resulting from Israeli aggression and atrocities as random acts of violence ascribable to defects in Arab character and culture, if not racial deficiencies. Subsequent U.S. commentary on terrorism fulfills these expectations with some precision, a major propaganda coup for state terrorists in Jerusalem and Washington.

The basic points are understood well enough in Israel. Prime Minister Yitzhak Shamir stated over Israeli television that Israel went to war because there was "a terrible danger . . . Not so much a military one as a political one," prompting the fine Israeli satirist, B. Michael, to write that "the lame excuse of a military danger or a danger to the Galilee is dead," once we "have removed the political danger" by striking first; now, "Thank God, there is no one to talk to." Columnist Aaron Bachar comments that "it is easy to understand the mood of the Israeli leadership. Arafat has been accused of steadily moving towards some kind of political accommodation with Israel" and "in the eyes of the Israeli Administration, this is the worst possible threat" – including Labor as well as Likud. Journalist/historian Benny Morris observes that "the PLO held its fire along the northern border for a whole year, on a number of occasions omitting completely to react to Israeli actions (designed specifically to draw PLO fire on the North)." For the senior IDF officers, he continues, "the war's inevitability rested on the PLO as a political threat to Israel and to Israel's hold on the occupied territories," since "Palestinian hopes inside and outside the occupied territories for the maturation of nationalist aspirations rested on and revolved about the PLO." Like every sane commentator, he ridicules the hysterical talk about captured weapons and the PLO military threat, and predicts that "the Shi'ites of West Beirut, many of them refugees from previous Israeli bombardments of Southern Lebanon in the 1970s, will probably remember the IDF siege of June–August [1982] for a long time," with long-term repercussions in "Shi'ite terrorism against Israeli targets."[54]

On the right wing, Likud Knesset member Ehud Olmert commented that "the danger posed by the PLO to Israel did not lie in its extremism, but in the fictitious moderation Arafat managed to display without ever losing sight of his ultimate aim, which is the destruction of Israel" (arguably true, in the sense in which David Ben-Gurion, while in power, never lost sight of his ultimate aim of expanding to "the limits of Zionist aspirations," including much of the surrounding countries and on some occasions, the "biblical borders" from the Nile to Iraq, while the native population would somehow be transferred). Former West Bank Administrator Professor Menachem Milson states that "it is a mistake to think that the threat to Israel represented by the PLO is essentially a military one; rather, it is a political and ideological one." Defense Minister Ariel Sharon explained just before the invasion that "quiet on the West Bank" requires "the destruction of the PLO in Lebanon," and his ultra-right cohort, Chief of Staff Rafael Eitan, commented afterwards that the war was a success, because it severely weakened "the political status" of the PLO and "the struggle of the PLO for a Palestinian state" while enforcing Israel's capacity "to block any such purpose." Commenting on such statements, Israeli military historian Uri Milshtein (a supporter of Labor's "Jordanian solution") observes that among the goals of the invasion in the Sharon-Eitan conception were: "to establish a New Order[55] in Lebanon and the Middle East," "to advance the process of Sadatization in several Arab states," "to guarantee the annexation of Judea and Samaria [the West Bank] to the state of Israel," and "perhaps a solution of the Palestinian problem."

Knesset Member Amnon Rubinstein, much admired in the U.S. for his liberal and dovish stance, writes that even though the cease-fire had been observed "more or less" (to translate: observed by the PLO but not by Israel), nevertheless the invasion of Lebanon was "justified" because of a potential, not actual military threat: the arms and ammunition in southern Lebanon were intended for eventual use against Israel. Consider the implications of this argument in other contexts, even if we were to take seriously the claims about a potential PLO military threat to Israel.[56]

Note that Rubinstein anticipated the interesting doctrine enunciated by the Reagan Administration in justifying its April 1986 bombing of Libya in "self-defense against future attack," to which we turn in the next chapter.

American supporters of Israeli atrocities occasionally acknowledge the same truths. Just before the invasion, *New Republic* editor Martin Peretz, echoing Sharon and Eitan, urged that Israel should administer to the PLO a "lasting military defeat" in Lebanon that "will clarify to the Palestinians in the West Bank that their struggle for an independent state has suffered a setback of many years," so that "the Palestinians will be turned into just another crushed nation, like the Kurds or the Afghans." And Democratic Socialist Michael Walzer, who sees the solution for Palestinian Arabs – within Israel as well – in transfer of those "marginal to the nation" (essentially, the position of the racist Rabbi Kahane; see chapter 1, note 7), explained in the *New Republic* after the war that "I certainly welcome the political *defeat* of the PLO, and I believe that the limited military operation required to inflict that defeat can be defended under the theory of just war."[57]

It is of some interest to observe the convergence on these issues between the Israeli ultra-right and American left-liberalism.

In short, the goals of the war were political, the occupied territories being one prime target, the "New Order" in Lebanon being another. The tale about protecting the border from terrorism is Agitprop. If Palestinian terrorism can be revived, so much the better. And if we can't pin the blame on Arafat, he can at least be stigmatized as "the founding father of contemporary Palestinian violence" (*New Republic*) so that his efforts at political settlement can be evaded.

The problem of evading a political settlement did not, however, end with the destruction of the political base for the PLO, as had been hoped, so it remained necessary to be on the alert to combat the threat and defend the doctrinal truth that the U.S. and Israel seek peace but are blocked by Arab rejectionism. Thus, in April–May 1984, Arafat made a series of statements in Europe and Asia calling for negotiations with Israel leading to mutual recognition. The offer was immediately rejected by Israel, ignored by the U.S. A UPI story on Arafat's proposals was the featured front-page story in the *San Francisco Examiner*, and the facts were reported without prominence in the local quality press. The national press suppressed the story outright, apart from a bare mention in the *Washington Post* some weeks later. The *New York Times* even banned letters referring to the facts, while continuing (along with others) to denounce Arafat for his unwillingness to pursue a diplomatic course. In general, the more influential the journal, the more it was determined to suppress the facts, an entirely natural stance given the position of the U.S. government on the issues.[58]

Knowledgeable Israelis are of course aware of Arafat's stand. Former chief of military intelligence General (ret.) Yehoshaphat Harkabi, an Arabist and well-known hawk for many years, notes that "the PLO wishes a political settlement because it knows that the alternative is terrible and will lead to total destruction." "Arafat, like Hussein and the Arabs of the West Bank, is afraid that if there will not be a settlement, Israel will explode, and with it all its neighbors, including the Palestinians." Therefore "Arafat adopts relatively moderate positions with regard to Israel."[59]

These observations underscore several points: 1) there is a crucial political context in which terrorism must be understood, if we are to be serious about it; 2) it is the other fellow's crimes, not our own comparable or worse ones, that constitute "terrorism" – in this case, Palestinian but not Israeli or American crimes; 3) the concepts of "terrorism" and "retaliation" are used as terms of propaganda, not description. Crucially, the hysteria fanned over carefully selected acts of terrorism – those by Arabs, whether Palestinians, Lebanese Shi'ites, Libyans, Syrians, or even Iranians, who can count as Arabs for this purpose since 1979 – is designed to achieve certain specific political goals. Further inquiry reinforces these conclusions.

Consider again the matter of retaliation. The first post-1981 rocket attack by Shi'ites against Qiryat Shemona was in December 1985, after over three years of a military occupation of extreme brutality, which reached its peak during the Iron Fist operations under Shimon Peres in early 1985. But the occasionally reported savagery of the occupiers fails to convey anything like the full story, since it ignores the day-to-day reality; the same is true of the occasional reporting of Israeli atrocities in the occupied territories, which fails to convey the true picture of brutal degradation, repression, exploitation of cheap (including child) labor, harsh control over political and cultural life and curtailment of economic development. A more instructive picture is given by Julie Flint, recounting "the story of life, and death, in one southern Lebanese village" of Shi'ites a month before the rocket attack. Kfar Roummane had been "a prosperous agricultural town of 8,000 people" near Nabatiya during the period when southern Lebanon was subjected only to PLO terror, according to official history (see note 37). After what the *New York Times* called its "liberation" from PLO rule, it was surrounded by "two huge fortifications built by the Israelis and their Lebanese proxy, the South Lebanon Army," from which there is constant sniping and shelling, "sometimes from dawn to dusk, sometimes only for a few hours," with many casualties, leading to the flight of 6,000 people and leaving three-fourths of the town uninhabitable in this "dying village" where there is no sign of resistance activities, and little likelihood of it among the apolitical farmers on a bare expanse of flat hillside.[60]

Was the shelling of Qiryat Shemona "unprovoked terrorism" or "retaliation," even putting aside the murderous atrocities of the Peres–Rabin Iron Fist operations?

A look at the lives of the terrorists is also instructive. One was interviewed by the *Washington Post* in a five-part series on terrorism, selective in the conventional way. Serving an 18-year sentence in an Israeli jail, he was chosen as "in many ways typical of terrorists now in jail from London to Kuwait." "In his life, a personal tragedy (the death of his father in a bomb blast in Jerusalem in 1946) combined with the discovery of a system of belief (Marxism) to plunge him into a world of cold-blooded political murder." "The bomb that killed his father and more than 90 other persons was set by the Irgun Zionist underground group, led by Menachem Begin, at British military headquarters in what is now the King David Hotel" – as it was then.[61] He "was introduced to Marxism, he said, by the 'reality' of conditions in Palestinian camps" in the occupied West Bank. The "reality" of the occupied territories, not only in the camps, is quite real, and is bitter and cruel, outside of the editorial pages of the nation's press, where we can learn that the occupation was "a model of future cooperation" and an "experiment in Arab-Israeli coexistence."[62] To explain is not to justify, but plainly some questions arise about the easy use of such terms as "retaliation."

Or consider Suleiman Khater, the Egyptian soldier who murdered seven Israeli tourists on a Sinai beach on October 5, 1985. The Egyptian press reported that his mother said she was "happy that these Jews had died" and a doctor in his village of Baher al-Bakr described the shootings as a warning against the "illusory peace" between Egypt and Israel. Why this shocking reaction to an unspeakable crime? The Tunis bombing a few days earlier might suggest a reason, but there may be others. In 1970, Israeli warplanes bombed Baher al-Bakr, killing 47 schoolchildren, during the "war of attrition," when extensive Israeli bombing, some deep inside Egypt, drove a million and a half civilians from the Suez Canal area, threatening general war when Soviet-piloted MIGs defending inner Egypt were shot down by newly acquired Israeli Phantom jets over Egyptian territory.[63]

Something is perhaps missing, then, when the *Times* Israel correspondent blandly reports that Khater "acted out of motives that were nationalist and anti-Israel"[64] – something that would surely not have been ignored had the situation been reversed.

David Hirst observes that "the main, or the really significant center of international terrorism [in the Western sense of the term] is Lebanon. It either breeds its own terrorists, or serves as a congenial home for imported ones," either Palestinians, who "have known little but bombardment, murder, massacre and mutilation, encircling hatred, fear and insecurity," or Lebanese whose society was given its final blow by the U.S.-backed Israeli aggression and its aftermath; ". . . one conviction is rooted in the minds of the youth of today" among these groups: "that under President Reagan, who has carried his country's traditional partisanship with Israel to unprecedented lengths, the U.S. is the incorrigible upholder of a whole existing order so intolerable that any means now justifies its destruction. The terrorist impulse may be strongest among the Palestinians, but it can also be Lebanese, Arab, or – in its most spectacular manifestation – Shi'ite."

The essential point was expressed by Yehoshaphat Harkabi: "To offer an honorable solution to the Palestinians respecting their right to self-determination: that is the solution of the problem of terrorism. When the swamp disappears, there will be no more mosquitoes."[65]

U.S.–Israeli wholesale terrorism and aggression have surely contributed to the situation Hirst describes, predictably and perhaps consciously so (see above), and both terrorist states are presumably satisfied with the outcome, which provides them with a justification to persist in their course of rejectionism and violence. Furthermore, the retail terrorism to which they have contributed can be exploited to induce a proper sense of fear and mobilization among the population, as required for more general ends. All that is necessary is a doctrinal system that will shriek in chorus when necessary and suppress any understanding of U.S. initiatives, their pattern, their sources, and their motivation. On this score, policy-makers need have few concerns, the record shows.

Terrorist acts are characteristically described by their perpetrators as "retaliatory" (or, in the case of U.S. and Israeli terrorism, as "preemptive"). Thus the bombing of Tunis was in alleged retaliation for the murders in Larnaca, as noted, though there was barely a pretense that the victims of the Tunis bombing had any connection with the Larnaca atrocity. The latter was also justified as "retaliatory," a response to Israeli hijacking of ships travelling from Cyprus to Lebanon.[66] The former claim was accepted in the U.S. as legitimate, the latter ignored or derided, a distinction based on ideological commitment, as is the norm.

Putting aside the justifications offered for terrorist violence and keeping to the factual record, there is no doubt that Israel *has* been carrying out hijacking operations and kidnapping at sea for many years, with little notice and no concern in the U.S. over this crime, which arouses great passion and anger when the perpetrators are Arabs. It was not even deemed necessary to report the fact that the Israeli High Court in effect gave its stamp of approval to this procedure. In the case of an Arab who appealed against his imprisonment on grounds that he was captured outside of Israeli territorial waters, the High Court ruled that "the legality of sentencing and imprisonment is unaffected by the means whereby the suspect was brought to Israeli territory," and held (once again) that an Israeli court may sentence a person for actions outside of Israel that it regards as criminal. In this case, the Court stated that "security reasons" made it necessary to keep the appellant in prison.[67]

Turning to the historical record, in 1976, according to Knesset member (General, ret.) Mattityahu Peled, the Israeli Navy began to capture boats belonging to Lebanese Muslims – turning them over to Israel's Lebanese Christian allies, who killed them – in an effort to abort steps towards conciliation that had been arranged between the PLO and Israel. Prime Minister Rabin conceded the facts but said that the boats were captured prior to these arrangements, while Defense Minister Shimon Peres refused to comment. After a prisoner exchange in November 1983, a front-page story in the *Times* mentioned in its eighteenth paragraph that 37 of the Arab prisoners, who had been held at the notorious Ansar prison camp, "had been seized recently by the Israeli Navy as they tried to make their way from Cyprus to Tripoli," north of Beirut, an observation that merited no comment there or elsewhere.[68] By the same logic, British forces could have sent agents to kidnap Zionists in the United States or on the high seas in 1947, placing them in prison camps without charge or convicting them of support for terrorism.

In June, 1984, Israel hijacked a ferryboat operating between Cyprus and Lebanon five miles off the Lebanese coast with a burst of machinegun fire and forced it to Haifa, where nine people were removed and held, eight Lebanese and the ninth Syrian. Five were freed after interrogation and four held, including one woman and a schoolboy returning from England for a holiday in Beirut; two were released two weeks later, while the fate of the others remains unreported. The matter was considered so insignificant that one has to search for tiny items in the back pages even to learn this much about the fate of the kidnapped passengers. The London *Observer* suggested a "political motive": to compel passengers to use the ferry operating from the Maronite port of Jounieh instead of Muslim West Beirut or to signal to the Lebanese that they are "powerless" and must come to terms with Israel. Lebanon denounced this "act of piracy," which Godfrey Jansen described as "another item" in Israel's "long list of international thuggery." "To maintain the maritime terrorist fiction," he adds, "the Israelis then bombed and bombarded a small island off Tripoli which was said to be a base for PLO seaborne operations," a claim that he dismisses as "absurd." The Lebanese police reported that 15 were killed, 20 wounded and 20 missing, all Lebanese, fishermen and children at a Sunni boy scout camp which was the "worst hit" target.[69]

In its report on the Israeli "interception" (more accurately, hijacking) of the ferryboat, the *Times* observes that prior to the 1982 war, "the Israeli Navy regularly intercepted ships bound for or leaving the ports of Tyre and Sidon in the south and searched them for guerrillas," as usual accepting Israeli claims at face value; Syrian "interception" of civilian Israeli ships on a similar pretext might be regarded a bit differently. Similarly, Israel's hijacking of a Libyan civilian jet on February 4, 1986 was accepted with equanimity, criticized, if at all, as an error based on faulty intelligence.[70] On April 25, 1985, several Palestinians were kidnapped from civilian boats operating between Lebanon and Cyprus and sent to secret destinations in Israel, a fact that became public knowledge (in Israel) when one was interviewed on Israeli television, leading to an appeal to the High Court of Justice for information; presumably there are others, unknown.[71]

None of these cases, most of them known only through incidental comment, arouses any interest or concern, any more than when it is reported in passing that Arab "security prisoners" released in an exchange with Syria were in fact "Druze residents of villages in the Israeli-annexed portion of the strategic Golan Heights."[72] It is considered Israel's prerogative to carry out hijacking of ships and kidnappings, at will, as well as bombardment of what it will call "terrorist targets," with the approval of articulate opinion in the United States, whatever the facts may be.

We might tarry a moment over the Israeli attack on the island off Tripoli north of Beirut, in which Lebanese fishermen and boy scouts at a camp were killed. This received scant notice, but that is the norm in the case of such regular Israeli terrorist atrocities, of which this is far from the most serious. Palestinian attacks fare differently. None is remembered with more horror than the atrocity at Ma'alot in 1974, where 22 members of a paramilitary youth group were killed in an exchange of fire after Moshe Dayan had refused, over the objections of General Mordechai Gur, to consider negotiations on the terrorists' demands for the release of Palestinian prisoners.[73] One might ask why the murder of Lebanese boy scouts is a lesser atrocity – in fact, none at all, since it was perpetrated by "a country that cares for human life" (*Washington Post*) with a "high moral purpose" (*Time*) perhaps unique in history.[74]

Two days before the Ma'alot attack, Israeli jets had bombed the Lebanese village of El-Kfeir, killing four civilians. According to Edward Said, the Ma'alot attack was "preceded by weeks of sustained Israeli napalm bombing of Palestinian refugee camps in southern Lebanon," with over 200 killed. At the time, Israel was engaged in large-scale scorched earth operations in southern Lebanon, with air, artillery and gunboat attacks and commando operations using shells, bombs, anti-personnel weapons and napalm, with probably thousands killed (the West could not be troubled, so no accurate figures are available here) and hundreds of thousands driven north to slums around Beirut.[75] Interest was slight and reporting scanty. None of this is recorded in the annals of terrorism; nor did it even happen, as far as sanitized history is concerned, though the murderous Palestinian terrorist attacks of the early 1970s were (rightly of course) bitterly condemned, and still stand as proof that the Palestinians cannot be a partner to negotiations over their fate. Meanwhile the media are regularly condemned as overly critical of Israel and even "pro-PLO" – a propaganda coup of quite monumental proportions.

We might note the interpretation of these events offered by Israeli leaders honored as moderates, for example Yitzhak Rabin, who was Ambassador to Washington and then Prime Minister during the period of the worst Israeli atrocities in Lebanon, pre-Camp David 1978: "we could not ignore the plight of the civil population in southern Lebanon . . . It was our humanitarian duty to aid the population of the area and prevent it from being wiped out by the hostile terrorists."[76] Reviewers of Rabin's memoirs found nothing amiss in these words, so effectively has an ideologically serviceable history been constructed, and so profound is anti-Arab racism in the West.

It should also be noted that Israel is not alone in enjoying the right of piracy and hijacking. A Tass report condemning the *Achille Lauro* hijacking in October 1985 accused the United States of hypocrisy because two men who hijacked a Soviet airliner, killing a stewardess and wounding other crew members, were given refuge in the U.S., which refused extradition.[77]

The case is not exactly well known, and the charge of hypocrisy might appear to have a certain merit. The case is also not unique. Abraham Sofaer, legal advisor to the State Department, observes that "During the 1950s, despite America's strong opposition to aircraft hijackings, the United States and its Western allies refused requests from Czechoslovakia, the U.S.S.R., Poland, Yugoslavia and other communist regimes for the return of persons who hijacked planes, trains and ships to escape." Sofaer claims that the U.S. "reexamined its policy" in the late 1960s and early 1970s "when aircraft hijacking reached epidemic proportions" and was posing "too serious a problem and too great a threat to the safety of innocent passengers to be tolerated."[78] Filling in the blanks, hijacking began to be directed against the U.S. and its allies and thus fell under the category of terrorism instead of heroic resistance to oppression.

One might also mention the first airplane hijacking in the Middle East, which is also not familiar fare. It was carried out by Israel in December 1954, when a Syrian airways civilian jet was intercepted by Israeli fighters and forced to land at Lydda airport. Chief of Staff Moshe Dayan's intent was "to get hostages in order to obtain the release of our prisoners in Damascus," Prime Minister Moshe Sharett wrote in his personal diary. The prisoners were Israeli soldiers who had been captured on a spy mission inside Syria; it was Dayan, we recall, who, 20 years later, ordered the rescue attempt that led to the death of Israeli teenagers in Ma'alot who had been taken hostage in an effort to obtain the release of Palestinian prisoners in Israel. Sharett wrote privately that "we had no justification whatsoever to seize the plane" and that he had "no reason to doubt the truth of the factual affirmation of the U.S. State Department that our action was without precedent in the history of international practice." But the incident has disappeared from history, so that Israeli UN Ambassador Benjamin Netanyahu, now a much-admired commentator on international terrorism, may appear on national television and accuse the PLO of "inventing" the hijacking of airplanes and even the killing of diplomats, with no fear of contradiction.[79]

As for the killing of diplomats, we might only recall the assassination of UN Mediator Folke Bernadotte in 1948 by a terrorist group led by Netanyahu's immediate superior, Foreign Minister Yitzhak Shamir, one of the three commanders who gave the orders for the assassination (a second, now dead, was a respected commentator in the Israeli press for many years, as is the third). A close friend of David Ben-Gurion privately confessed that he was one of the assassins, but Ben-Gurion kept it secret, and the Israeli government arranged for the escape from prison and departure from the country of those responsible. In his eyewitness account, Zionist historian Jon Kimche writes that "there was no nation-wide outcry or determination to catch the perpetrators" and "not much moral indignation." "The attitude of the majority was that another enemy of the Jews had fallen by the wayside." The assassination "was condemned, regretted and deplored because it would cast reflections on Israel, and make the work of her diplomats more difficult; not because it was wrong in itself to resort to assassination."[80]

Honoring of terrorists who took part in national struggles is quite standard, of course, in the U.S. as well. But in the contrived selective memory, only the actions of enemies find a place as "the evil scourge of terrorism."

After the hijacking of the *Achille Lauro* in retaliation for the Tunis bombing, the issue of ship hijacking became a major Western concern. A study by Reuters news agency concluded that "there have been just a handful of ship hijackings since 1961," giving a few examples by Muslims; the Israeli hijackings were not on the list.[81]

Hijacking is not the only form of terrorism that escapes this category when it is carried out by our friends. UN Ambassador Jeane Kirkpatrick explained that the blowing up of the Greenpeace anti-nuclear protest ship *Rainbow Warrior* by French agents with one man murdered was not terrorism: "I'd like to say that the French clearly did not intend to attack civilians and bystanders and maim, torture or kill," an appeal that other terrorists could offer with ease. In its lead editorial, under the title "Mitterrand's Finest Hour," the *Asian Wall St. Journal* wrote that "The Greenpeace campaign is fundamentally violent and dangerous . . . That the French government was prepared to use force against the *Rainbow Warrior* . . . suggests that the government had its priorities straight." In the *New York Times*, David Housego reviews a book on the affair, criticizing the French for "blunders" and "a bad mistake"; "there was no need" to blow up the ship and the French could have "gained the same objective with far less unfavorable publicity." There is no hint that some harsher words might be in order. Given these "blunders," Housego concludes that "it was difficult to justify not incriminating [Defense Minister] Mr. Hernu and hard to blame the New Zealanders for imprisoning the French officers."[82] Housego discusses the comparison with Watergate, missing the major analogy: in that case too there was a great hullabaloo about "blunders" and petty criminality, and much self-congratulation on the part of the media, while both Congress and the media ignored as irrelevant the far more serious crimes of the Nixon Administration and its predecessors revealed at the same time.[83] The emperor is exempt from the charge of terrorism or other crimes, and his allies often share the same privilege. They are guilty at worst of "blunders."

George Shultz may well deserve a prize for hypocrisy on this score. While urging an "active" drive on terrorism, he described as "insidious" the claim that "one man's terrorist is another man's freedom fighter":

> Freedom fighters or revolutionaries don't blow up buses containing non-combatants. Terrorist murderers do. Freedom fighters don't assassinate innocent businessmen or hijack innocent men, women and children. Terrorist murderers do . . . The resistance fighters in Afghanistan do not destroy villages or kill the helpless. The Contras in Nicaragua do not blow up school buses or hold mass executions of civilians.

In fact, the terrorists Shultz commands in Nicaragua, as he knows, specialize precisely in murderous attacks on civilians, with torture, rape, mutilation; their odious record of terror is well documented, though ignored and quickly forgotten, even denied by terrorist apologists (see note 16). The resistance fighters in Afghanistan have also carried out brutal atrocities of a sort that would evoke fevered denunciations in the West if the attacking forces (who would then be called "liberators" acting in "self-defense") were American or Israeli. Only a few months before he spoke, Shultz's UNITA friends in Angola were boasting of having shot down civilian airliners with 266 people killed and had released 26 hostages who had been held as long as nine months, including 21 Portuguese, and Spanish and Latin American missionaries; they had also announced "a new campaign of urban terror," Associated Press reported, noting a bombing in Luanda in which 30 people were killed and more than 70 injured when a jeep loaded with dynamite exploded in the city. They had also captured European teachers, doctors, and others; some 140 foreigners the press reported, including 16 British technicians "taken hostage," Jonas Savimbi stated, and not to "be released until Prime Minister Thatcher offered his organization some kind of recognition." Such actions continue regularly, e.g., the blowing up of a hotel in April 1986 with 17 foreign civilians killed and many wounded. Savimbi "is one of the few authentic heroes of our times," Jeane Kirkpatrick declaimed at a Conservative Political Action convention where Savimbi "received enthusiastic applause after vowing to attack American oil installations in his country," a plan to kill Americans that did not prompt the U.S. to invoke the doctrine of "self-defense against future attack" employed to justify the bombing of "mad dog" Qaddafi, just as there was no bombing of Johannesburg when South African mercenaries were captured in May 1985 in northern Angola on a mission to destroy these facilities and kill Americans. A terrorist state must exercise subtle judgments.[84] Savimbi qualifies as a freedom fighter for Shultz, Kirkpatrick and other leading terrorist commanders and advocates primarily because "UNITA is the most extensively backed of South Africa's client groups used to destabilise the neighbouring states."[85]

As for Shultz's *Contra* armies, their prime task, as noted earlier, is to hold the entire civilian population of Nicaragua hostage under the threat of sadistic terror to compel the government to abandon any commitment to the needs of the poor majority, in preference to the "moderate" and "democratic" policy of addressing the transcendent needs of U.S. business and its local associates as in more properly behaved states under the U.S. aegis. But in the cultural climate in which terrorist commanders and apologists thrive, Shultz's statements and others like them pass with barely a raised eyebrow.

Taking of hostages plainly falls under the rubric of terrorism. There is no doubt, then, that Israel was guilty of a serious act of international terrorism when it removed some 1,200 prisoners, mainly Lebanese Shi'ites, to Israel in violation of international law in the course of its retreat from Lebanon, explaining that they would be released "on an unspecified schedule to be determined by the security situation in southern Lebanon" – that is, making it quite clear that they were to be held as hostages, pending a demonstration of "good behavior" on the part of the local population kept under guard by Israeli forces and their mercenaries in the "security zone" in southern Lebanon and in surrounding areas. As Mary McGrory observed in a rare departure from general conformity, the prisoners were "hostages in Israeli jails"; "They are not criminals; they were scooped up as insurance against attack when the Israelis were finally quitting Lebanon." In fact, there was no intention to quit southern Lebanon, where Israel retained its "security zone," and even the partial withdrawal was the achievement of the Lebanese resistance. One hundred and forty prisoners had been secretly removed to Israel in November 1983 in violation of an agreement with the Red Cross to release them in a prisoner exchange, after the closing (temporary, as it turned out) of the Ansar prison camp, the scene of brutal atrocities, frequently described as a "concentration camp" by Israelis who served or visited there and were sickened by the barbarous behavior of the captors. The prisoners were refused even Red Cross visits until July 1984. Israeli Defense Ministry spokesman Nachman Shai stated that 400 of the 766 still in custody in June 1985 had been arrested for "terrorist activities" – meaning resistance to the Israeli military occupation – while "the rest were arrested for less violent forms of political activism or organizing activities designed to undermine the Israeli Army presence in Lebanon, Mr. Shai indicated."[86]

Israel had promised to release 340 of the hostages on June 10, "but canceled the release at the last minute for security reasons that were never fully explained."[87] Four days later, Lebanese Shi'ites, reported to be friends and relatives of the Israeli-held hostages,[88] hijacked TWA flight 847, taking hostages in an attempt to free the hostages held by Israel, evoking another bout of well-orchestrated hysteria in the United States, with overt racist undertones and numerous condemnations of the media for allowing the hijackers an occasional opportunity to explain their position, thus interfering with the discipline deemed appropriate within a free society. The Israeli kidnappers needed no special access to the U.S. media, which were delighted to deliver their message for them, often as "news."

The media are commonly condemned for "supporting terrorism" by allowing terrorists to express their position; the reference is not to the regular appearance of Ronald Reagan, George Shultz, Elliott Abrams and other leading commanders or advocates of terrorism, who present their messages without any rebuttal or comment, providing the framework of concepts and assumptions for news reporting and commentary.

The press dismissed with ridicule the statements of the TWA 847 hijackers that they wished to secure the release of the Israeli-held hostages – who were not hostages in U.S. parlance, since they were held by "our side." The absurdity of the Shi'ite pretense was easily exposed. The distinguished commentator Flora Lewis explained that "it is out of character for militant Shi'ites, who extol martyrdom and show little reluctance to take the lives of others, to be so concerned with the timing of the prisoners' return," another version of the useful concept that the lower orders feel no pain. Citing no evidence, the *Times* editors alleged that "Israel had planned to appease the resentful Shi'ites last week [that is, a few days prior to the TWA hijacking], but was delayed by the kidnapping of some Finnish U.N. troops in Lebanon"; in a 90-word news item, the *Times* had noted the charge by Finland that during this entirely unrelated event, "Israeli officers had watched Lebanese militiamen beat up kidnapped Finnish soldiers serving with the United Nations in Lebanon, but had done nothing to help them" while they "were beaten with iron bars, water hoses and rifles by members of the South Lebanon Army." "There are crimes aplenty here," the *Times* thundered, denouncing the TWA hijackers, the Greek authorities (for their laxity), and even the United States – for "having failed to punish Iran for sheltering the killers of two Americans in a hijacking last year" (see note 77). But the Israeli hostage-taking was not one of these crimes.[89]

Princeton Middle East historian Bernard Lewis, his scholarly reputation rendering evidence irrelevant, asserted unequivocally that "the hijackers or those who sent them must have known perfectly well that the Israelis were already planning to release the Shi'ite and other Lebanese captives, and that a public challenge of this kind could only delay, rather than accelerate, their release." They could proceed "to challenge America, to humiliate Americans" because they knew that the supine media would "provide them with unlimited publicity and perhaps even some form of advocacy." Recall that this is the voice of a respected scholar in a respected journal, a fact that once again yields some insight into the reigning intellectual culture. The editors of the *New Republic* dismissed the Shi'ite plea for release of the Israeli-held hostages as "perfect rubbish": "Hijacking, kidnapping, murder, and massacre are the way Shi'ites and other factions in Lebanon do their political business," and "Everyone knew" that the Israeli-held prisoners were scheduled for release – when Israel was good and ready, if ever. President Reagan escalated the hysteria yet another notch, explaining that the "real goal" of the terrorists is "to expel America from the world," no less. Norman Podhoretz, noting that use of force would probably have led to the death of American hostages, denounced Reagan for failing "to risk life itself [namely, the lives of others] in defense of the national honor"; New York Mayor Edward Koch called for the bombing of Lebanon and Iran, and others struck appropriate heroic poses.[90]

Meanwhile, the careful reader could discover buried in news reports on the hostage crisis that 2,000 Lebanese Shi'ites, including 700 children, fled their homes under shelling by Israel's South Lebanon Army, who also shot at jeeps of the UN peacekeeping forces, while "a combined force of Israeli troops and Christian-led militiamen swept into a south Lebanese village today and seized 19 Shi'ite men, a United Nations spokesman announced."[91]

After the hijacking, Israel began to release its hostages according to its own timetable, perhaps accelerated because the TWA hijacking had focused international attention on its own vastly more significant kidnapping operations. When 300 were released on July 3, Associated Press reported their testimony that they were tortured and starved, while Thomas Friedman of the *Times* heard only that "we were treated well by the Israelis . . ." Reagan wrote a letter to Shimon Peres "saying that the Beirut hostage crisis has strengthened relations between their countries"; nothing was said about the other "hostage crisis," which has been deleted from official history.[92]

The Israeli actions would qualify as hostage-taking were it not that as a client of the emperor who molests the world, Israel is exempt from this charge. But it is important to stress, repeatedly, the nature of the Orwellian concepts of contemporary political discourse, in which such terms as "terrorism" and "hostage" are construed so as to exclude some of the most extreme examples, as in Nicaragua or southern Lebanon, where entire populations are held hostage to ensure obedience to the foreign master.

Keeping just to the Middle East, we should recognize that at some level the matter is well understood by the organizers of international terrorism. The reason for the savage attack on southern Lebanon through the 1970s was explained by the Israeli diplomat Abba Eban, considered a leading dove: "there was a rational prospect, ultimately fulfilled, that affected populations would exert pressure for the cessation of hostilities." Translating into plain language: the population of southern Lebanon was being held hostage to exert pressure on them to compel the Palestinians to accept the status assigned to them by the Labor government represented by Eban, who had declared that the Palestinians "have no role to play" in any peace settlement.[93] Chief of Staff Mordechai Gur explained in 1978 that "For 30 years . . . we have been fighting against a population that lives in villages and cities." He noted such incidents as the bombing of the Jordanian city of Irbid and the expulsion by bombing of tens of thousands of inhabitants of the Jordan valley and a million and a half civilians from the Suez Canal, among other examples, all part of the program of holding civilian populations hostage in an effort to prevent resistance to the political settlement that Israel imposed by force, and then proceeded to maintain while rejecting the possibility of political settlement, for example, Sadat's offer of a full peace treaty on the internationally recognized Egypt–Israel border in 1971. Israel's regular practice of "retaliation" against defenseless civilian targets unrelated to the source of terrorist acts (themselves, often retaliation for earlier Israeli terrorism, and so on, through the familiar, ugly cycle) also reflects the same conception, a departure, by the early 1950s, from Ben-Gurion's earlier dictum that "reaction is inefficient" unless it is precisely focused: "If we know the family – [we must] strike mercilessly, women and children included."[94]

Gur's understanding of Israel's wars is widely shared among the military command. During the Iron Fist operations of early 1985, Defense Minister Yitzhak Rabin warned that if necessary, Israel would conduct "a policy of scorched earth as was the case in the Jordan Valley during the war of attrition" with Egypt. "Lebanon is a more serious source of terror than it was in 1982," he added, with Shi'ite terrorists now holding Western Europe in fear (they did not do so prior to the Israeli invasion of 1982, for unexplained reasons), so that Israel must maintain a zone in the south in which "we may intervene." The veteran paratroop commander Dubik Tamari, who gave the orders to level the Palestinian camp of Ain el-Hilweh by air and artillery bombardment "to save lives" of troops under his command (another exercise of the fabled "purity of arms"), justified the action with the comment that "the State of Israel has been killing civilians from 1947," "purposely killing civilians" as "one goal among others."[95]

Tamari cited as an example the attack on Qibya in 1953, when Ariel Sharon's Unit 101 killed some 70 Arab villagers in their homes in alleged retaliation for a terrorist attack with which they had no connection whatsoever; Ben-Gurion pretended on Israeli radio that the villagers were killed by Israeli civilians enraged by Arab terror, "mostly refugees, people from Arab countries and survivors from the Nazi concentration camps," dismissing the "fantastic allegation" that Israeli military forces were involved – a brazen lie which, furthermore, placed Israeli settlements under threat of retaliation for this cold-blooded massacre. Less known is the fact that a month before the Qibya massacre, Moshe Dayan had sent Unit 101 to drive 4,000 Bedouins of the Azzazma and Tarbin tribes across the Egyptian border, another step in expulsions that had been proceeding from 1950, shortly after the cease-fire. In March 1954, eleven Israelis were murdered in an ambush of a bus in the Eastern Negev by members of the Azzazma tribe ("unprovoked terrorism"), evoking an Israeli raid on the completely unrelated Jordanian village of Nahaleen with nine villagers killed ("retaliation"). In August 1953, Sharon's Unit 101 had killed 20 people, two-thirds of whom were women and children, at the al-Bureig refugee camp in the Gaza Strip, in "retaliation" for infiltration.[96]

The cycle of "retaliation" (by Israel) and "terror" (by Palestinians) can be traced back step-by-step for many years, an exercise that will quickly reveal that the terminology belongs to the realm of propaganda, not factual description.

Here too we might note how effectively history has been reconstructed in a more serviceable form. Thus Thomas Friedman, reviewing "Israel's counterterrorism" strategy, writes that "the first period, from 1948 to 1956, might best be described as the era of counterterrorism-through-retaliation, or negative feedback," though "at least one of these retaliations became highly controversial, involving civilian casualties," the reference presumably being to Qibya. The record of scholarship on terrorism is often hardly different.[97]

The Iron Fist operations of the Israeli Army in southern Lebanon in early 1985 were also guided by the logic outlined by Eban. The civilian population were held hostage under the threat of terror to ensure that they accept the political arrangements dictated by Israel in southern Lebanon and the occupied territories. The warnings remain in effect; the population remain hostages, with no concern in the superpower that finances these operations and bars any meaningful political settlement.

While wholesale terrorism, including the holding of hostages, is exempt from censure when conducted by an approved source, the same is true of smaller-scale operations, as already illustrated. To mention a few other cases, in November–December 1983, Israel "made it clear that it would not allow Arafat's forces to evacuate the city [Tripoli, in northern Lebanon, where they were under attack by Syrian-backed forces] as long as the fate of the Israeli prisoners was in doubt." Israel therefore bombed what were called "guerrilla positions," preventing the departure of Greek ships that were to evacuate Arafat loyalists. Druze spokesmen reported that a hospital was hit during the bombing and strafing of "what were described as Palestinian bases," east of Beirut, while in Tripoli, "One already-gutted cargo ship took a direct hit and sank" and "a freighter burst into flames when it was hit."[98]

Here too the population, as well as foreign vessels, were held hostage to ensure the release of Israeli prisoners captured in the course of Israel's aggression in Lebanon. There was no comment in the U.S. on this further atrocity.

In Lebanon and the Mediterranean Sea Israel carries out attacks with impunity and abandon. In mid-July 1985, Israeli warplanes bombed and strafed Palestinian camps near Tripoli, killing at least 20 people, most of them civilians, including six children under twelve. "Clouds of smoke and dust engulfed the Tripoli refugee camps, home to more than 25,000 Palestinians, for several hours after the 2:55 p.m. attack," which was assumed to be retaliation for two car-bomb attacks a few days earlier in Israel's "security zone" in southern Lebanon by a group aligned with Syria. Two weeks later, Israeli gunboats attacked a Honduran-registered cargo ship a mile from the port of Sidon, delivering cement according to its Greek captain, setting it ablaze with 30 shells and wounding civilians in subsequent shore bombardment when militiamen returned the fire. The mainstream press did not even bother to report that the following day Israeli gunboats sank a fishing boat and damaged three others, while a Sidon parliamentarian called on the UN to end U.S.-backed Israeli "piracy." The press did report what Israel called a "surgical" operation against "terrorist installations" near Baalbek in the Bekaa valley in January 1984, killing about 100 people, mostly civilians, with 400 wounded, including 150 children in a bombed-out schoolhouse. The "terrorist installations" also included a mosque, a hotel, a restaurant, stores and other buildings in the three Lebanese villages and Palestinian refugee camp that were attacked, while Beirut news reported that a cattle market and an industrial park were also struck with scores of houses destroyed. A Reuters reporter in the bombed villages said that a second round of bombing began ten minutes after the first, "adding to the number of those killed or wounded" since men and women had begun dragging dead and wounded from the wrecked buildings. He saw "lots of children" in hospitals while witnesses reported men and women rushing to schools in a frantic search for their children. The leader of Lebanon's Shi'ites denounced "Israeli barbarism," describing the attacks on "innocent civilians, hospitals and houses of worship" as an attempt "to terrorize the Lebanese people." But the incident passed without comment, in no way affecting Israel's status as "a country that cares for human life" (*Washington Post*), so we may conclude again that the victims of this surgical bombing were less than human.[99]

One may, again, imagine what the reaction would be in the West, including the "pro-Arab" media, if the PLO or Syria were to carry out a "surgical strike" against "terrorist installations" near Tel Aviv, killing 100 civilians and wounding 400 others, including 150 children in a bombed-out schoolhouse along with other civilian victims.

While the standard version in the United States is that Israeli violence, perhaps excessive at times, is "retaliation" for Arab atrocities, Israel, like the United States, claims much broader rights: the right to carry out terrorist attacks to prevent potential actions against it, as in the justification for the Lebanon war by the dovish Knesset member Amnon Rubinstein cited earlier. Israeli troops carry out what they call "preventative gunfire" as they patrol in Lebanon, spraying the terrain with machinegun fire, leading Irish peacekeeping forces to block the road in protest. Quite commonly, Israeli attacks in Lebanon were described as "preventive, not punitive," for example, the bombing and strafing of Palestinian refugee camps and nearby villages by 30 Israeli jets on December 2, 1975, apparently in retaliation for the decision of the UN Security Council to debate a peace proposal vetoed by the U.S., accordingly excised from history.[100] Similarly, when Israeli airborne and amphibious forces attacked Tripoli in northern Lebanon in February 1973, killing 31 people (mainly civilians) according to the Lebanese authorities, and destroying classrooms, clinics and other buildings, Israel justified the raid as "intended to forestall a number of planned terrorist attacks against Israelis overseas."[101]

The pattern is regular, and the justifications are accepted as legitimate, again reflecting the status of Israel as a useful client-state and the subhuman status of its victims.

The last case mentioned occurred on the day that Israel shot down a Libyan civilian airliner lost in a sandstorm two minutes' flight time from Cairo, towards which it was heading, with 110 people killed. The U.S. officially expressed its sympathy to the families of those involved, but the press spokesman "declined to discuss with reporters the Administration's feelings about the incident." Israel blamed the French pilot, with the *New York Times* dutifully in tow, accepting the Israeli claim that the pilot knew he had been ordered to land but instead resorted to "highly suspicious" evasive action – the justification offered by the USSR for downing KAL 007[102] – so that the Israeli act was "at worst . . . an act of callousness that not even the savagery of previous Arab actions can excuse."

The official Israeli reaction was given by Prime Minister Golda Meir: "the government of Israel expresses its deep sorrow for the loss of human life and is sorry that the Libyan [*sic*] pilot did not respond to the warnings given him in accordance with international practice," while Shimon Peres added that "Israel acted in accordance with international laws." Israel falsely claimed that the pilot was not authorized to fly the jet plane. "The press was forbidden to publish pictures of the destroyed plane, of the dead and the wounded," Amiram Cohen observes in a detailed analysis of the Israeli reaction (undertaken after the KAL 007 atrocity), and "journalists were not allowed to visit the hospital in Beersheba and to interview survivors," all part of a "disinformation" effort. The international reaction was dismissed by the Israeli press as yet another demonstration that "the spirit of anti-Semitism flourishes" in Europe, virtually a reflex response, in the U.S. as well, when someone dares to mention or criticize an Israeli crime. The Israeli press insisted that "Israel is not responsible" and that "one must blame the [French] pilot." It was "a mobilized press," firm in support of the justice of Israel's actions, Cohen observes. After numerous fabrications, Israel confirmed that there had been an "error of judgment," agreeing to make *ex gratia* payments to the families of victims "in deference to humanitarian considerations" while denying any "guilt" or Israeli responsibility.[103]

The incident was passed over quickly in the United States, with little criticism of the perpetrators of the crime. Prime Minister Golda Meir arrived in the U.S. four days later; she was troubled by few embarrassing questions by the press and returned home with new gifts of military aircraft. The reaction was slightly different when the Russians shot down KAL 007 in September 1983,[104] though it was comparable when Washington's UNITA friends claimed to have shot down two civilian airliners at the same time. It is not difficult to discern the criteria for "international terrorism."

The record of Israeli terrorism goes back to the origins of the state – indeed, long before – including the massacre of 250 civilians and brutal expulsion of 70,000 others from Lydda and Ramle in July 1948; the massacre of hundreds of others at the undefended village of Doueimah near Hebron in October 1948 in another of the numerous "land-clearing operations" conducted while the international propaganda apparatus was proclaiming, as it still does, that the Arabs were fleeing at the call of their leaders; the murder of several hundred Palestinians by the IDF after the conquest of the Gaza strip in 1956; the slaughters in Qibya, Kafr Kassem, and a string of other assassinated villages; the expulsion of thousands of Bedouins from the demilitarized zones shortly after the 1948 war and thousands more from northeastern Sinai in the early 1970s, their villages destroyed, to open the region for Jewish settlement; and on, and on. The victims, by definition, are "PLO partisans," hence terrorists. Thus the respected editor of *Ha'aretz*, Gershom Schocken, can write that Ariel Sharon "made a name for himself from the early 1950s as a ruthless fighter against Palestine Liberation Organization (PLO) partisans," referring to the slaughter of civilians he conducted at Al-Bureig and Qibya in 1953 (long before the PLO existed). And the victims in Lebanon and elsewhere are also "terrorists," as must be the case, or they could not have been killed by a state that is so devoted to "purity of arms" and is held to a "higher law" by the "pro-Arab" American press.

The terrorist commanders are honored. When the leading contemporary U.S. terrorist took over the Presidency in 1981, Israel's Prime Minister and Foreign Minister were both notorious terrorist commanders while the highest position in the Jewish Agency was held by a man who had murdered several dozen civilians he was holding under guard in a mosque in a Lebanese town during yet another land-clearing operation in 1948, to be quickly amnestied, all trace of the crime removed from the record, and granted a lawyer's license on the grounds that "no stigma" could be attached to his act.[105]

Even terrorism against Americans is tolerable. The Israeli terrorist attacks against U.S. installations (also, public places) in Egypt in 1954 in an attempt to exacerbate U.S.–Egyptian relations and abort secret peace negotiations then in progress were ignored at the time and are barely remembered, much as in the case of the attempt to sink the U.S. spy ship *Liberty* in international waters in 1967 by Israeli bombers and torpedo boats that even shot lifeboats out of the water in an effort to ensure that no one would escape, with 34 crewmen killed and 171 injured, the worst peacetime U.S. naval disaster of the century, but dismissed as an "error" – a transparent absurdity – and barely known.[106] Similarly, torture of Americans by the Israeli Army in the West Bank and southern Lebanon is barely noted in the media, with Israeli denials highlighted and verification by the U.S. Ambassador in Israel ignored.[107] The fact that the victims were Arab-Americans no doubt serves as justification, by the operative standards.

What is striking about this record, which includes ample terrorism against Jews as well from the earliest days, is that it in no way sullies Israel's reputation in the United States for moral standards unequalled in history. Each new act of terrorism, if noted at all, is quickly dismissed and forgotten, or described as a temporary deviation, to be explained by the hideous nature of the enemy which is forcing Israel to depart, if only for a moment, from its path of righteousness. Meanwhile the media are regularly denounced for their "double standard" as they ignore Arab crimes while holding Israel to impossible standards, and respected scholars inform us soberly that "numerous public figures in the West, even a number of Western governments" (naturally, all unnamed) have encouraged the PLO to destroy Israel.[108] Across the political spectrum in the United States and among the educated classes with remarkable uniformity and only the most marginal of exceptions, the prevailing doctrine is that it is the terrorism of the Palestinians and their Arab allies, urged on by the Kremlin, their unremitting commitment to kill Jews and destroy Israel and their refusal to consider any political settlement, that is the root cause of the endless Arab–Israeli conflict, of which Israel is the pathetic victim. As for the United States, it is courageously struggling against "the evil scourge of terrorism," from Central America to Lebanon and beyond.

The Jewish national movement and the state that developed from it have broken no new ground in their record of terrorist atrocities, apart from the immunity they enjoy in enlightened Western opinion. For Americans, it suffices to recall "that Adolf Hitler chose to praise the United States . . . for 'solving the problem' of the native races,"[109] as do some of those who live by Hitler's code in Central America today, with U.S. support. But the recent commentary on "terrorism" in the "civilized countries" reeks of hypocrisy, and can only be an object of contempt among decent people.

3 Libya in U.S. Demonology (1986)

Within the American doctrinal system, no one so epitomizes "the evil scourge of terrorism" as Muammar Qaddafi, the "mad dog" of the Arab world; and Libya under his leadership has become the very model of a terrorist state.

The description of Libya under Qaddafi as a terrorist state is certainly just. Reviewing the major acts of terrorism plausibly attributed to Libya, the latest Amnesty International (AI) Report lists the killings of 14 Libyan citizens by this terrorist state, four abroad, through 1985.[1] In the course of the hysteria orchestrated to serve other ends, all sorts of charges have been made, but the record confirms the April 1986 statement of a senior U.S. intelligence official that until "a few weeks ago, [Qaddafi] had used his people primarily to assassinate Libyan dissidents."[2] "A few weeks ago," this intelligence official continues, Qaddafi "made a clear decision to target Americans." This alleged decision, which has assumed the aura of indubitable fact though no credible evidence has yet been provided to substantiate it, followed the Gulf of Sidra incident, when a U.S. air and naval armada sank Libyan vessels off the coast of Libya with many killed. Furthermore, the alleged Libyan decision would be entirely legitimate, indeed laudable and much belated, under the doctrines professed by the U.S. executive and endorsed by respected commentators, some already cited, others to which we turn directly.

AI reports that Libya's terrorist killings began in early 1980, at the time when Jimmy Carter was overseeing the escalation of the terrorist war in El Salvador, with José Napoleon Duarte joining as a cover to ensure that arms would flow to the killers. While Libya was killing 14 of its own citizens, along with a handful of others, the U.S. client regime of El Salvador killed some 50,000 of its citizens in the course of what Bishop Rivera y Damas, who succeeded the assassinated Archbishop Romero, described in October 1980, after seven months of terror, as "a war of extermination and genocide against a defenseless civilian population."[3] The security forces who perform these necessary chores were hailed by Duarte, a few weeks later, for their "valiant service alongside the people against subversion" while he conceded that "the masses were with the guerrillas" when this exercise began under the Carter–Duarte alliance. Duarte expressed this praise for the mass murderers as he was sworn in as President of the Junta in an effort to lend it legitimacy after the murder of four American churchwomen, an act generally regarded as improper, though justifications were offered even for that crime by Jeane Kirkpatrick and Alexander Haig. Meanwhile the media assured us that "There is no real argument that most of the estimated 10,000 political fatalities in 1980 were victims of government forces or irregulars associated with them" (*Washington Post*), though it was later quietly conceded that at the time, officials of the Carter Administration were informing the media that "security forces were responsible for 90 percent of the atrocities," not "'uncontrollable' right-wing bands" as the press had been reporting.[4] From the earliest days of the Carter–Reagan terrorist operations in El Salvador, Duarte's primary role had been to ensure that there will be no impediment to the slaughter while denying well-documented atrocities or justifying them on the grounds that the victims are "Communists." He played this role to mounting applause in the United States as the savage assault against the civilian population had its intended effect of destroying the threat of meaningful democracy that had arisen in the 1970s with the rise of church-based self-help groups, peasant associations, unions, and other "popular organizations." The conservative Central America correspondent of the London *Spectator* observes that the death squads "did exactly what they were supposed to do: they decapitated the trade unions and mass organisations" and caused the survivors "either to flee the country or to join the guerrillas," at which point the U.S. war against the rural population moved into high gear, with ample terror and massacre. It is only natural, then, that the editors of the *New Republic*, who had urged Reagan to pursue the slaughter with no concern for human rights ("there are higher American priorities") and "regardless of how many are murdered," should look with pleasure at these accomplishments in El Salvador, which is "the real model for supporting the push toward democracy in our sphere." The continuing terror, documented by Americas Watch, AI, and – very rarely – by the media, is a matter of indifference.[5]

The slaughter in El Salvador is not mere state terrorism on a remarkable scale, but international terrorism, given the organization, supply, training and direct participation by the ruler of the hemisphere. The same is true of the massacre of some 70,000

Guatemalans in the same years, when U.S. arms to the murderers flowed at close to the normal level contrary to what is commonly alleged, though it was necessary to call in U.S. proxies – neo-Nazi Argentine generals, Taiwan, and Israel – to implement the slaughter more efficiently; the U.S. government also constructed an arms pipeline involving Belgium and other collaborators, under the illegal direction of the Pentagon and the CIA, as a supplement. Meanwhile, as the terror reached its peak of savagery, Reagan and his associates extolled the killers and torturers for their human rights improvements and "total dedication to democracy," dismissing the flood of documentation on atrocities as a "bum rap."[6]

U.S. international terrorism in El Salvador is hailed as a substantial achievement because it laid the basis for the preferred version of "democracy": the rule of groups serving U.S. requirements with the public reduced to occasional ratification of elite decision now that the popular organizations, which might have provided a basis for meaningful democracy, have been "decapitated" and decimated. In 1982 and 1984 the United States organized what Edward Herman and Frank Brodhead call "demonstration elections" to pacify the home front, carried out in an atmosphere of "terror and despair, macabre rumor and grisly reality," in the words of the observers of the British Parliamentary Human Rights Group, while U.S. commentators lauded this demonstration of commitment to democracy.[7] Guatemala is also considered a success, for similar reasons. When half the population is virtually marched to the polls after it has been properly traumatized by U.S.-backed violence, enlightened commentators are overjoyed at this renewed demonstration of our love for democracy, untroubled by the rise in death squad killings and the open recognition by the newly elected president that he can do nothing given the roots of actual power in the military and the oligarchy and that the civilian government are merely "the managers of bankruptcy and misery."[8]

These two examples represent only a part of the U.S. role in international terrorism during the 1980s, and the grisly record goes back many years.

"The striking feature of Libyan atrocities," two commentators observe in reviewing the AI study of state terror, "is that they are the only ones whose numbers are sufficiently limited that the individual cases can be enumerated," in striking contrast to Argentina, Indonesia, or the Central American states where the emperor molests the world.[9]

In short, Libya is indeed a terrorist state, but in the world of international terrorism, it is a bit player.

Those who believe that it is possible to find a level of vulgarity and apologetics for mass slaughter and terror that will not be reached in respectable Western publications can be disabused of such illusions by consideration of numerous examples during the worst years of the terror in Central America,[10] or by turning to the neoconservative journal *The National Interest*, where they can read, in a critique of the *Washington Post* for being soft on Libya, that "There is no doubt that if, for example, the government of Jose Napoleon Duarte in El Salvador or any recent government in Turkey had carried out anywhere near the number of executions that Qaddafi has, the *Post* would have provided us with great detail, and would have reported the existence of considerable opposition."[11]

Not only is "terrorism" defined for ideological serviceability, as discussed earlier, but standards of evidence are also set so as to achieve the emperor's goals. To demonstrate Libya's role as a state terrorist, the flimsiest evidence, or none at all, will suffice. The headline of a *New York Times* editorial justifying the terrorist attack that killed some 100 people in Libya (according to press reports from the scene at the time) reads: "To Save the Next Natasha Simpson." The reference is to the eleven-year-old American girl who was one of the victims of the terrorist attacks in the Rome and Vienna air terminals on December 27, 1985; these victims entitle us to bomb Libyan cities "to discourage state-supported terrorism," the editors of the *Times* solemnly declare. It is only a minor defect that no evidence has been presented to implicate Libya in these actions. The Italian and Austrian governments stated that the terrorists were trained in Syrian-controlled areas of Lebanon and had come via Damascus, a conclusion reiterated by Israeli Defense Minister Yitzhak Rabin. Four months later, in response to U.S. claims about Libyan involvement in the Vienna attack, the Austrian Minister of Interior stated that "there is not the slightest evidence to implicate Libya," again citing Syria as the connection and adding that Washington had never presented the evidence of Libyan complicity it had promised to provide to the Austrian authorities. He also added the correct but – in the U.S. – inexpressible comment that the problem of Lebanese-based terrorism lies largely in the failure to solve the Palestine problem, which has led desperate people to turn to violence, the result perhaps intended by U.S.–Israeli terrorism, as discussed in chapter 2.[12]

A few months later, Italy's Interior Minister, while signing an agreement with the U.S. for cooperation in "the fight against terrorism," reiterated the position expressed by Italy "since January" that they suspected a Syrian source for the Rome and Vienna attacks. The *Times* reported his statement without, however, feeling any need to comment on the righteous blow of retaliation against Libya that they had applauded in April.[13]

If an individual implicated in a terrorist act once paid a visit to Libya, or is alleged to have received training or funds from Libya in the past, that suffices for condemnation of Qaddafi as a "mad dog" who must be eradicated. The same standards would implicate the CIA in the murderous exploits of Cuban exiles, among numerous others. Keeping just to 1985, one of the suspects in the bombing of the Air India jumbo jet near Ireland that was the year's worst terrorist act, killing 329 people, was apparently trained in a training camp for mercenaries in Alabama. U.S. Attorney-General Meese, visiting India nine months later, made a barely reported statement that the U.S. was taking steps "to prevent terrorists from obtaining training or resources in the United States," referring to the private military training camps that India has charged have trained Sikh extremists; no evidence has been produced to support Meese's promise, nor has there been any investigation, to my knowledge.[14] The terrorist action that took the most lives in the Middle East was a car-bombing in Beirut in March that killed 80 people and wounded several hundred, carried out by a Lebanese intelligence unit trained and supported by the CIA, in an effort to kill a Shi'ite leader who was believed to have been involved in "terrorist attacks against U.S. installations" in Beirut;[15] the term "terrorism" is commonly used by foreign forces in reference to actions against them by the local population that sees them as occupiers attempting to impose a detested political settlement instituted by a foreign invasion, in this case, Israel's "New Order." By the standards of evidence used in the case of Libya, one would have to conclude that the U.S. was once again the world's leading terrorist power in 1985, even if we exclude the wholesale terrorism ruled ineligible by the doctrinal system.

Continuing to 1986, among the most serious terrorist acts in the Middle East/Mediterranean region as of the time of writing, apart from Israel's continuing terrorism in southern Lebanon, are the U.S. bombing of Libya and the bombings in Syria which, according to the radio station of Lebanon President Amin Gemayel's Phalangist party, killed more than 150 people in April, blamed by Syria on Israeli agents with no reported evidence, but no less credibility than similar U.S. charges against whoever happens to be the villain of the day – and, incidentally, not falling within "the evil scourge of terrorism."[16]

The U.S., of course, disclaims responsibility for the actions of terrorists it has trained: Cubans, Lebanese, mass murderers such as Rios Montt in Guatemala, and numerous others in Latin America and elsewhere. In the case of the Lebanon bombing, for example, the CIA denied involvement though this denial was "disputed by some Administration and Congressional officials who said that the agency was working with the group at the time of the bombing," a conclusion also drawn by a *Washington Post* inquiry, which determined that Washington cancelled the covert operation after the bombing, conducted without CIA authorization.[17] Even if we accept the claim that the CIA did not authorize the bombing and was no longer involved with the terrorist group it had trained, the government's excuse is readily dismissed by the standards applied to official enemies by apologists for U.S. and Israeli terrorism, both in the government and the media. Recall that "the larger moral responsibility for atrocities . . . is *all* Yasir Arafat's" because "he was, and remains, the founding father of contemporary Palestinian violence," and thus the U.S. will hold Arafat "accountable for acts of international terrorism" quite generally, whether he is involved or not.[18] By the same logic, we must conclude that "the larger moral responsibility" in the cases mentioned and much else is "*all* Washington's," which must be held accountable whatever the facts about direct involvement.

As noted in the preface, the Reagan campaign against "international terrorism" was a natural choice for the doctrinal system in furtherance of its basic agenda: expansion of the state sector of the economy, transfer of resources from the poor to the rich, and a more "activist" foreign policy. Such policies are facilitated if the public can be frightened into obedience by some terrible enemy threatening to destroy us, though it is necessary to avoid, as too dangerous, direct confrontation with the Great Satan himself. International terrorism by the Evil Empire's proxies is an obvious candidate, and the Administration's PR specialists turned at once to the task of concocting the appropriate web of half-truths and deceit, anticipating that the charade would be taken seriously.

Libya fits the need perfectly. Qaddafi is easy to hate, particularly against the background of rampant anti-Arab racism in the United States and the commitment of the political class and articulate intellectuals to U.S.–Israeli rejectionism. He has created an ugly and repressive society, and is indeed guilty of terrorism, primarily against Libyans, so it appears. Qaddafi's execution of Libyan dissidents, his major recorded terrorist acts, might have been prevented according to U.S. and Israeli intelligence analysts, but with the possible consequence of revealing that the (apparently quite transparent) Libyan codes had been broken. "An Israeli analyst put it more bluntly: 'Why expose our sources and methods for the sake of some Libyans?'"[19]

Furthermore, Libya is weak and defenseless so that martial flourishes and, when needed, murder of Libyans can be conducted with impunity. The glorious military victory in Grenada, a culmination of the hostility and aggressiveness of the Carter–Reagan Administrations after the Bishop government threatened to consider the needs of the poor majority, served similar ends. The point is readily perceived abroad. American journalist Donald Neff, writing in a British publication about the March 1986 Gulf of Sidra incident, comments that

> this was less of a Rambo-style operation than a demonstration of the bully on the block picking a fight. It was typical of Reagan. In his five years in office, he has repeatedly got away with lording it over little guys. He did this time too.

It is an interesting fact that this regular show of cowardice and two-bit thuggery seems to strike a responsive chord, sometimes abroad as well. British commentator Paul Johnson denounces the "distasteful whiff of pure cowardice in the air" as "the wimps" raise doubts about the U.S. bombing of "terrorist bases" (that is, civilian targets) in Libya. He gushes with admiration for "the strength of the Cowboy," who demonstrates his courage by sending his bombers to murder defenseless civilians.[20]

The PR specialists of the Reagan Administration understood the utility of the Libyan enemy and wasted little time in confronting this ominous foe. Libya was at once designated as a prime agent of the Soviet-inspired "terror network," and in July 1981, a CIA plan to overthrow and possibly kill Qaddafi with a paramilitary campaign of terror within Libya was leaked to the press.[21]

We may note parenthetically that by U.S. standards, this plan authorized Qaddafi to carry out acts of terror against American targets in "self-defense against future attack," the words of White House spokesman Larry Speakes presenting the official justification for the bombing of Tripoli and Benghazi. The same justification was reiterated at the United Nations by Vernon Walters and Herbert Okun. The Administration even went so far as to argue that this stance – which if adopted by other violent states would tear to shreds what little remains of global order and international law – is in accord with the United Nations Charter. No form of legal sophistry can bridge that gap, but the Administration assumed that "it would play well in Peoria" – or at least in Cambridge, New York and Washington. At the extreme left-liberal end of the permissible spectrum, Reagan was duly acclaimed by *New York Times* legal specialist Anthony Lewis for his reliance "on a legal argument that violence against the perpetrators of repeated violence is justified as an act of self-defense."

The reason why the U.S. justified the bombing of Libya "on the basis of pre-empting an attack, which could be seen as a form of self-defense, [rather] than as a retaliatory action" was explained by a State Department official, who noted that the UN Charter expressly forbids the use of force except in self-defense – more accurately, self-defense until the UN acts after a formal request to the Security Council by the country that regards itself as the victim of a sudden and overwhelming armed attack. While the "legal argument" was admired at home, it was generally dismissed abroad, where few could be found who would disagree with Canada's former UN Ambassador George Ignatieff, a member of Canada's first delegation to the UN and now Chancellor of the University of Toronto, who rejected the appeal to the right of self-defense established in the UN Charter as without merit.[22]

In August 1981, the anti-Qaddafi message "was reinforced by the trap laid for Libya in the Gulf of Sidra," a trap "elaborately planned on the U.S. side" with the intent of a confrontation in which Libyan jets could be shot down, as they were, Edward Haley observes in his bitterly anti-Qaddafi study of U.S. relations with Libya. One specific purpose, Haley plausibly argues, was to "exploit the 'Libyan menace' in order to win support for steps [the Administration] wished to take in pursuit of Secretary Haig's 'strategic consensus' against the Soviet Union, and as an element in the arrangements necessary for the creation of a Rapid Deployment force," an intervention force targeted primarily at the Middle East.

In November, the Administration concocted an amusing tale about Libyan hit-men roaming the streets of Washington to assassinate Our Leader, eliciting feverish media commentary along with some skepticism, quite limited at the time. When questioned about the plot, Reagan stated: "We have the evidence, and [Qaddafi] knows it."[23] The story faded away when its purpose had been served, and the press was sufficiently disciplined so as not to report the exposure that the "assassins" on the official U.S. list, leaked in England, were prominent members of the (passionately anti-Libyan) Lebanese Amal, including its leader Nabih Berri and the elderly religious leader of the Shi'ite community.[24]

Other dramatic discoveries included a Libyan threat to invade the Sudan across 600 miles of desert (with the Egyptian and U.S. air forces helpless to impede this outrage) and a plot to overthrow the government of the Sudan in February 1983, unearthed at a moment when the Administration's reactionary constituency was charging it with insufficient militancy – a plot so subtle that Sudanese and Egyptian intelligence knew nothing about it, as quickly discovered by U.S. reporters who took the trouble to go to Khartoum to investigate. The U.S. responded to this awesome plot with an elaborate show of force, enabling Secretary of State Shultz, who had been denounced as too faint-hearted, to strike heroic poses on television while announcing that Qaddafi "is back in his box where he belongs" because Reagan acted "quickly and decisively" against this threat to world order, demonstrating again "the strength of the cowboy." This episode too was forgotten once its purposes had been served. There have been a series of similar examples. The media have generally played their appointed role, with only occasional demurrers.[25]

The events of March–April 1986 fit the familiar pattern. The Gulf of Sidra operation in March was plainly timed to stir up jingoist hysteria just prior to the crucial Senate vote on Contra aid, coinciding with a fabricated Nicaraguan "invasion" of Honduras, an inspired PR operation that succeeded brilliantly as demonstrated by the enraged reaction of Congressional doves and the media fairly generally, and the Senate vote (see chapter 2). The charade also permitted the Administration to provide $20 million of military aid to Honduras, which Honduras officially maintains that it did not request, and which has no doubt been conveniently "lost" in the Contra camps, yet another method by which the lawless band in Washington evades the weak Congressional restrictions on their thuggery.[26]

The Gulf of Sidra provocation was at least a partial success as well, enabling U.S. forces to sink several Libyan boats, killing more than 50 Libyans, presumably with the expectation that it might incite Qaddafi to acts of terror against Americans, as was subsequently claimed. The effort is reported to have caused considerable frustration in Washington over Qaddafi's failure to rise to the bait with some terrorist atrocity that could be used as a pretext for the next phase in the terrorist campaign against Libya.[27]

While U.S. forces were successful in killing many Libyans, they were singularly unable to rescue survivors. The task was apparently not impossible; 16 survivors of the U.S. attack were rescued from a lifeboat by a Spanish oil tanker.[28]

The official purpose of the U.S. military operation was to establish the right of passage in the Gulf of Sidra. Dispatch of a naval flotilla was hardly the necessary or appropriate means to achieve this end: a declaration would have sufficed. Were further steps deemed necessary for some reason, lawful means were readily available. If someone has a dispute with his neighbor over rights to some property, there are two ways to proceed: one is to take the matter to the Courts, the second is to pick up a gun and kill the neighbor. The first option was surely available in the case of the Gulf of Sidra. Since there is plainly no urgency, it was possible to resort to legal means to establish the right of innocent passage. But a lawless and violent state will naturally observe different priorities. Asked why the U.S. did not take the issue to the World Court, Brian Hoyle, director of the Office of Ocean Law and Policy at the State Department, said that the case "would have taken years and years. I don't think we could live with this"[29] – given the evident necessity for U.S. naval armadas to operate in the Gulf of Sidra, at once, if the United States is to survive as a nation.

The U.S. position is dubious on narrower grounds. The press continually speaks of "the law of the sea," but the United States is hardly on firm grounds in appealing to this doctrine if only because the Reagan Administration rejected the Law of the Sea Treaty. Furthermore, Libya shot at U.S. planes, not U.S. ships, and "the law of the air" is far from well established. States make various claims in this regard. The U.S., for example, claims a 200-mile Air Defense Identification Zone within which it has the right to exercise "self-defense" against intruding aircraft judged to be hostile. There is no doubt that U.S. aircraft were well within 200 miles of Libyan territory – 40 miles, the Pentagon claims – and that they were hostile, so that by U.S. standards, Libya was within its rights to intercept them. The point was noted by the conservative legal scholar Alfred Rubin of the Fletcher School at Tufts University, who commented that "by sending in aircraft we went beyond what we were clearly authorized to do under the Law of the Sea" in "an unnecessary provocation."[30] But for a gangster state, such matters are irrelevant, and the exercise was a success, among the intended domestic circles at least.

The extent and meaning of the provocation in the Gulf of Sidra were made clear by Pentagon spokesman Robert Sims, who "said that U.S. policy is to shoot at any Libyan boat that enters international waters in the Gulf of Sidra for as long as the U.S. naval exercise in that region continues – no matter how far away the boat might be from U.S. ships." "Given the 'hostile intent' displayed by Libya when it tried to shoot down U.S. warplanes," Sims stated, any Libyan military vessel is "a threat to our forces."[31] In short, the U.S. maintains the right to fire in "self-defense" at any Libyan vessel that approaches its naval armada off the Libyan coast, but Libya does not have a right of self-defense in air space off its own coast, even a fraction of that declared by the U.S. for itself.

There is more to the story. British correspondent David Blundy interviewed British engineers in Tripoli who were repairing the Russian-installed radar system there. One, who says he was monitoring the incident throughout on the radar screens (which, contrary to Pentagon claims, were not rendered inoperative), reports that he "saw American warplanes cross not only into the 12 miles of Libyan territorial waters, but over Libyan land as well." "'I watched the planes fly approximately eight miles into Libyan air space,' he said. 'I don't think the Libyans had any choice but to hit back. In my opinion they were reluctant to do so.'" The engineer added, "American warplanes made their approach using a normal civil airline traffic route and followed in the wake of a Libyan airliner, so that its radar blip would mask them on the Libyan radar screen."[32]

No hint of this information appeared in the U.S. media, to my knowledge, apart from an informative report by Alexander Cockburn, playing his usual role of personal antidote to media subservience and distortion. Blundy's article was not mysteriously missed by the U.S. press. It was cited by Joseph Lelyveld of the *Times*, but with its crucial contents omitted.[33]

One likely – and probably eagerly awaited – consequence of the Gulf of Sidra operation was to elicit acts of Libyan terrorism in retaliation. These would then have the effect of inducing a state of terror in the United States and, with some luck, in Europe as well, setting the stage for the next escalation. The bombing of the "La Belle" discotheque in West Berlin on April 5, with one black American soldier and one Turk killed,[34] was immediately blamed on Libya, then used as the pretext for the April 14 bombing of Tripoli and Benghazi, with many Libyans killed, apparently mostly civilians (about 100, according to the Western press; 60 according to the official Libyan report). The bombing was neatly timed the day before the expected House vote on Contra aid. In case the audience missed the point, Reagan's speechwriters made it explicit. Addressing the American Business Conference on April 15, Reagan said: "And I would remind the House voting this week that this arch-terrorist has sent $400 million and an arsenal of weapons and advisers into Nicaragua to bring his war home to the United States. He has bragged that he is helping the Nicaraguans because they fight America on its own ground."[55]

The idea that the "mad dog" is bringing his war home to the U.S. by providing arms to a country the U.S. is attacking with its terrorist proxy army was a nice touch, which passed without notable comment, but the PR operation did not, for once, succeed in steamrollering Congress, though the bombing of Libya did enflame chauvinist passions, a consequence largely attributable, perhaps, to the prevailing anti-Arab racism and the relative absence of any sane reaction to earlier episodes of manufactured hysteria over Qaddafi's real or alleged crimes.

The April 14 attack was the first bombing in history staged for prime time television. The bombing raids were carefully planned so that they would begin precisely at 7 p.m. Eastern Standard Time;[36] that is, precisely at the moment when all three national television channels broadcast their major news programs, which were preempted as agitated anchor men switched to Tripoli for direct eyewitness reports of the exciting events. That was no small logistical feat for a seven-hour flight from London. As soon as the raids ended, the White House had Larry Speakes address a press conference, followed by other dignitaries, ensuring total domination of the information system during the crucial early hours.

One might argue that the Administration took a gamble in this transparent PR operation, since journalists might have asked some obvious questions, but the White House was confident that nothing untoward would occur and its faith in the self-discipline of the media proved to be warranted.

Quite apart from matters of timing and advance notice, other questions could have been raised. To mention only one, Speakes stated that the U.S. knew on April 4 that the East Berlin Libyan "People's Bureau" had informed Tripoli that an attack would take place in Berlin the following day, and that it then informed Tripoli that the "La Belle" discotheque bombing had taken place, as planned. Thus the U.S. knew on April 4–5 – with certainty, the White House declared – that Libya was directly responsible for the disco bombing. One might have asked, then, why the reports of U.S. and West German investigations from April 5 to the moment of the attack consistently stated that there were at most suspicions of Libyan involvement. In fact, every journalist listening to the Administration story had in his or her hands – unless we assume the most astonishing incompetence on the part of the news rooms – an Associated Press report from Berlin which came across the wires at 6:28 p.m. EST, a half-hour before the bombing, stating that "the Allied military command [in West Berlin] reported no developments in the investigation of the disco bombing" and that "U.S. and West German officials have said Libya – *possibly* through its embassy in Communist-ruled East Berlin – is *suspected* of involvement in the bombing of the La Belle nightclub" (my emphasis).[37] Someone might have asked, then, how it is that a few minutes prior to the attack, the U.S. and West Germany still had at most suspicions of Libyan involvement – as throughout the preceding period – while on April 4–5, ten days earlier, they had certain knowledge of it. But no embarrassing questions were asked, and the relevant facts have been largely suppressed.

Reagan stated on the evening of April 14 that "our evidence is direct, it is precise, it is irrefutable" – just as "We have the evidence, and [Qaddafi] knows it" in the case of the Libyan hit-men prowling the streets of Washington, not to speak of the Sandinista involvement in drug-peddling, their announcement of a "revolution without frontiers," the support of Helmut Kohl and Bettino Craxi for the Libyan attack (angrily denied by "shocked" officials in Germany and Italy),[38] and numerous other productions of an Administration that has well surpassed the usual standards of deceit, and continues "to commit any crime, to lie, to cheat" – in the words of the titular leadership, referring to his official enemy – to achieve its ends, confident that the occasional exposure in the small print, well after the fact, will not prevent the regular stream of lies from setting the terms of debate and leaving the appropriate impressions firmly implanted.

Beyond the borders, discipline did not reign, however. In Germany, a week after Washington had stated its certain knowledge ten days earlier (April 4–5) of Libyan responsibility for the disco bombing, *Der Spiegel* (April 21) reported that the famed telephone intercepts apparently do not exist and that West Berlin intelligence has only suspicions about Libyan involvement, also suspecting "rival groups of drug dealers" among other possibilities (including Klan or neo-Nazi groups, some suspected; the disco was frequented by black GIs and Third World immigrants). Washington's war is "a means of politics," *Der Spiegel* continued, "insofar as the enemy is as small as Grenada and Libya – and the adversary is as ideal a scoundrel as Qaddafi"; and no European leader should have any illusions that Europe's concerns or interests will be considered if the U.S. decides to escalate international violence, even to the level of a final World War, editor Rudolf Augstein added.[39]

In an interview on April 28 with a reporter for the U.S. Army journal *Stars And Stripes*, Manfred Ganschow, chief of the Berlin Staatschutz (domestic intelligence) and head of the 100-man team investigating the disco bombing, stated that "I have no more evidence that Libya was connected to the bombing than I had when you first called me two days after the act. Which is none." He agreed that it was "a highly political case" and hinted at considerable skepticism about what "the politicians" were saying and would say about it.[40]

The U.S. press concealed the doubts expressed in Germany by the media and the investigating team, but the discerning reader will be able to detect them in the reports of the continuing investigation, as suspects alleged to have Syrian and other connections are investigated, and Washington's claims of "certain knowledge" on April 4–5 were qualified with such terms as "reportedly" and "alleged."[41] The hesitancy, the qualifications, the backing off from the former confident assertion, and the indirect citation of evidence that undermines Administration claims – these are the devices used by the media to signal that they are well aware that there was little merit to the case they enthusiastically endorsed when called upon to rally round the flag.

In the *New York Review of Books*, Shaul Bakhash asserts that the Jordanian Hindawi brothers were "responsible for the bombing of the night club in West Berlin" and that "there is now persuasive evidence" that they "were recruited by Syria (not by Libya as one might have thought from some official statements at the time)."[42] Apart from the fact that he goes well beyond available evidence, this is a curious formulation. It was not a matter of "some official statements" from which "one might have thought" that Libya was involved; rather *all* official statements, presented with certainty and no qualifications and repeated in this manner by the media until the case began to unravel, confidently asserted Libyan responsibility and justified the bombing and killing of Libyan civilians on this basis. Furthermore, neither the media backtracking nor this statement draw the immediate conclusion: if the Reagan Administration was lying about its "direct," "precise" and "irrefutable" evidence, then the bombing was simply unprovoked state terrorism (instead of state terrorism with a pretext) – covered up by the loyal media, which avoided the obvious questions at the time of their enthusiastic endorsement of the attack while offering absurd pretexts (e.g., the *Times* editors' tale about "the next Natasha Simpson") in justifying their complicity in terrorism.

The PR operation was surely a success, at least in the short term, at home, "playing well in Peoria" as the press put it, hence a successful example of "the engineering of democratic consent" that should "strengthen President Reagan's hand in dealing with Congress on issues like the military budget and aid to Nicaraguan 'contras.'"[43]

For much of the world, the U.S. has become an object of considerable fear, as the "bizarre cowboy leader" who so enraptures Paul Johnson and the like engages in acts of "madness" in organizing a "band of cut-throats" to attack Nicaragua and playing mad bomber elsewhere, in the words of Canada's leading journal, generally restrained and quite pro-U.S. in tendency.[44] The Reagan Administration is cultivating these fears, exploiting the "madman" strategy attributed to Richard Nixon. At the Tokyo Summit of the advanced industrial democracies in May, the Administration circulated a position paper in which it stated that one reason why Europe would be wise to line up in the U.S. crusade is "the need to do something so that the crazy Americans won't take matters into their own hands again." The threat succeeded in eliciting a statement against terrorism mentioning only Libya by name.[45] This explicit threat was ignored as commentators exulted in the success of the Libya bombing in bringing European "wimps" finally to take the measures required to counter the Libyan threat to Western civilization.

The reaction to the bombing of Libya was sharply different at home and abroad. The twelve-member European Economic Community called upon the U.S. to avoid "further escalation of military tension in the region with all the inherent dangers." A few hours later, U.S. warplanes struck, as West German Foreign Minister Hans-Dietrich Genscher was on his way to Washington to explain the EEC position. His spokesman stated that "We want to do everything we can to avoid a military escalation." The bombing aroused extensive protest throughout most of Europe, including large-scale demonstrations, and evoked editorial condemnation in much of the world. Spain's major newspaper *El Pais* condemned the raid, writing that "The military action of the United States is not only an offense against international law and grave threat to peace in the Mediterranean, but a mockery of its European allies, who did not find motives for economic sanctions against Libya in a meeting Monday, despite being previously and unsuccessfully pressured to adopt sanctions." The *South China Morning Post* in Hong Kong wrote that "President Reagan's cure for the 'mad dog of the Middle East' may prove more lethal than the disease," and his action "may also have lit the fuse to a wider conflagration" in the region. In Mexico City, *El Universal* wrote that the U.S. "has no right to set itself up as the defender of world freedom," urging recourse to legal means through the United Nations. There were many similar reactions.

The U.S. press, in contrast, was overwhelmingly favorable. The *New York Times* wrote that "even the most scrupulous citizen can only approve and applaud the American attacks on Libya," describing this as a just verdict and sentence: "the United States has prosecuted [Qaddafi] carefully, proportionately – and justly." The evidence for Libyan responsibility for the disco bombing has been "now laid out clearly to the public," at least to the satisfaction of the editors, though they did not see fit to publish it. "Then came the jury, the European governments to which the United States went out of its way to send emissaries to share evidence and urge concerted action against the Libyan leader." It is irrelevant, apparently, that the jury was hardly convinced, and issued a "judgment" calling on the executioner to refrain from any action – just as it is unnecessary to comment editorially on the fact, later tacitly recognized, that the evidence was of little merit.

Most governments also condemned the action, though not all. Britain and Canada went along, though the public response was sharply different, and there was support from France in its current mood of Reaganite enthusiasm. The government-controlled South African Broadcasting Corporation said the attack "underlines the commitment the leader of the Western world has made to taking positive action against terrorism"; the U.S. was justified in attacking Qaddafi, "whose name is virtually synonymous with international terrorism." In Israel, Prime Minister Shimon Peres stated that the U.S.

action was clearly justified "in self-defense": "If the Libyan Government issues orders to murder American soldiers in Beirut in cold blood, in the middle of the night, what do you expect the United States to do? Sing Hallelujah? Or take action in her defense?" The idea that the U.S. was acting in "self-defense" against an attack on her forces in Beirut two and a half years earlier is an intriguing innovation, even putting aside the circumstances of that earlier act.[46]

In the U.S., Senator Mark Hatfield, one of the few political figures in the country who merits the honorable term "conservative," denounced the U.S. bombing raid "on a nearly deserted Senate floor," and in a letter to the *Times*. Leaders of several major Christian denominations condemned the bombing, but Jewish leaders generally praised it, among them Rabbi Alexander Schindler, president of the Union of American Hebrew Congregations, who "said the U.S. government 'properly and vigorously responded' to the 'mindless terrorism'" of Qaddafi. Harvard international affairs professor Joseph Nye said Reagan had to respond "to the smoking gun of that Berlin thing. What else do you do about state-supported terrorism?" – such as U.S.-supported terrorism in Central America and southern Lebanon, for example, where the "smoking gun" is rather more clearly in evidence. Eugene Rostow supported the bombing as "inevitable and overdue" as part of a "more active defense against the process of Soviet expansion." The "forcible removal of the Qaddafi regime," he explained, "would be fully justified under the existing rules of international law," since Qaddafi "has flagrantly and continually violated these rules." "That being the case, every state injured by Libya's actions has the right, alone or with others, to use whatever force is reasonably necessary to put an end to Libya's illegal behavior. Libya is in the legal position of the Barbary pirates."[47] He urged NATO to "issue a declaration on the responsibility of states for illegal acts committed from their territory."[48]

A fortiori, then, NATO should condemn the emperor, not just the pirate, and states from Indochina to Central America to the Middle East, among others, should organize to use whatever force is necessary to attack the United States, Israel and other terrorist states, following the Rostow doctrine.

For ABC correspondent Charles Glass, who reported the bombing and aftermath from the scene, the event was symbolized by the handwritten letter of a seven-year-old girl, dug out of the rubble of her home, whose American-educated family he visited. The letter reads:

Dear Mr Reagan

Why did you kill my only sister Rafa and my friend Racha, she is only nine, and my baby doll Strawberry. Is it true you want to kill us all because my father is Palestinian and you want to kill Kadafi because he wants to help us go back to my father's home and land.

My name is Kinda

A facsimile of the original was submitted to the press in the U.S. as a letter to the editor, but not considered fit for publication. It was published by Alexander Cockburn, with a suggestion to President and Mrs. Reagan that since they "are fond of reading out messages from small children, they might care to deliver this one on the next appropriate occasion."[49]

Others saw the matter differently. Michael Walzer took issue with Europeans who criticized the bombing of Libya as a case of "state terrorism." It was not, he declared, "for it was aimed at specific military targets, and the pilots took some risks in their effort to hit those targets and nothing else," as he presumably knows from secret Pentagon briefings. If night bombing of a city happens to strike densely populated residential sections of Tripoli, killing Rafa and Racha and many other civilians, that is just the way the cookie crumbles.[50] Perhaps this is what we should expect from the highly regarded moralist and theorist of just war who assured us that the Israeli invasion of Lebanon can be defended under this concept, that Israel's military operations in southern Lebanon were "a good example of proportionate warfare," and that if civilians were "at risk" during the Israeli bombing of Beirut, then "the responsibility for the risks lies with the PLO."[51]

Media complicity in this act of state terrorism did not end with the patriotic behavior at the time of the bombing, a natural sequel to earlier endorsement of whatever tales the Administration chose to concoct. It was also necessary to show that the bombing was a success in curbing Libyan terrorism, as proven by the absence of terrorist actions attributed to Qaddafi after the bombing. To establish the thesis, it is necessary to suppress the fact that there were also no credible attributions prior to the bombing apart from those mentioned earlier, which are clearly irrelevant. No such problems interfered with the task at hand.

The editors of the *Washington Post* extolled the Libya bombing on the grounds that "No new acts of terrorism have been attributed to"

Colonel Qaddafi, who has now been reduced to a "subdued policy." Still more important is the impact on Western allies, most of whom "needed the shock" delivered by "the example of decisiveness, the undeniable precision of the intelligence, the subsequent demonstration of Libya's isolation and, not least, the fall in tourism" – not to speak of the threat that the "crazy Americans" might flail away with abandon somewhere else, a threat underscored by the dispatch of U.S. naval vessels to within a few miles of the Soviet coastline in the Black Sea at the same time;[52] note that the editors still find it possible to refer to "the undeniable precision of the intelligence," which the journal had ample reason to question, and later proceeded to reject, as noted. David Ignatius writes that the bombing "worked surprisingly well against Libya's Moammar Gadhafi," accomplishing "some startling – and very beneficial – changes in Libya, the Mideast and Europe." It proved that Qaddafi was "weak, isolated and vulnerable," "so vulnerable, in fact, that American warplanes were able to operate freely within his own, heavily defended airspace" – a glorious victory indeed, and a most surprising discovery about the Libyan colossus. To demonstrate "the psychology that had allowed Gadhafi to intimidate much of the world," Ignatius cites no acts – for there are no credible examples – but rather states that even if "Libyans may engage in terrorism again, it won't be on the scale they seemed to be embarking on early this year," when "U.S. intelligence learned that Libya had ordered its 'Peoples Bureaus' to mount terrorist attacks in about a dozen cities." A highly competent journalist, Ignatius knows that government claims about what intelligence had "learned" are worthless; his demonstration of the "success" of the operation in terms of alleged plans aborted is his circumspect way of saying that the consequences were undetectable.[53]

Similarly, George Moffett noted that Libyan terrorist attacks "have all but ceased" – that is, they have reduced from near zero to near zero – one of the "positive developments" that "appear to vindicate the Reagan Administration's policy of military retaliation." His colleague John Hughes observed triumphantly that "since the punitive air strikes against Libya . . . there have been no major terrorist attacks on Americans directed by Col. Muammar Qaddafi" – just as there were none before, so far as is known.[54]

The message to the state terrorists in Washington is clear: We will follow your dictates when you concoct a record of enemy terrorism that you claim has intimidated the world, when you carry out a major terrorist act to punish the outrage you have constructed, and when you announce that as a result of your heroism, the fearsome monster is subdued. Mere facts will never deter us from our obedient service.

For the record, "there have been some 18 anti-American terrorist incidents in Western Europe and the Middle East in the three months since the Libyan raid, compared with about 15 during the 3½ months before it" while "In the world as a whole, the rate of anti-American terrorism looks like being little different from last year," the *Economist* observed (while lauding Reagan's act of courage); and the Rand Corporation's leading specialist on terrorism noted that terrorist attacks after the raid persisted at about the same level as before.[55]

Completing the record, on July 3 the FBI released a 41-page report reviewing terrorist incidents within the United States in 1985. Seven were listed, with two people killed. In 1984, there had been 13 terrorist acts. The number has dropped each year since 1982, when 51 terrorist incidents were recorded.[56]

The FBI report received some coverage. The *Toronto Globe & Mail* ran an Assoicated Press story under the headline: "Jewish extremists blamed in 2 deaths." The lead paragraph reads: "Jewish extremists committed four of the seven terrorist acts that killed two people in the United States in 1985, the Federal Bureau of Investigation reported yesterday." The report goes on to provide details of the "incidents attributed to Jewish extremists" which "killed two people and injured nine, the report said," along with the other incidents. The *New York Times* ran no story on the FBI report, though there is a reference to it in the 11th paragraph of a column several weeks later, reading: "According to the F.B.I.'s annual report on terrorism, four of seven instances of domestic terrorism in 1985 were believed to involve 'Jewish terrorist groups.' No indictments have resulted from any [of] the investigations." The second national newspaper, the *Washington Post*, ran a story on the FBI report headlined "Domestic Terrorism Declined Last Year, FBI Report Shows." It is noted within that "both killings and nine of the injuries were attributed to four terrorist acts by Jewish extremists" (of the seven reported); this is repeated in a later story on the FBI investigation of the murder of Alex Odeh, noting that "Jewish extremist groups are suspects."[57]

These three sentences constitute the coverage in the national press of the conclusions of the FBI report on sources of domestic terrorism in 1985. I noticed no editorials or other comments calling upon the United States to bomb Tel Aviv or Jerusalem to excise the "cancer" and "subdue" the "mad dogs" who have brought "the evil scourge of terrorism" to our own shores. One may ask why not. Quite properly, Israel disclaims responsibility for the actions of "Jewish extremists." It also condemns the terrorist actions, as does Knesset Member Rabbi Kahane, whose former associates of the Jewish Defense League are suspected by the FBI of carrying out the actions. With rather less warrant, Washington disclaims responsibility for the terrorist acts of those it has trained and encouraged. But as I have already mentioned, these excuses amount to naught by the standards applied to Muammar Qaddafi and Yasser Arafat, who also condemn terrorist actions and deny responsibility for them. Recall again the doctrine that "the larger moral responsibility for atrocities . . . is *all* Yasir Arafat's" because "he was, and remains, the founding father of contemporary Palestinian violence," and thus the U.S. will hold Arafat "accountable for acts of international terrorism" quite generally, whether he is involved or not.[58] By the same logic, "the larger moral responsibility" for the acts of Zionist extremists is *all* Israel's.

The press has regularly dismissed Arafat's condemnation of Palestinian terrorist actions. To mention one critical case, on June 3, 1982, the terrorist group headed by Abu Nidal, who was at war with the PLO and had been condemned to death by them years earlier, attempted to assassinate Israeli Ambassador Shlomo Argov in London, the event that precipitated Israel's invasion of Lebanon, a "retaliation" considered legitimate by the U.S. government, the media, and educated opinion generally. The *Washington Post* commented that the Argov assassination attempt was an "embarrassment" for the PLO, which "claims to represent all Palestinians, but . . . tends to be selective about accepting responsibility for acts of Palestinian violence."[59] If a terrorist act by a Palestinian group at war with the PLO is an "embarrassment" for the PLO on these grounds, then plainly terrorist acts by Zionist extremists in the U.S., killing two and wounding nine, are an "embarrassment" for Israel, which is, by law, "the State of the Jewish people," including those in the Diaspora (not the state of its citizens, one-sixth of whom are non-Jews). Hence by the logic of the U.S. government, noted commentators, and the media quite generally, the U.S. is certainly entitled, if not obligated, to bomb Tel Aviv "in self-defense against future attacks."

One may imagine the reaction had the majority of terrorist actions in the U.S., including all fatalities, been committed by Arab-Americans associated with extremist elements of the PLO or suspected of being part of a terrorist group founded by a member of the Libyan government.

The U.S. bombing of Libya had nothing to do with "terrorism," even in the cynical Western sense of the word. In fact, it was clear enough that the Gulf of Sidra operation and the bombing of Libyan cities would if anything incite such retail terrorism, one major reason why the likely targets in Europe pleaded with the U.S. to refrain from such action.

This is hardly the first time that violent actions have been executed with the expectation that they would incite retail terrorism. The U.S.-backed Israeli invasion of Lebanon in 1982 is another case, as discussed in chapter 2. The attack on Libya may also sooner or later inspire terrorist acts, which will serve to mobilize domestic and foreign opinion in support of U.S. plans at home and abroad. If Americans react by general hysteria, including fear of travelling to Europe where visitors will be far safer than in any American city, this too is a net benefit, for the same reasons.

The real reasons for the U.S. attack on Libya have nothing to do with self-defense against "terrorist attacks" on U.S. forces in Beirut in October 1983, as Shimon Peres would have it, or any of the other actions attributed rightly or wrongly to Libya, or "self-defense against future attack" in accord with the doctrine proclaimed by the Reagan Administration to much domestic acclaim. Libya's terrorism is a minor irritant, but Qaddafi has stood in the way of U.S. plans in North Africa, the Middle East and elsewhere. He has supported Polisario and groups in the Sudan that the U.S. opposes, forged a union with Morocco contrary to U.S. wishes, intervened in Chad (following the dispatch of French Foreign Legion forces, advisors and aircraft, but French intervention is laudable because French forces help "keep West Africa safe for French, American, and other foreign oilmen" and perform similar services elsewhere),[60] and in general interfered with U.S. efforts to forge a "strategic consensus" in the region and to impose its will elsewhere. These are real crimes, which must be punished.

Furthermore, the Libyan attack had the purpose, and the effect, of preparing opinion at home and abroad for further acts of U.S. violence. The immediate response might be negative, but once absorbed, the level of expectation is heightened and the U.S. executive can proceed to further escalation if the necessity arises.

The cynicism of the propaganda campaign about "international terrorism" has been exposed to audiences that can be reached by dissident opinion in the United States, but the campaign itself has been a remarkable public relations achievement, and the prospects for future successes remain impressive, thanks to the generally uncritical and loyal reaction of articulate sectors. This service of the educated classes to international terrorism contributes to massive suffering and brutality, and in the longer term, carries with it dangers of superpower confrontation and terminal nuclear war. But such considerations count for little in comparison with the need to ensure that no threat to "stability" and "order" can arise, no challenge to privilege and power.

There is little here to surprise any honest student of history.

4 The U.S. Role in the Middle East (November 15, 1986)

It would only be proper for me to begin by presenting my credentials to talk to you on this topic, and since it would be unfair to present my own version, or even to rely on the very kind introductory remarks, let me read a letter of recommendation for me that was sent to a small journal in England, *Index on Censorship*, where I had a brief article on some aspects of our present topic.[1]

> Dear Dan:
>
> Forgive me for writing to you again in your capacity as a Director and Member of the Editorial Board of *Index on Censorship*, but I can't resist. In the latest issue which I have, July/August 1986, there appears a truly astonishing article, beginning on p. 2 and continuing at great length. This article is an attack on the United States, the United States Government, and the United States press by Noam Chomsky.
>
> You probably know about Chomsky: he is a fanatical defender of the PLO who has set new standards for intellectual dishonesty and personal vindictiveness in his writings about the Middle East. There really isn't anyone left in the U.S. – without regard to politics – who takes Chomsky seriously in view of his astonishing record. I therefore find it inexplicable that he is given fully three pages to go on with his attack on one of the freest presses in the world. Clearly giving him this much space lends a certain respectability to his disreputable efforts. Can it be that your editors simply do not know who Chomsky is and are unfamiliar with his record? Can it be that, fully familiar with him, they nevertheless decided to give him this platform? If so, why?

Signed "Elliott," that is, Elliott Abrams, Assistant Secretary of State for Inter-American Affairs, July 29, 1986, on official State Department stationery, and therefore counts, I presume, as a public document (some personal remarks omitted).

I cite this letter for two reasons. One, because I naturally treasure it, just as I treasure, for precisely the same reasons, the efforts of

Soviet advisors in the Third World to have my books banned (as they have been for years in the USSR)[2] and the rejection of my only visa application to Eastern Europe. The reactions of the commissars often indicate that one is probably on the right course. But beyond that, the letter is germane to our topic. It gives a revealing (and not untypical) insight into the mentality of the Reagan Administration and also of the Israeli lobby – I should mention that Abrams's letter was only one part of an impressive barrage launched against the journal for daring to publish remarks on the U.S. and Israel that were deemed improper by the guardians of the faith.[3] These are phenomena with which many of you have personal familiarity, a fact also germane to our topic, for obvious reasons.

Let me put aside the remarkable lack of a sense of irony; recall that this is a journal devoted to *censorship*, now under attack because it permitted brief expression of fact and analysis that is not to the taste of the commissars. What the letter reveals is the deep totalitarian streak in the mentality of leading figures in the Reagan Administration: not even the tiniest opening must be allowed to unacceptable thought. I do not want to suggest that it is outside the spectrum of American politics. Unfortunately, it is not. But in its practices, its style and its commitments, the Reagan Administration does represent an extreme position within this spectrum, an extreme of reactionary jingoism – which has misappropriated the honorable term "conservative" – marked by dedicated lying, lawlessness, enhancement of state power and violence, attacks on personal freedom and civil liberties, all developments that are ominous in character and important for the future of American politics and society, hence for the Middle East, and for the world, given the awesome scale of American power.

These features of the Reagan Administration have not gone unnoticed, and have naturally aroused concern among genuine conservatives here – of whom there are very few in government or the media – and abroad. Three years ago, David Watt, Director of the Royal Institute of International Affairs in London, writing in *Foreign Affairs*, commented on

> the chasm that lies between current American perceptions of the world and the world's perception of America . . . [W]ith the possible exceptions of the Israelis, the South Africans, President Marcos of the Philippines and a few right-wing governments in Central and South America, [most of the world believes] that the

> Reagan administration has vastly overreacted to the Soviet threat, thereby distorting the American (and hence the world) economy, quickening the arms race, warping its own judgment about events in the Third World, and further debasing the language of international intercourse with feverish rhetoric.

He adds that "it is in my experience almost impossible to convey even to the most experienced Americans just how deeply rooted and widely spread the critical view has become" – also an important fact. As if to confirm this judgment, in a companion article on the current international scene, *Foreign Affairs* editor William Bundy writes that with regard to the "degree of threat from the Soviet Union . . . the Reagan administration's broad view seems to this observer nearer to reality than the often excessively sanguine and parochial stated positions of other major nations."[4]

Watt in fact exaggerates the "chasm." European elites are not so removed from Reaganite hysteria as he indicates, and the "exceptions" go beyond those he mentioned, including particularly France, where many Paris intellectuals have adopted Reaganite fanaticism as their current fad. Furthermore, as Bundy's comment indicates, what Watt is describing represents elite opinion in the U.S. well beyond the Reagan Administration; Bundy writes from near the opposite end of the elite spectrum. Watt is describing the extreme version of a general elite reaction to the problems caused by the Vietnam war, including the harm caused to the U.S. economy and the benefits to its industrial rivals, and the breakdown of discipline both in the Third World and at home, factors that require stern state action and thus an appeal to the ever-useful Russian threat, regularly invoked in such situations. But Watts's essential point is accurate enough.

The isolation of the U.S. has since increased, as revealed for example by votes in the United Nations on a wide range of issues. Within just the last few weeks, the General Assembly voted 124 to 1 in favor of a South Atlantic zone of peace and 94 to 3 calling on the U.S. to comply with the World Court ruling ordering cessation of the U.S. attack against Nicaragua; in the latter case, the U.S. was joined by two client-states, El Salvador (which is "independent" in the sense in which Poland is independent of the USSR) and Israel, which has chosen to become an armed mercenary of the United States. U.S. isolation on Middle East votes is notorious, but the phenomenon is much more general. In 1980–85 alone the U.S.

resorted to 27 vetoes in the Security Council, as compared to 15 in the earlier history of the UN (all since 1966) and four vetoes for the USSR in the 1980s.[5]

The reaction is interesting. In the early days of the UN, when it was firmly under U.S. control and could be used for Cold War purposes, the general attitude towards the organization was highly favorable and there was much earnest debate over what caused the USSR, then almost isolated, to be so negative; perhaps this resulted from the use of swaddling clothes for infants, which reinforced "negativism," some suggested – a doctrine that a few skeptics called "diaperology." As U.S. global dominance declined from its quite phenomenal postwar peak and the relative independence of members of the UN increased, attitudes towards the UN became more critical, and by now are extremely hostile. We no longer read disquisitions on the curious negativism of the Russians, but rather on the equally curious fact that the world is out of step, as *New York Times* UN correspondent Richard Bernstein thoughtfully explains.[6]

Opinion polls in Europe show similar results. A recent classified USIA poll shows that outside of France, European opinion trusts Mikhail Gorbachev on arms control far more than Reagan, by four to one in England and seven to one in Germany.[7]

The international isolation is of little concern to the Reagan Administration. They have shown a shrewd understanding of the efficacy of violence and intimidation. Like some of their predecessors and models elsewhere in the world, they are well aware that cheap victories over weak and defenseless enemies can be manipulated to arouse jingoist sentiments and popular enthusiasm at home, if the population can be properly terrified by grave threats to its existence; among earlier examples that come to mind are Hitler's warnings of the encirclement of Germany by hostile states bent on its destruction, the Czech "dagger pointed at the heart of Germany," the aggressiveness and terror of the Czechs and Poles, and above all, the threat of the international Jewish conspiracy. The Reaganites understand very well what H. L. Mencken called "the whole aim of practical politics": "to keep the public alarmed (and hence clamorous to be led to safety) by menacing it with an endless series of hobgoblins, all of them imaginary." As for the rest of the world, U.S. cultural hegemony is sufficiently great so that doctrines contrived for domestic purposes will be adopted or taken seriously, however ludicrous they may be; and if not, the threat of escalated violence if

U.S. allies prove intransigent, and its potential costs to them, remain credible and have been effectively exploited.

The propaganda campaign about international terrorism is one example of the skillful use of these techniques, both at home and abroad. Policy-makers of the Reagan Administration know that liberal elements in Congress and the media can easily be cowed by the charge that they are soft and insufficiently militant in the face of whatever hobgoblin happens to be the monster of the day, and hence will line up obediently in the "crusade against terrorism." They also understand that the overwhelming resources of violence at their command allow disdain for world opinion. In fact, they regularly exploit concerns over their violence, as in the Tokyo summit after the Libya bombings, when the Reaganites rallied Western elites by warning them that unless they fell in line, there is no telling what the "crazy Americans" might do next.[8]

The disdainful attitude towards Congress as well is revealed at every turn. For example, last month, in the military authorization bill, both houses of Congress insisted upon wording that called upon the Executive to comply with SALT II, in the interest of national security. A few weeks later, the Administration announced that it was proceeding to exceed the SALT II limits. An Administration spokesman explained that "Congress is out of town and the summit in Iceland is past. [Gorbachev] is not expected to come here for some time. So what's holding us back?"[9] In other words, the cop is looking the other way, so why not rob the store? In actual fact, Congress has been out of town even when it is in town, as the Administration knows very well, and it has not proven too difficult for a gang of street toughs to ride roughshod over the generally pathetic opposition.

The attitude towards the public is revealed by what one Reagan official called "a vast psychological warfare operation" designed to set the agenda for debate over Nicaragua – a disinformation campaign called "Operation Truth"; Goebbels and Stalin would have been amused.[10] Disinformation has been an Administration specialty since the earliest days, though the media and Congress always profess to be shocked when a new example is exposed, recently during the 1986 disinformation campaign concerning Libya (see chapter 3). In this case, the display of outraged surprise necessitated a slight case of amnesia; as early as August 1981, *Newsweek* had reported a government "disinformation program designed to embarrass Qaddafi and his government" along with assorted acts of U.S. terrorism within Libya to try to "demonstrate that Qaddafi was opposed by an indigenous political force." There have also been extensive disinformation campaigns, quite successful thanks to media cooperation, on the arms race and numerous other matters.[11]

We derive further insights from current revelations about the sophisticated program to evade Congressional restrictions on military aid to the terrorist proxy army attacking Nicaragua – or the "resistance," as it is termed by the government and the loyal press, a "resistance" organized by the Hemispheric Enforcer to attack Nicaragua from bases established outside its borders (the term "proxy army," in contrast, is used in internal White House documents, and its terrorism is also not concealed in secret reports). To mention one illustration of the careful planning that lies behind the terrorist operations, consider the decision of the Reagan Administration to sell (probably quite useless) AWACs to Saudi Arabia in 1981. This was a politically unpopular move, and it was not clear at the time why the Administration was so determined to pursue it. Some likely reasons have since emerged. The Reagan planners evidently anticipated potential difficulties in funding their proxy army, and when Congress, responding to public pressure, later sought to limit the terrorist war against Nicaragua, Saudi Arabia was called upon to repay its debt and to fund shipments of arms to the contras, apparently Soviet arms that Israel had captured during its Reagan-backed aggression in Lebanon.[12]

These are the machinations of sophisticated international terrorists, with a global vision. Now that they have finally surpassed the point where they can be easily suppressed, the partial exposures will elicit the pretense that the Reagan policy-makers are incompetent bunglers; the invariable elite response to failure of state plans is to focus attention on alleged personal inadequacies, so as to avert the threat that the public may come to understand the systematic nature of policy, the general support for it within elite circles (tactics aside), and the institutional roots of these commitments. But no one should be deluded into believing that we are witnessing the operations of fools and bunglers; their achievements in organizing efficient international terrorism are impressive, from the Middle East to Central America, and beyond.

Another crucial fact should also be kept in mind: the current scandals are a great tribute to the popular movements of the 1960s and since, which forced the state to resort to clandestine operations to conceal its terrorism and violence, operations so complex that finally they could not be entirely kept from public view. Had the public been apathetic and quiescent, as in earlier years, Reagan could have emulated the practices of John F. Kennedy when he simply sent the U.S. Air Force to carry out large-scale bombing and initiated defoliation and crop destruction missions in South Vietnam from 1961–62, or Lyndon Johnson when he escalated the aggression against South Vietnam by land and air, extending it to the north as well, and sent 23,000 Marines to the Dominican Republic to avert the threat of democracy there, all in early 1965, with very little protest at the time. Clandestine operations carry the risk of exposure, and of undermining the rhetorical pose of the government (for example, "combating terrorism"). This may inhibit the terrorist commanders, for a time at least. These facts serve to show that even in a generally depoliticized society like the United States, with no political parties or major media outside of the narrow business-based elite consensus, significant public action is quite possible and may influence policy, though indirectly, as during the Vietnam years and since. These are important facts to bear in mind in connection with the Middle East as well.

One element of the U.S.-organized international terror network is the World Anti-Communist League, a collection of Nazis, anti-Semites, death squad assassins, and some of the worst killers and thugs around the world, mobilized by the Reagan Administration into an effective network of murderers and torturers, worldwide in scope. Last month, the League attracted some attention in the course of the Hasenfus affair in Nicaragua. The *New York Times*, as usual reporting government propaganda as fact, claimed that the League had been purged of its more nefarious elements when General Singlaub took it over in the 1980s. The World Anti-Communist League had just then completed its annual conference in Europe (not reported in the media here to my knowledge). The leading Nazis were present, given respectful applause when their leaders – Nazi killers from the days of Hitler – mounted the podium to address the audience. The Latin American death squad leaders, allegedly expelled in 1984, reappeared at once in 1984–85 conferences sponsored by the U.S. affiliate – a tax-exempt "educational" organization. The League continues to include Nazis, racists of various assortments and killers from around the world. It is supported by the U.S. and several of its client-states, particularly Taiwan and South Korea, but also reportedly by Syria and other Arab states; and its workings are concealed by the Israeli lobby here. In the introduction to their recent book on the League, Scott Anderson and John Anderson comment that the Anti-Defamation League of B'nai Brith, a leading component of the domestic Israeli lobby, refused to provide them with information on this notorious collection of anti-Semites, who now serve a useful purpose within the Reaganite international terror network that they generally support.[13]

All of this, and much more, reveals a sophisticated understanding of how to conduct international terrorism, on a scale with few historical precedents.

The sordid record of the World Anti-Communist League should remind us that while Reaganite thuggery is unusual, it is not unique in U.S. history. Immediately after World War II, the U.S. turned to the task of suppressing the anti-fascist resistance throughout much of the world, often in favor of fascists and collaborators. One component of this global program was the recruitment of Nazi gangsters such as Klaus Barbie, "the Butcher of Lyons," who had been responsible for horrendous atrocities in France and was duly placed in charge of spying on the French for American intelligence. A far more important example was Reinhard Gehlen, in charge of Hitler's East European intelligence operations and quickly assigned the same tasks under the CIA, in West German intelligence. His organization was responsible for U.S. support for military actions within the USSR and Eastern Europe, in conjunction with armies that had been encouraged by Hitler. These operations were run out of George Kennan's office in the State Department according to John Loftus, who investigated these matters for the U.S. Justice department. Later, when many of these useful folk could no longer be protected in Europe, the U.S. authorities brought them here or to Latin America with the aid of the Vatican and fascist priests. They have continued to serve U.S. government interests, training torturers in methods devised by the Gestapo, helping establish the neo-Nazi National Security states in Latin America and the Central American death squad apparatus within the framework of the U.S.-trained security forces, and so on.[14]

We will understand very little about the world if we neglect the relevant historical context, commonly ignored or suppressed in official doctrine.

The same is true when we turn directly to the Middle East. Consider U.S. relations with Iran, now in the news, but with the historical context largely excised, as is usually the case when it teaches inconvenient lessons. The Reagan Administration argues that the recently reported arms shipments to Iran via an Israeli connection are part of an effort to establish contacts with "moderate" elements in Iran. There is a sense in which this claim is true; namely, if we enter the domain of conventional Newspeak, in which the term "moderate" is used to refer to elements that are properly obedient to U.S. orders and demands; it is counterpoised to "radical," used to refer to those who do not follow orders properly. Notice that the terminology has nothing to do with the commitment to violence and terror of these groups, or even their social and political goals, apart from the crucial defining feature; thus the mass murderer Suharto in Indonesia is a respected "moderate," but a peasant self-help group organized by the Church in El Salvador is "radical," and must be exterminated by Pol Pot-style terror conducted by the U.S. mercenary forces.

In Iran, the U.S. restored "moderates" to power with a CIA coup in what the *New York Times* (August 6, 1954) described as an "object lesson" to "underdeveloped countries with rich resources," an "object lesson in the cost that must be paid by one of their number which goes berserk with fanatical nationalism" and tries to take control of their own resources, thus becoming "radical." Iran remained "moderate" until the fall of the Shah in 1979 while compiling one of the worst human rights records in the world, as Amnesty International and other human rights groups regularly documented, not affecting the classification of the Shah as a "moderate" or the applause for him among U.S. elites. The Shah was supported by the Carter Administration to the very end of his bloody rule. The U.S. then apparently looked into the possibility of a military coup, but without success. Since that time, a flow of arms to Iran has been maintained, in part via Israel, which had very close relations with the Shah and his military.

Notice that very much the same was true in the case of Somoza in Nicaragua, who fell at about the same time. The Carter Administration also backed him until the end, with Israel providing the arms, surely with tacit U.S. backing, while he was killing tens of thousands in a last paroxysm of fury. Carter attempted to impose the rule of the National Guard when Somoza could no longer be maintained. Shortly after, remnants of the Guard were reestablished in Honduras and Costa Rica with the aid of U.S. proxies such as Argentina (then under the neo-Nazi generals, and thus a useful "moderate" client-state), and were then taken over directly by the U.S. and organized as a terrorist proxy army dedicated to preventing the threat of social reform in Nicaragua.

Meanwhile, U.S. elites underwent a magical conversion; they became profoundly concerned, for the first time, with human rights and "democracy" in Nicaragua and Iran, a sudden moral awakening that failed to elicit the contempt it richly merits.[15]

Returning to Iran, according to Israel's Ambassador to the U.S. Moshe Arens, in October 1982, Israel's supply of arms to Iran after the fall of the Shah was carried out "in coordination with the U.S. government . . . at almost the highest of levels." The objective "was to see if we could not find some areas of contact with the Iranian military, to bring down the Khomeini regime," or at least "to make contact with some military officers who some day might be in a position of power in Iran." Yaakov Nimrodi, the Israeli arms salesman and intelligence official who was under cover as military attaché in Iran during the Shah's reign, described this plan in a BBC broadcast in 1982. Former Israeli de facto Ambassador to Iran Uri Lubrani of the Labor Party added further details, in the same program:

> I very strongly believe that Tehran can be taken over by a very relatively small force, determined, ruthless, cruel. I mean the men who would lead that force will have to be emotionally geared to the possibility that they'd have to kill ten thousand people.

– demonstrating that they are "moderates," in the technical sense. Similar ideas were expressed by David Kimche, head of Israel's Foreign Office and former deputy director of the Mossad. Kimche and Nimrodi are now identified in the media as among those who initiated the mid-1980s program of U.S. military aid to Iran via Israel in connection with U.S. hostages and the "search for moderates." The publicized views of the Israelis concerned with these programs – long before there were any hostages – are suppressed, however. At the same time – early 1982 – these plans were generally endorsed, with varying degrees of skepticism as to their feasibility, by Richard Helms (ex-director of the CIA and former Ambassador to Iran), Robert Komer (a leading candidate for war crimes trials in the late 1960s and a high Pentagon official under Carter, one of the architects of the Rapid Deployment Force which, he suggested, could be used to support "moderates" after a military coup), and others.[16] All this too is now suppressed.

Essentially the same facts were also reported more recently, though ignored, well before the scandals erupted, for example, by

Israeli senior Foreign Ministry spokesman Avi Pazner, who confirmed in an interview that in 1982 Israel had sent Iran military supplies with the approval of the U.S., including spare parts for U.S.-made jet fighters.[17]

The arms flow to Iran through Israel (and probably other avenues) has very likely continued at a level sufficient to keep contacts with the proper elements of the Iranian military, though the U.S. is opposed to sending sufficient arms to enable Iran to win the Iran–Iraq war, which would be a disaster for the U.S. policy of support for Saddam Hussein. Thus the U.S. blocked a major Iranian arms deal with Israel last April, arresting an Israeli ex-general, among others.[18]

None of this is a discovery of late 1986, as these earlier references indicate. In 1982, a front-page story by current *New York Times* editor Leslie Gelb reported that half of the arms to Iran were "being supplied or arranged by Israel" – surely with U.S. knowledge and at least tacit authorization – "and the rest by free-lance arms merchants, some of whom may also have connections with Israeli intelligence," while the CIA was carrying out covert actions against the Khomeini regime from its bases in eastern Turkey.[19] And Arens's disclosures were prominently reported in the *Boston Globe* on successive days, among other cases. In more recent months, well before the "scandals," additional information surfaced. Thus in May, Patrick Seale reported that "Israeli and European arms dealers are rushing war supplies to Iran" as Israel now dispenses with "the usual roundabout arms routes"; "for example, a ship now at sea, carrying more than 25,000 tonnes of Israeli artillery, ammunition, gun barrels, aircraft parts and other war supplies" was ordered to proceed directly to Iran instead of transshipping through Zaire.[20] It is hard to take very seriously the current show of surprise on these matters.

Note again the continuing similarity between U.S. policy towards Iran and towards Nicaragua. There too, it is difficult to take seriously the current show of surprise over the fact that the Reagan Administration has been actively engaged in arranging military support for its proxy army, circumventing Congressional legislation, not to speak of the World Court ruling, irrelevant to a terrorist state, and laws going back to the eighteenth-century Neutrality Act.

We can learn more about these matters by attending to recent history. Notice first that the pattern of arms sales to Iran is a classic one, another crucial fact evaded in current commentary. For example, relations between the U.S. and Indonesia became bitterly hostile 30 years ago, so much so that the CIA sponsored a failed military rebellion in Indonesia in 1958. During the period of hostility, the U.S. continued to provide arms to the Sukarno regime. In late 1965, the pro-American General Suharto carried out a military coup, leading to the slaughter of several hundred thousand people, mostly landless peasants, and the destruction of the only mass-based political organization in Indonesia, the Indonesian Communist Party. Indonesia was thus restored to the Free World, opened to robbery and exploitation by U.S., Canadian, European and Japanese corporations, impeded only by the rapacity of the ruling generals, who imposed a corrupt and brutal dictatorship.

These developments were warmly welcomed by enlightened opinion in the West, and regarded as a vindication of U.S. aggression against South Vietnam (called "defense of South Vietnam" within the propaganda system), which provided a "shield" that encouraged the generals to carry out the necessary purge of their society. In Senate testimony after the slaughter, Defense Secretary McNamara was asked to explain the supply of arms to Indonesia during the period of intense hostility between the two countries. He was asked whether this arms supply had "paid dividends" and agreed that it had – including some 700,000 corpses at that point according to his Indonesian friends. A Congressional report held that training and maintaining communication with military officers paid "enormous dividends" in overthrowing Sukarno. Similarly, according to Pentagon sources, "United States military influence on local commanders was widely considered as an element in the coup d'état that deposed Brazil's leftist President João Goulart in 1964,"[21] installing a National Security State complete with torture, repression, and profits for the foreign investor, also greeted with acclaim by Kennedy liberals. The story was reenacted in Chile a few years later. During the Allende regime, the U.S. continued to supply arms while doing its best to bring down the regime, and was rewarded with the Pinochet coup, which again it welcomed.

The Iranian operations conform to a familiar pattern of policy planning, which is understandable and sometimes realistic. One can understand easily why it was publicly endorsed by Richard Helms and others in 1982.

The nature of U.S.–Iran relations under the Shah must also be recalled, in this connection. Iran was assigned a central role in controlling the Middle East under the Nixon doctrine, which was based upon the recognition that the U.S. did not have the capacity to enforce its will everywhere and must therefore rely on local "cops on the beat" (as Defense Secretary Melvin Laird put it), local proxies that would carry out their "regional responsibilities" within the "overall framework of order" maintained by the United States, in Henry Kissinger's phrase at the time. A (partially tacit) tripartite alliance was constructed linking Iran, Saudi Arabia and Israel under the U.S. aegis, committed to "defending" U.S. domination of the world's major energy reserves and protecting them from the primary enemy, the indigenous population, which might be infected with the "radical" idea that they should have a share in controlling our resources which happen to be in their lands. This is, incidentally, only one example of a worldwide pattern.[22]

It is in this context that the "special relationship" with Israel developed as well. In 1958, the National Security Council noted that a "logical corollary" of opposition to radical Arab nationalism (in the technical sense of the term) "would be to support Israel as the only strong pro-West power left in the Near East." According to David Ben-Gurion's biographer, Michael Bar-Zohar, at that time Israel concluded a "periphery pact," which was "long-lasting," with Iran, Turkey and Ethiopia, encouraged by U.S. Secretary of State John Foster Dulles. Through the 1960s, U.S. intelligence regarded Israel as a barrier to "radical nationalist" pressures against Saudi Arabia, and the conception of Israel as a "strategic asset" became institutionalized in U.S. policy after the U.S.-backed Israeli victory in 1967, and particularly after Israel's moves to block Syrian support for Palestinians being massacred in Jordan in 1970 at a time when the U.S. was unable to intervene directly for domestic reasons. The fall of the Shah enhanced Israel's role as a "strategic asset" serving as a base for enforcing U.S. interests in the region. Meanwhile, Israel increasingly provided subsidiary services to the U.S. in southern Africa, Asia and Latin America.[23]

About 1970, a split developed among U.S. elites over U.S. policy in the region. This was symbolized by the controversy between Secretary of State William Rogers, who advanced a plan for a political settlement of the Arab–Israel conflict along the lines of the international consensus of the time, and Henry Kissinger, who argued that we must maintain a "stalemate," his reason for backing Israel's rejection of Sadat's February 1971 offer of a full peace settlement along the general lines of official U.S. policy. Kissinger's views prevailed. Since that time his confrontationist, hard-line opposition to a genuine political settlement has dominated U.S. policy, which has preferred to see an Israeli "strategic asset" playing its role in U.S.

control of the region by the threat or use of force. This explains the continued U.S. commitment to block a political settlement, that would probably lead to Israel's integration into the region.[24]

The U.S. has consistently sought to maintain the military confrontation and to ensure that Israel remains a "strategic asset." In this conception, Israel is to be highly militarized, technologically advanced, a pariah state with little in the way of an independent economy apart from high tech production (often in coordination with the U.S.), utterly dependent on the United States and hence dependable, serving U.S. needs as a local "cop on the beat" and as a mercenary state employed for U.S. purposes elsewhere, for example, in support of near-genocide in Guatemala when domestic factors prevented Washington from participating as fully as it would have liked in this enterprise.[25]

What about U.S. relations with the Arab world? First, the U.S. will act to ensure that it controls the major energy resources of the Arabian peninsula: this is a central principle of U.S. foreign policy, as it has been throughout the post-World War II period. The U.S. will therefore support "moderate nationalists," such as the ruling elites in Saudi Arabia, well known for their "moderation." Saudi Arabia too is called upon to enlist in support of U.S. international terrorism, as already noted, and there should be little surprise at the revelation that it is deeply involved in the supply of arms to Iran along with its tacit Israeli ally and in U.S. terrorist activities in Central America, and probably elsewhere as well: southern Africa, for example. At the same time, the U.S. will consistently oppose "radical nationalists" who stand in the way of U.S. objectives. Libya is a case in point. While the U.S. appears to have supported Qaddafi's effort to raise oil prices in the early 1970s "in order to strengthen the position of the 'moderates,' such as Iran, Kuwait, and Saudi Arabia,"[26] Libya has increasingly been an obstacle to U.S. objectives, and was designated as a prime target from the earliest days of the Reagan Administration under the pretext of a "war against international terrorism."[27]

In this connection, we should bear in mind that the Reagan Administration faced a rather serious problem, from the outset. Contrary to many illusions, its major policies have quite generally been unpopular. The population continues, as before, to support social rather than military spending and to oppose the program of enhancing state power and converting the state, even more than before, into a welfare state for the rich – one major function of the Pentagon system, which provides a forced public subsidy to high-technology industry in the system of public subsidy and private profit called "free enterprise." The public has also generally opposed the "activist" foreign policy of subversion, intervention, international terrorism and aggression hailed as "the Reagan doctrine." There is a classic means to deal with the problem of bringing a reluctant population to accept policies to which it is opposed: induce fear, in accord with Mencken's dictum, quoted earlier. Therefore, we must have confrontations with the Evil Empire bent on our destruction, "the monolithic and ruthless conspiracy" committed to thwart our global benevolence and to destroy us, in John F. Kennedy's phrase during a rather similar period of U.S. history. But a problem arises: confrontations with the Evil Empire are too dangerous. They might be costly to us, and therefore cannot be undertaken. The solution to the dilemma is to create "proxies" of the Evil Empire, which can be attacked with impunity, since they are weak and defenseless. Libya is perfect for the role, particularly against the background of rampant anti-Arab racism in the United States, and within the general context of the "campaign against international terrorism" – that plague of the modern age from which the terrorist commanders in Washington must defend us, according to various "Operation Truths" conducted by the ideological institutions. It is quite easy to kill many Libyans without cost to ourselves – indeed with many cheers at home, including enlightened liberal opinion – as we defend ourselves against the "evil scourge of terrorism."

The next two years could be dangerous. The Reaganites want to leave a permanent stamp on American politics, whatever the outcome of the next elections. They want to prove that violence pays. They want to overcome "the sickly inhibitions against the use of military force" (Norman Podhoretz). The propaganda system has constructed a series of demons: the Sandinistas, who are a "cancer" that must be destroyed (George Shultz); Qaddafi, the "mad dog of the Middle East"; Arafat, "the father of modern terrorism"; Castro, who threatens to take over the Western Hemisphere in the service of the USSR; etc. If they can be destroyed by violence, the long-term effects on American culture will be profound. There will be no more "wimps" making treaties and entering into negotiations, no concern for political settlement, international law and similar tommy rot. Rather, the political system will be dominated by men lacking "sickly inhibitions" who get their kicks out of sending their client military forces and goon squads to torture people who cannot fight back – what is called "conservatism" in contemporary Newspeak.

5 International Terrorism: Image and Reality (1989)

There are two ways to approach the study of terrorism. One may adopt a *literal approach*, taking the topic seriously, or a *propagandistic approach*, construing the concept of terrorism as a weapon to be exploited in the service of some system of power. In each case it is clear how to proceed. Pursuing the literal approach, we begin by determining what constitutes terrorism. We then seek instances of the phenomenon – concentrating on the major examples, if we are serious – and try to determine causes and remedies. The propagandistic approach dictates a different course. We begin with the thesis that terrorism is the responsibility of some officially designated enemy. We then designate terrorist acts as "terrorist" just in case they can be attributed (whether plausibly or not) to the required source; otherwise they are to be ignored, suppressed or termed "retaliation" or "self-defense."

It comes as no surprise that the propagandistic approach is adopted by governments generally, and by their instruments in totalitarian states. More interesting is the fact that the same is largely true of the media and scholarship on terror in the Western industrial democracies, as has been documented in extensive detail.[1]

"We must recognise," Michael Stohl observes, "that by convention – and it must be emphasised *only* by convention – great power use and the threat of the use of force is normally described as coercive diplomacy and not as a form of terrorism," though it commonly involves "the threat and often the use of violence for what would be described as terroristic purposes were it not great powers who were pursuing the very same tactic."[2] Only one qualification must be added: the term "great powers" is restricted to favored states; in the Western conventions under discussion here, the Soviet Union is granted no such rhetorical license, and indeed can be charged and convicted on the flimsiest evidence, the mirror-image of Soviet practice.

Terrorism became a major public issue in the 1980s. The Reagan Administration took office announcing its dedication to stamp out what the president called "the evil scourge of terrorism," a plague spread by "depraved opponents of civilization itself" in "a return to barbarism in the modern age" (Secretary of State George Shultz). The campaign focused on a particularly virulent form of the plague: state-directed international terrorism. The central thesis attributed responsibility to a Soviet-based "worldwide terror network aimed at the destabilization of Western democratic society," in the words of Claire Sterling, whose highly praised book *The Terror Network* became the Bible of the Administration and the founding document of the new discipline of terrorology. It was taken to have provided "ample evidence" that terrorism occurs "almost exclusively in democratic or relatively democratic societies" (Walter Laqueur), leaving little doubt about the origins of the plague. The book was soon exposed as a worthless propaganda tract, but the thesis remained intact, dominating mainstream reporting, commentary and scholarship.

Concern over international terrorism peaked in the mid-1980s. Mideast/Mediterranean terrorism was selected by editors as the lead story of 1985 in an Associated Press poll, and a year later the tourism industry in Europe collapsed as Americans stayed away in fear of Arab terrorists infesting European cities. The plague then subsided, the monster having been tamed by "the strength of the cowboy," according to the approved version.

Shifting to the literal approach, we first define the concept of terrorism, and then investigate its application, letting the chips fall where they may. Let us see where this course leads.

THE CONCEPT OF TERRORISM

Concepts of political discourse are hardly models of clarity, but there is general agreement as to what constitutes terrorism. As a point of departure we may take the official United States Code: "'act of terrorism' means an activity that –

> (A) involves a violent act or an act dangerous to human life that is a violation of the criminal laws of the United States or any State, or that would be a criminal violation if committed within the jurisdiction of the United States or of any State; and (B) appears to be intended (i) to intimidate or coerce a civilian population; (ii) to influence the policy of a government by intimidation or coercion; or (iii) to affect the conduct of a government by assassination or kidnapping."[3]

The concept is not precisely delimited. First, the boundary between international terrorism and aggression is not always clear.

On this matter, let us give the benefit of the doubt to the United States and its clients: if they reject the charge of aggression in the case of some act of international violence, we will take it to fall under the lesser crime of terrorism. There is also disagreement over the distinction between terrorism and retaliation or legitimate resistance, to which we return.

U.S. sources also provide more succinct definitions of "terrorism." A U.S. Army manual on countering terrorism defines it as "the calculated use of violence or threat of violence to attain goals that are political, religious, or ideological in nature. This is done through intimidation, coercion, or instilling fear." Still simpler is the characterization in a Pentagon-commissioned study by noted terrorologist Robert Kupperman, which refers to the threat or use of force "to achieve political objectives without the full-scale commitment of resources."[4]

Kupperman, however, is not discussing terrorism; rather, low intensity conflict (LIC), a central doctrine of the Reagan Administration. Note that as the description indicates and practice confirms, LIC – much like its predecessor "counterinsurgency" – is hardly more than a euphemism for state-directed international terrorism, that is, reliance on force that does not reach the level of the war crime of aggression.

The point is recognized within the scholarly discipline, though with the usual doctrinal twist. One leading Israeli specialist, Professor Yonah Alexander, observes that "state-sponsored terrorism is a form of low-intensity conflict that states undertake when they find it convenient to engage in 'war' without being held accountable for their actions."[5] Alexander restricts his attention to the Kremlin conspiracy to destabilize the West with "surrogate groups," offering such examples as "an extensive PLO training programme . . . provided for Nicaragua." In this conception, "the PLO, which maintains a special relationship with Moscow," serves its Soviet master by passing on the "specialized training" in terrorism it acquires in the Soviet Union to Nicaragua, which is therefore able to conduct LIC against the United States and its interests. He also suggests ways in which "the Eastern Bloc's sincerity must be tested"; for example, "Showing willingness to stop propaganda campaigns linking the U.S. and its allies to terrorism."

As the examples illustrate, it would take a fertile imagination to conjure up a thought so outlandish as to ruffle the composure of the fraternity, as long as doctrinal purity is preserved.

TERRORISM AND THE POLITICAL CULTURE

There are many terrorist states in the world, but the United States is unusual in that it is *officially* committed to international terrorism, and on a scale that puts its rivals to shame. Thus Iran is surely a terrorist state, as Western governments and media rightly proclaim. Its major known contribution to international terrorism was revealed during the Iran–Contra inquiries: namely, Iran's perhaps inadvertent involvement in the U.S. proxy war against Nicaragua. This fact is unacceptable, therefore unnoticed, though the Iranian connection in U.S.-directed international terrorism was exposed at a time of impassioned denunciation of Iranian terrorism.

The same inquiries revealed that under the Reagan Doctrine, the U.S. had forged new paths in international terrorism. Some states employ individual terrorists and criminals to carry out violent acts abroad. But in the Reagan years, the U.S. went further, not only constructing a semi-private international terrorist network, but also an array of client and mercenary *states* – Argentina (under the Generals), Taiwan, South Korea, Israel, Saudi Arabia, and others – to finance and implement its terrorist operations. This advance in international terrorism was revealed during the period of maximal anguish over the plague, but did not enter into the discussion and debate.

The U.S. commitment to international terrorism reaches to fine detail. Thus the proxy forces attacking Nicaragua were directed by their CIA and Pentagon commanders to attack "soft targets," that is, barely defended civilian targets, and not to "duke it out" with the army. The State Department specifically authorized attacks on agricultural cooperatives – exactly what we denounce with horror when the agent is Abu Nidal. Media doves expressed thoughtful approval of this stand. *New Republic* editor Michael Kinsley, at the liberal extreme of mainstream commentary, argued that we should not be too quick to dismiss State Department justifications for terrorist attacks on farming cooperatives: a "sensible policy" must "meet the test of cost-benefit analysis," an analysis of "the amount of blood and misery that will be poured in, and the likelihood that democracy will emerge at the other end." It is understood that U.S. elites have the right to conduct the analysis and pursue the project if it passes their tests.[6]

When a Contra supply plane was shot down in October 1986 with an American mercenary on board, it became impossible to suppress the evidence of illegal CIA supply flights to the proxy forces. The

Iran–Contra hearings ensued, focusing much attention on these topics. A few days after they ended, the Central American presidents signed the Esquipulas II peace agreement. The U.S. undertook at once to subvert it. The agreement identified one factor as "an indispensable element to achieving a stable and lasting peace in the region," namely, termination of any form of aid "to irregular forces or insurgent movements" on the part of "regional or extraregional" governments. In response, the U.S. moved at once to escalate the attacks on soft targets in Nicaragua. Congress and the media kept their eyes scrupulously averted from the rapid increase in CIA supply flights to several a day, while cooperating with the White House program of dismantling the unwanted accords, a goal finally achieved in January 1988, though further steps were required to subvert a follow-up agreement of the Central American presidents in February 1989.[7]

As supply and surveillance flights for the proxy forces increased, so did violence and terror, as intended. This too passed largely unnoticed, though an occasional reference can be found. The *Los Angeles Times* reported in October 1987 that "Western military analysts say the Contras have been stashing tons of newly airdropped weapons lately while trying to avoid heavy combat . . . Meanwhile, they have stepped up attacks on easy government targets like the La Patriota farm cooperative . . . where several militiamen, an elderly woman and her year-old grandson died in a pre-dawn shelling." To select virtually at random from the many cases deemed unworthy of notice, on November 21, 150 Contras attacked two villages in the southern province of Rio San Juan with 88 mm mortars and rocket-propelled grenades, killing six children and six adults and injuring 30 others. Even cooperatives of religious pacifists who refused to bear arms were destroyed by the U.S. terrorist forces. In El Salvador too, the military forces armed and trained by the U.S. attack cooperatives, killing, raping and abducting members, among routine terrorist atrocities.[8]

The decision of the International Court of Justice in June 1986 condemning the United States for the "unlawful use of force" and illegal economic warfare was dismissed as an irrelevant pronouncement by a "hostile forum" (*New York Times*). Little notice was taken when the U.S. vetoed a Security Council resolution endorsing the ruling and calling on all states to observe international law, and voted against General Assembly resolutions to the same effect (with Israel and El Salvador in 1986; with Israel alone in 1987). Also ignored was the Court ruling that all aid to the Contras is military, not humanitarian; it continued to be designated "humanitarian aid" in the media. The guiding principle, it appears, is that the U.S. is a lawless terrorist state and *this is right and just*, whatever the world may think, whatever international institutions may declare.

A corollary is the doctrine that no state has the right to defend itself from U.S. attack. The broad acquiescence in this remarkable doctrine was revealed as Reagan Administration Agitprop floated periodic stories about Nicaraguan plans to obtain jet interceptors. There was some criticism of the media for uncritically swallowing the disinformation, but a more significant fact was ignored: the general agreement that such behavior on the part of Nicaragua would be entirely unacceptable. When the tale was concocted to divert attention from the Nicaraguan elections of 1984, Senator Paul Tsongas of Massachusetts, with the support of other leading doves, warned that the U.S. would have to bomb Nicaragua if it obtained vintage 1950s MIGs, because "they're also capable against the United States," hence a threat to its security[9] – as distinct, say, from U.S. nuclear missiles on alert status in countries surrounding Russia, no threat to it because they are purely for defensive purposes. It is understood that jet interceptors might enable Nicaragua to protect its territory from the CIA supply flights that keep the U.S. proxy forces in the field and the surveillance flights that provide them with up-to-the-minute information on the disposition of Nicaraguan troops, so that they can safely attack soft targets. Understood, but scarcely mentioned.[10] And it seems that no one in the mainstream released the open secret that Nicaragua would happily accept French planes instead of MIGs if the U.S. had not pressured its allies to bar military aid so that we might cower in fear of "the Soviet-supplied Sandinistas."

The same issue arose in August 1988, when congressional doves effusively supported the Byrd Amendment on "Assistance for the Nicaraguan Resistance." Three days before, the Contras had attacked the passenger vessel *Mission of Peace*, killing two people and wounding 27, all civilians, including a Baptist minister from New Jersey who headed a U.S. religious delegation. The incident was unmentioned in the Senate debate on the Byrd Amendment. Rather, congressional doves warned that if the Nicaraguan Army carried out "an unprovoked military attack" or "any other hostile action" against the perpetrators of such terrorist atrocities, then Congress would respond with vigor and righteousness by renewing official military aid to them. Media coverage and other commentary found nothing odd or noteworthy in this stance.

The message is clear: no one has the right of self-defense against U.S. terrorist attack. The U.S. is a terrorist state *by right*. That is unchallengeable doctrine, so firmly established that in responsible discourse it cannot even be discussed, only presupposed, much like the doctrine that the U.S. attack against South Vietnam was the "defense of South Vietnam" against "internal aggression," perhaps unwise, the doves came to believe.

Accordingly, organization of a terrorist proxy army to subdue some recalcitrant population is a legitimate task. On the right, Jeane Kirkpatrick explained that "forceful intervention in the affairs of another nation" is neither "impractical" nor "immoral" – merely illegal, a crime for which people were hanged at Nuremberg and Tokyo with ringing declarations that this was not "victor's justice" because, as Justice Robert Jackson stated: "If certain acts and violations of treaties are crimes, they are crimes whether the United States does them or whether Germany does them. We are not prepared to lay down a rule of criminal conduct against others which we would not be willing to have invoked against us."[11]

Countering any such thoughts, Irving Kristol explains that "The argument from international law lacks all credibility." True, "a great power should not ordinarily intervene in the domestic affairs of a smaller nation," but this principle is overcome if "another great power has previously breached this rule." Since it is "beyond dispute" that "the Soviet Union has intervened in Nicaragua" by providing arms and technicians "in both the military and civilian spheres," then the U.S. has the right to send its proxy army to attack Nicaragua. By the same argument, the Soviet Union has a perfect right to attack Turkey or Denmark – far more of a security threat to it than Nicaragua is to the United States – since it is "beyond dispute" that the U.S. provides them with assistance, and would go well beyond that, surely, if the USSR were to exercise the right of aggression accorded it by Kristol's logic.

Kristol might, however, counter this argument too by invoking a crucial distinction that he has drawn elsewhere in connection with the right of forceful intervention by the United States: "insignificant nations, like insignificant people, can quickly experience delusions of significance," he explained. And when they do, these delusions must be driven from their minds by force: "In truth, the days of 'gunboat diplomacy' are never over . . . Gunboats are as necessary for international order as police cars are for domestic order." It presumably follows, then, that the U.S. is entitled to use violence against Nicaragua, an insignificant nation, though the USSR lacks this right in the case of Turkey or Denmark.[12]

The overwhelming endorsement for U.S.-directed international terrorism should not be obscured by the wide elite opposition to the Contra war. By 1986, polls showed that 80 percent of "leaders" opposed aid to the Contras, and there was vigorous debate in Congress and the media about the program. But it is important to attend to the terms of the debate. At the dissident extreme, Tom Wicker of the *New York Times* observed that "Mr. Reagan's policy of supporting [the contras] is a clear failure," so we should "acquiesce in some negotiated regional arrangement that would be enforced by Nicaragua's neighbors" – if they can take time away from slaughtering their own populations, a feature of these terror states that does not exclude them from the role of enforcing regional arrangements on the errant Sandinistas, against whom no remotely comparable charge could credibly be made. Expressing the same thought, the editors of the *Washington Post* saw the Contras as "an imperfect instrument," so that other means must be sought to "fit Nicaragua back into a Central American mode" and impose "reasonable conduct by a regional standard," the standard of Washington's terror states. Senate Majority Whip Alan Cranston, a leading dove, recognized that "the Contra effort is woefully inadequate to achieve . . . democracy in Nicaragua" (the U.S. aim by doctrinal fiat, whatever the facts may be), so the U.S. must find other means to "isolate" the "reprehensible" government in Managua and "leave it to fester in its own juices." No such strictures hold for Washington's murderous clients.

In short, there is little deviation from the basic terms of Michael Kinsley's "sensible policy." The questions have to do with efficacy, not principle. Our own state has the right to use violence as deemed appropriate.[13]

The motivation for the resort to international terrorism in the case of Nicaragua has been candidly explained. High Administration officials observed that the goal of the attack was "forcing [the Sandinistas] to divert scarce resources to the war and away from social programs." This was the basic thrust of the 1981 CIA program endorsed by the Administration. As outlined by former CIA analyst David MacMichael in his testimony before the World Court, this program had as its purpose: to use the proxy army to "provoke cross-border attacks by Nicaraguan forces and thus serve to demonstrate Nicaragua's aggressive nature," to pressure the Nicaraguan government to "clamp down on civil liberties within Nicaragua itself, arresting its opposition, demonstrating its allegedly inherent totalitarian nature and thus increase domestic dissent within the country," and to undermine the shattered economy. Discussing the strategy of maintaining a terrorist force within Nicaragua after the huge CIA supply operation was theoretically cancelled by Congress in February 1988 (and the proxy forces largely fled), a Defense Department official explained:

> Those 2000 hard-core guys could keep some pressure on the Nicaraguan government, force them to use their economic resources for the military, and prevent them from solving their economic problems – and that's a plus . . . Anything that puts pressure on the Sandinista regime, calls attention to its lack of democracy, and prevents the Sandinistas from solving their economic problems is a plus.

Viron Vaky, Assistant Secretary of State for Interamerican Affairs in the Carter Administration, observed that the principal argument for the terrorist attack is that "a longer war of attrition will so weaken the regime, provoke such a radical hardening of repression, and win sufficient support from Nicaragua's discontented population that sooner or later the regime will be overthrown by popular revolt, self-destruct by means of internal coups or leadership splits, or simply capitulate to salvage what it can." As a dove, Vaky regards the conception as "flawed" but in no way wrong.[14]

The terrorist forces fully understand their directives, as we learn from the most important defector of the 1980s, the head of intelligence of the main Contra force (FDN), Horacio Arce, whose *nom de guerre* was "Mercenario"; talk of "democrats" and "freedom fighters" is for home consumption. Sandinista defectors are eagerly exploited by the White House and the media, and the Contras generally received extensive coverage. But Contra *defectors* are another matter, particularly when they have unwelcome stories to relate. Arce was ignored in the U.S. when he defected in late 1988. In interviews in Mexico before returning to Managua to accept amnesty, Arce described his illegal training in an airforce base in the southern United States, identified by name the CIA agents who provided support for the Contras under an AID cover in the Honduran

Embassy in Tegucigalpa, outlined how the Honduran Army provides intelligence and support for Contra military activities, and discussed the immense corruption of the proxy forces and their sale of arms to the Honduran arms bazaar, where they then reach Salvadoran guerrillas. U.S. intelligence on "non-military targets" was particularly useful, he explains, because: "We attack a lot of schools, health centers, and those sort of things. We have tried to make it so that the Nicaraguan government cannot provide social services for the peasants, cannot develop its project . . . that's the idea." The effectiveness of the U.S. training is amply confirmed by the record.[15]

The Contra war easily qualifies as "state-sponsored terrorism," as former CIA director Stansfield Turner testified before Congress in April 1985. But one might argue that it should be termed outright aggression. That might be taken to be the import of the 1986 World Court decision. Let us, however, continue to give the U.S. the benefit of the doubt, thus assigning its actions against Nicaragua to the category of international terrorism.

INTERNATIONAL TERRORISM IN THE 1980S

During the 1980s, the primary locus of international terrorism was Central America. In Nicaragua the U.S. proxy forces left a trail of murder, torture, rape, mutilation, kidnapping and destruction, but were impeded because civilians had an army to defend them. No comparable problems arose in the U.S. client-states, where the main terrorist force attacking the civilian population *was* the army and other state security forces. In El Salvador, tens of thousands were slaughtered in what the Archbishop in October 1980, shortly after the operations moved into high gear, described as "a war of extermination and genocide against a defenseless civilian population." This exercise in state terror sought "to destroy the people's organizations fighting to defend their fundamental human rights," as Archbishop Oscar Romero warned shortly before his assassination while vainly pleading with President Carter not to send aid to the armed forces who, he continued, "know only how to repress the people and defend the interests of the Salvadorean oligarchy." The goals were largely achieved during the Reagan Administration, which escalated the savagery of the assault against the population to new heights. When it seemed that the U.S. might be drawn into an invasion that would be harmful to its own interests, there was some concern and protest in elite circles, but that abated as state terror appeared successful, with the popular organizations decimated and "decapitated." After elections under conditions of violence and repression guaranteeing victory to privileged elements acceptable to the U.S., the issue largely passed below the threshold.

Little notice was taken of the significant increase in state terror after the Esquipulas II accords; or of an Amnesty International report entitled *El Salvador: "Death Squads" – A Government Strategy* (October 1988), reporting the "alarming rise" in killings by official death squads as part of the government strategy of intimidating any potential opposition by "killing and mutilating victims in the most macabre way," leaving victims "mutilated, decapitated, dismembered, strangled or showing marks of torture . . . or rape." Since the goal of the government strategy is "to intimidate or coerce a civilian population" (that is, terrorism, as officially defined in the U.S. Code), it is not enough simply to kill. Rather, bodies must be left dismembered by the roadside, and women must be found hanging from trees by their hair with their faces painted red and their breasts cut off, while domestic elites pretend not to see as they continue to fund, train, and support the murderers and torturers.

In the same years, a massacre of even greater scale took place in Guatemala, also supported throughout by the United States and its mercenary states. Here too, terror increased after the Esquipulas II peace agreement in order to guard against steps towards democracy, social reform and protection of human rights called for in the accords. As in El Salvador, these developments were virtually ignored; the assigned task was to focus attention on Nicaragua and to express vast outrage when Nicaragua occasionally approached the lesser abuses that are regular practice in the U.S. client-states. Since the goal is to restore Nicaragua to "the Central American mode" and ensure that it observes the "regional standards" satisfied by El Salvador and Guatemala, terror in client-states is of no real concern, unless it becomes so visible as to endanger the flow of aid to the killers.[16]

Notice crucially that all of this is *international* terrorism, supported or directly organized in Washington with the assistance of its international network of mercenary states.

Well after the 1984 elections that were hailed for having brought democracy to El Salvador, the Church-based human rights organization *Socorro Juridico*, operating under the protection of the Archdiocese of San Salvador, described the results of the continuing terror, still conducted by "the same members of the armed forces who enjoy official approval and are adequately trained to carry out these acts of collective suffering," in the following terms:

> Salvadoran society, affected by terror and panic, a result of the persistent violation of basic human rights, shows the following traits: collective intimidation and generalized fear, on the one hand, and on the other the internalized acceptance of the terror because of the daily and frequent use of violent means. In general, society accepts the frequent appearance of tortured bodies, because basic rights, the right to life, has absolutely no overriding value for society.[17]

The same comment applies to the societies that oversee these operations, or simply look the other way.

BEFORE THE OFFICIAL PLAGUE

International terrorism is, of course, not an invention of the 1980s. In the previous two decades, its major victims were Cuba and Lebanon.

Anti-Cuban terrorism was directed by a secret Special Group established in November 1961 under the code name "Mongoose," involving 400 Americans, 2,000 Cubans, a private navy of fast boats, and a $50 million annual budget, run in part by a Miami CIA station functioning in violation of the Neutrality Act and, presumably, the law banning CIA operations in the United States.[18] These operations included bombing of hotels and industrial installations, sinking of fishing boats, poisoning of crops and livestock, contamination of sugar exports, etc. Not all of these actions were specifically authorized by the CIA, but no such considerations absolve official enemies.

Several of these terrorist operations took place at the time of the Cuban missile crisis of October–November 1962. In the weeks before, Garthoff reports, a Cuban terrorist group operating from Florida with U.S. government authorization carried out "a daring speedboat strafing attack on a Cuban seaside hotel near Havana where Soviet military technicians were known to congregate, killing a score of Russians and Cubans"; and shortly after, attacked British and Cuban cargo ships and again raided Cuba among other actions that were stepped up in early October. At a tense moment of the missile crisis, on November 8, a terrorist team dispatched from the United States blew up a Cuban industrial facility after the Mongoose operations had been officially suspended. Fidel Castro alleged that 400 workers had been killed in this operation, guided by "photographs taken by spying planes." This terrorist act, which might have set off a global nuclear war, evoked little comment when it was revealed. Attempts to assassinate Castro and other terror continued immediately after the crisis terminated, and were escalated by Nixon in 1969.[19]

Such operations continued after the Nixon years. In 1976, for example, two Cuban fishing vessels were attacked in April by boats from Miami, the main center of anti-Cuban terrorism worldwide. A few weeks later, the Cuban embassy in Portugal was bombed with two killed. In July, the Cuban mission to the UN in New York was bombed and there were bombings aimed at Cuban targets in the Caribbean and Colombia, along with the attempted bombing of a pro-Cuban meeting at the Academy of Music in New York. In August, two officials of the Cuban embassy in Argentina were kidnapped and Cubana airline offices in Panama were bombed. The Cuban embassy in Venezuela was fired upon in October and the embassy in Madrid was bombed in November. In October, CIA-trained Cuban exiles bombed a Cubana civilian airliner, killing all 73 aboard, including Cuba's gold medal-winning international fencing team. One of the agents of this terrorist operation, Bay of Pigs veteran Luis Posada Carriles, was sprung from the Venezuelan jail where he was held for the bombing; he found his way to El Salvador, where he was put to work at the Ilopango military airbase to help organize the U.S. terrorist operations in Nicaragua. The CIA attributed 89 terrorist operations in the U.S. and the Caribbean area for 1969–79 to Cuban exile groups, and the major one, OMEGA 7, was identified by the FBI as the most dangerous terrorist group operating in the U.S. during much of the 1970s.[20]

Cuba figures heavily in scholarly work on international terrorism. Walter Laqueur's standard work (see note 1) contains many innuendoes about possible Cuban sponsorship of terrorism, though little evidence. There is not a word, however, on the terrorist operations *against* Cuba. He writes that in "recent decades . . . the more oppressive regimes are not only free from terror, they have helped to launch it against more permissive societies." The intended meaning is that the United States, a "permissive society," is one of the victims of international terrorism, while Cuba, an "oppressive regime," is one of the agents. To establish the conclusion it is necessary to suppress the fact that the U.S. has undeniably launched major terrorist attacks against Cuba and is relatively free from terror itself; and if there is a case to be made against Cuba, Laqueur has signally failed to present it.

Turning to the second major example of the pre-Reagan period, in southern Lebanon from the early 1970s the population was held hostage with the "rational prospect, ultimately fulfilled, that affected populations would exert pressure for the cessation of hostilities" and acceptance of Israeli arrangements for the region (Abba Eban, commenting on Prime Minister Menachem Begin's account of atrocities in Lebanon committed under the Labor government in the style "of regimes which neither Mr. Begin nor I would dare to mention by name," Eban observed, acknowledging the accuracy of the account).[21] Notice that this justification, offered by a respected Labor Party dove, places these actions squarely under the rubric of international terrorism (if not aggression).

Thousands were killed and hundreds of thousands driven from their homes in these attacks. Little is known because the matter was of no interest; PLO attacks against Israel in the same years, barbaric but at a far lesser scale, elicited great indignation and extensive coverage. ABC correspondent Charles Glass, then a journalist in Lebanon, found "little American editorial interest in the conditions of the south Lebanese. The Israeli raids and shelling of their villages, their gradual exodus from south Lebanon to the growing slums on the outskirts of Beirut were nothing compared to the lurid tales of the 'terrorists' who threatened Israel, hijacked aeroplanes and seized embassies." The reaction was much the same, he continues, when Israeli death squads were operating in southern Lebanon after the 1982 Israeli invasion. One could read about them in the London *Times*, but U.S. editors were not interested. Had the media reported the operations of "these death squads of plainclothes Shin Beth [secret police] men who assassinated suspects in the villages and camps of south Lebanon . . . stirring up the Shi'ite Muslim population and helping to make the Marine presence untenable," there might have been some appreciation of the plight of the U.S. Marines deployed in Lebanon. They seemed to have no idea why they were there apart from "the black enlisted men: almost all of them said, though sadly never on camera, that they had been sent to protect the rich against the poor." "The only people in Lebanon they identified with were the poor Shi'ite refugees who lived all around their base at the Beirut airport; it is sad that it was probably one of these poor Shi'ites . . . who killed 241 of them on 23 October 1983." If any of these matters had been reported, it might have been possible to avert, or at the very least to comprehend, the bombing in which the Marines were killed, victims of a policy that "the press could not explain to the public and their information officers could not explain to the Marines themselves."[22]

In 1976, Syria entered Lebanon with U.S. approval and helped implement further massacres, the major one at the Palestinian refugee camp of Tel Al-Zaater, where thousands were murdered by Syrian-backed Christian forces with Israeli arms.[23]

Without proceeding further, it is clear that the plague of state-directed international terrorism was rampant well before it was converted into a major issue by the "public diplomacy" of the Reagan Administration.

THE CANON: RETAIL TERRORISM

Wholesale terrorism of the kind reviewed here has largely been excluded from the discussion of "the evil scourge of terrorism." Let us then turn to the smaller-scale acts of terror that fall within the canon.

Here too, the record goes back well before the 1980s, though the literature is too selective to be very useful. To mention a few examples not found in Laqueur's standard source, while he refers to the use of letter bombs and "a primitive book bomb" used by approved villains, there is no mention of the sophisticated book bomb used by Israeli intelligence to kill General Mustapha Hafez in Gaza in 1956 at a time when he was responsible for preventing Palestinian Fedayeen from infiltrating to attack Israeli targets.[24] Laqueur's review of the use of letter bombs does not include the testimony of Ya'akov Eliav, who claims to have been the first to use letter bombs when he served as a commander of the terrorist group headed by the current Prime Minister of Israel, Yitzhak Shamir (Lehi, the "Stern Gang"). Working from Paris in 1946, he arranged to have 70 such bombs sent in official British government envelopes to all members of the British cabinet, the heads of the Tory opposition, and several military commanders. In June 1947, he and an accomplice were caught by Belgian police while attempting to send these letter bombs, and all were intercepted.[25]

The standard record of hijacking and bombing of airliners also avoids some important topics, among them, the U.S. refusal of requests from communist countries in the 1950s to return "persons who hijacked planes, trains, and ships to escape" (State Department legal advisor Abraham Sofaer, who notes that the policy was "reexamined" from the late 1960s – when the U.S. and its allies were targeted). The first airplane hijacking in the Middle East also falls outside the canon: Israel's hijacking of a Syrian airways civilian jet in 1954, with the intent "to get hostages in order to obtain the release of our prisoners in Damascus," who had been captured on a spy mission in Syria (Prime Minister Moshe Sharett). Also excluded is the shooting down of an unarmed Egyptian civilian plane by the Israeli air force in October 1956, killing 16 people including four journalists, in a failed attempt to assassinate Field Marshall Abdul Hakim Amar, second to President Nasser, at a time when the two countries were not in a state of war. This was a pre-planned operation, thus unlike Israel's downing of a Libyan civilian airliner with 110 killed as it was lost in a sandstorm two minutes' flight time from Cairo, towards which it was heading. This February 1973 action took place while Israeli airborne and amphibious forces were attacking Tripoli in northern Lebanon, killing 31 people (mainly civilians) and destroying classrooms, clinics and other buildings in a raid justified as preemptive.[26]

Such matters were (and are) dismissed as insignificant, if even noticed. The reaction to Arab terrorism is quite different.

Turning to the 1980s, consider 1985, when media concern peaked. The major single terrorist act of the year was the blowing up of an Air India flight, killing 329 people. The terrorists had reportedly been trained in a paramilitary camp in Alabama run by Frank Camper, where mercenaries were trained for terrorist acts in Central America and elsewhere. According to ex-mercenaries, Camper had close ties to U.S. intelligence and was personally involved in the Air India bombing, allegedly a "sting" operation that got out of control. On a visit to India, Attorney-General Edwin Meese conceded in a backhanded way that the terrorist operations originated in a U.S. terrorist training camp.[27] Any connection of a terrorist to Libya, however frail, suffices to demonstrate that Qaddafi is a "mad dog" who must be eliminated.

In the Middle East, the main center of international terrorism according to the canon, the worst single terrorist act of 1985 was a car bombing in Beirut on March 8 that killed 80 people and wounded 256. "About 250 girls and women in flowing black chadors, pouring out of Friday prayers at the Imam Rida Mosque, took the brunt of the blast," Nora Boustany reported three years later: "At least 40 of them were killed and many more were maimed."

The bomb also "burned babies in their beds," "killed a bride buying her trousseau," and "blew away three children as they walked home from the mosque" as it "devastated the main street of the densely populated" West Beirut suburb. The target was the Shi'ite leader Sheikh Fadlallah, accused of complicity in terrorism, but he escaped. The attack was arranged by the CIA and its Saudi clients with the assistance of Lebanese intelligence and a British specialist, and specifically authorized by CIA director William Casey, according to Bob Woodward's account in his book on Casey and the CIA.[28]

Even under its chosen conventions, then, it seems that the United States wins the prize for acts of international terrorism in the peak year of the official plague. The U.S. client-state of Israel follows closely behind. Its Iron Fist operations in Lebanon were without parallel for the year as sustained acts of international terrorism in the Middle East, and the bombing of Tunis (with tacit U.S. support) wins second prize for single terrorist acts, unless we take this to be a case of actual aggression, as was determined by the U.N. Security Council.[29]

In 1986, the major single terrorist act was the U.S. bombing of Libya – assuming, again, that we do not assign this attack to the category of aggression.[30] For 1986 too the United States seems to place well in the competition for the prize for international terrorism, even apart from the wholesale terrorism it sponsored in Central America, where, in that year, Congress responded to the World Court call for an end to the "unlawful use of force" by voting $100 million of military aid to the U.S. proxy forces in what the Administration gleefully described as a virtual declaration of war.

TERROR AND RESISTANCE

Let us turn now to several contentious questions about the scope of terrorism, so far avoided.

Consider the boundary between terrorism and legitimate resistance. Sometimes, nationalist groups are prepared to describe their actions as terrorism, and some respected political leaders decline to condemn acts of terrorism in the national cause. An example particularly relevant to current discussion is the pre-state Zionist movement. Israel is the source of the 1980s "terrorism industry" (then transferred to the U.S. for further development), as an ideological weapon against Palestinians.[31] The PLO is anathema in the United States. A special act of Congress, the Anti-Terrorism

Act of 1987, "prohibits American citizens from receiving any assistance, funds, or 'anything of value except informational materials' from the PLO," which is not permitted to establish offices or other facilities to further its interests.[32] Palestinian violence has received worldwide condemnation.

The pre-state Zionist movement carried out extensive terror, killing many civilians, mainly Arabs, also murdering British diplomat Lord Moyne and U.N. mediator Folke Bernadotte (whose killers were protected after the state was established). In 1943, current Prime Minister Yitzhak Shamir wrote an article entitled "Terror" for the journal of the terrorist organization he headed (Lehi) in which he proposed to "dismiss all the 'phobia' and babble against terror with simple, obvious arguments." "Neither Jewish morality nor Jewish tradition can be used to disallow terror as a means of war," he wrote, and "We are very far from any moral hesitations when concerned with the national struggle." "First and foremost, terror is for us a part of the political war appropriate for the circumstances of today, and its task is a major one: it demonstrates in the clearest language, heard throughout the world including by our unfortunate brethren outside the gates of this country, our war against the occupier." As has been widely observed in Israel, the British occupation was far less repressive than Israel's rule in the occupied territories and faced a much more violent resistance.

Isaiah Berlin recalls that Chaim Weizmann, first president of Israel and one of the most revered figures of the national movement, "did not think it morally decent to denounce either the acts [of Jewish terrorism] or their perpetrators in public . . . he did not propose to speak out against acts, criminal as he thought them, which sprang from the tormented minds of men driven to desperation, and ready to give up their lives to save their brothers from what, he and they were equally convinced, was a betrayal and a destruction cynically prepared for them by the foreign offices of the western powers."[33]

The archives of the mainstream Zionist resistance group, Haganah, contain the names of 40 Jews killed by Menachem Begin's Irgun and Lehi. Yitzhak Shamir's personal assassination of a Lehi associate is a famous incident. The official Irgun history, while recalling with admiration many acts of terror against Arab civilians, also cites the murder of a Jewish member who, it was feared, would give information to the police if captured. Suspected collaborators were a particular target, from the earliest days. The official history of the Haganah, under "special activities," describes the assassination of the Dutch orthodox Jew Jacob de Haan by Haganah assassins in 1924 because he was seeking "to construct a united front of the old Yishuv [Jewish community] with the Arab Higher Committee against the new Yishuv and the Zionist enterprise." In later years the Haganah Special Actions Squads carried out "punitive actions" against Jewish informers. A Haganah prison in Haifa in the 1940s contained a torture chamber for interrogation of Jews suspected of collaboration with the British. In a 1988 interview, Dov Tsisis describes his work as a Haganah enforcer, "following orders, like the Nazis," to "eliminate" Jews interfering with the national struggle, "particularly informers." He also rejects the familiar charge that the murderous bombing of the King David Hotel was carried out by the Irgun alone, identifying himself as the special representative of Haganah commander Yitzhak Sadeh, who authorized it. He was later recommended by Moshe Dayan to replace him as commander of an elite unit.[34]

Anti-Nazi resisters also describe the murder of collaborators. Israel Shahak, one of Israel's foremost civil libertarians and a survivor of the Warsaw ghetto and Bergen-Belsen, recalls that "before the Warsaw ghetto revolt . . . the Jewish underground, with complete justification, killed every Jewish collaborator that they could find." He recalls a vivid childhood memory from February 1943, "when I danced and sang together with other children around the body [of a murdered Jewish collaborator], with blood still flowing from his body, and to the present I have no regrets about that; on the contrary." Citing the memoirs of Yitzhak (Antek) Zuckerman, the leader of the Warsaw Ghetto uprising, Leah Enbal writes that "Nine months before the outbreak of the Warsaw Ghetto uprising the Jewish underground initiated the systematic extermination of collaborators from the Judenrat and the Jewish police," sometimes with "collective killings." "It would have been impossible to fight the Germans without first finishing with the internal treachery," Zuckerman recalled. The killing of collaborators was regarded as legitimate revenge by the ordinary person. German collaborators, sometimes "Gestapo members," had to be "destroyed to the last one," including those "whose activities were in contradiction to Jewish interests." It was a "historic failure" to "delay too long" in killing Jewish collaborators, Zuckerman added: "Today, for example, I am certain that, wherever there is internal treachery, the war must begin with elimination of the internal treachery. [Delay in doing this] was our great failure, our disgrace."[35]

These comments appeared during a wave of intense criticism of Palestinians for killing collaborators with the Israeli secret police during the *Intifada*.

While frank avowal of terrorism of the Shamir variety can occasionally be found, the more normal pattern is for actions undertaken against oppressive regimes and occupying armies to be considered resistance by their perpetrators and terrorism by the rulers, even when they are nonviolent. What the Western democracies considered to be resistance in occupied Europe or Afghanistan, the Nazis and the USSR branded terror – in fact, terror inspired from abroad, therefore international terrorism. The U.S. took the same position towards the South Vietnamese who bore the brunt of the U.S. attack.

On similar grounds, the Apartheid regime of South Africa surely takes strong exception to the international conventions on terrorism: specifically, to the major U.N. General Assembly resolution condemning international terrorism and calling on all states to act to combat the plague. The reason is that the General Assembly:

> *Considers* that nothing in the present resolution could in any way prejudice the right to self-determination, freedom and independence, as derived from the Charter of the United Nations, of peoples forcibly deprived of that right . . . , particularly peoples under colonial and racist regimes and foreign occupation or other forms of colonial domination, nor . . . the right of these peoples to struggle to this end and to seek and receive support [in accordance with the Charter and other principles of international law].[36]

While this provision was endorsed by virtually the entire world, South Africa was not entirely alone in opposing it. The resolution passed 153 to two (Honduras alone abstaining). Explaining their negative votes, the U.S. and Israel referred to the cited paragraph, understood to refer to resistance to their South African ally by the African National Congress (one of the "more notorious terrorist groups" in the world, according to official Washington), and to Israel's military occupation of the West Bank and Gaza, then entering its third decade.[37] Washington's refusal to endorse the strongest UN resolution condemning the "return to barbarism in the modern age" at the peak of concern, and the reasons for it, elicited no comment.

The issue came to a head in late 1988 in connection with the Israel–Palestinian conflict. In November, the Palestine National

Council (PNC) declared an independent Palestinian state alongside of Israel, endorsing the UN terrorism resolution and other relevant UN resolutions. Yasser Arafat repeated the same positions in subsequent weeks in Europe, including a special session of the UN General Assembly convened in Geneva when he was barred from New York, in violation of legal obligations to the United Nations, on the grounds that his presence there would pose an unacceptable threat to the security of the United States. The reiteration by the PNC and Arafat of the UN terrorism resolution was denounced in the United States on the grounds that the Palestinian leadership had failed to meet Washington's conditions on good behavior, including "Rejection of terrorism in all its forms" without qualification.

The editors of the *New York Times* ridiculed the PNC endorsement of international conventions on terrorism as "the old Arafat hedge." Anthony Lewis, who is at the outer limits of tolerable dissent on these matters, wrote that Arafat was progressing, but not sufficiently: "the United States says correctly that the PLO must unambiguously renounce all terrorism before it can take part in negotiations," and this proper condition had not yet been met. The general reaction largely fell within these bounds.

The reasoning is straightforward. The PLO failed to join the U.S., Israel and Apartheid South Africa off the spectrum of world opinion, and therefore merits either derision (from the hardliners) or encouragement for its limited but insufficient progress (from the dissidents).

When the U.S. became isolated diplomatically by December 1988, Washington moved to a fallback position, pretending that Arafat had capitulated to U.S. demands, though his position had not changed in any substantive way – for years, in fact. With Arafat's capitulation to U.S. demands now official, by U.S. stipulation, he could be rewarded by discussions with the U.S. Ambassador in Tunis. As was underscored by Israeli Defense Minister Yitzhak Rabin, the U.S.–PLO discussions were designed to deflect diplomatic pressures for settlement and to grant Israel a year or more to suppress the Palestinian uprising (*Intifada*) by "harsh military and economic pressure" so that "they will be broken."[38]

The issue of terrorism versus resistance arose at once during the U.S.–PLO discussions. The protocols of the first meeting were leaked and published in the *Jerusalem Post*, which expressed its pleasure that "the American representative adopted the Israeli positions," stating two crucial conditions that the PLO must accept: the PLO must call off the *Intifada*, and must abandon the idea of an international conference. With regard to the *Intifada*, the U.S. stated its position as follows:

> Undoubtedly the internal struggles that we are witnessing in the occupied territories aim to undermine the security and stability of the State of Israel, and we therefore demand cessation of those riots, *which we view as terrorist acts against Israel*. This is especially true as we know you are directing, from outside the territories, those riots which are sometimes very violent.[39]

Once this "terrorism" is called off and the previous conditions of repression restored, the U.S. and Israel can proceed to settle matters to their satisfaction. Again, the resistance of an oppressed population to a brutal military occupation is "terror," from the point of view of the occupiers and their paymaster.

The same issue arose during the operations of the Israeli Army in southern Lebanon. These too were guided by the logic outlined by Abba Eban, cited earlier. The civilian population was held hostage under the threat of terror to ensure its acceptance of the political arrangements dictated by Israel for southern Lebanon and the occupied territories. The threat can be realized at will, and is, with extreme brutality.[40] But it does not count as terror, given the agent and its backer. Nor does it even merit mild reprimand. The acts fall under legitimate self-defense, by definition.

Adopting the same concepts, it is reasonable to report, without comment, that Secretary of State Shultz's concern over international terrorism became "his passion" after the suicide bombing of U.S. Marines in Lebanon in October 1983. There was no need to call upon witnesses from Nicaragua, Angola, Lebanon, the occupied territories, and elsewhere, to testify to Shultz's "passion," either then, or when renewing the praise for his "visceral contempt for terrorism" and "personal crusade" against it in explaining his refusal to admit Arafat to speak at the United Nations.[41]

Doubtless Syria too regards the Lebanese who resist its bloody rule as "terrorists," but such a claim would evoke the ridicule and contempt it merits. The reaction shifts along with the cast of characters.

TERROR AND RETALIATION

The concept of retaliation is a useful device of ideological warfare. Throughout a cycle of violent interaction, each side typically portrays its own acts as retaliation for the terrorism of the adversary. In the Middle East, the Israeli–Arab conflict provides many examples. Israel being a client-state, U.S. practice uncritically adopts the Israeli conventions.

To illustrate, consider the hijacking of the *Achille Lauro* and the murder of Leon Klinghoffer in 1985, doubtless a vile terrorist act. The hijackers, however, regarded their action not as terror but as retaliation for the Israeli bombing of Tunis a week earlier with U.S. support, either an "act of armed aggression" (as the Security Council determined) or only murderous international terrorism (giving the benefit of the doubt to the U.S. and its client). But for the perpetrators, the Tunis bombing was not terror or aggression, but rather legitimate retaliation for the cold-blooded murder of three Israelis in Larnaca, Cyprus (with no suspected connection to Tunis or the victims there). The perpetrators of the Larnaca killings, in turn, regarded their act not as terrorism, but as retaliation in response to Israeli terrorism in international waters for many years. The facts are not contested, and are even occasionally reported, but they do not constitute "terrorism" by definition, so the Larnaca crimes cannot be retaliation, as claimed. The Israeli operations are little discussed, and do not fall within the canon.[42]

There are many similar cases. The concepts of terrorism and retaliation are supple instruments, readily adapted to the needs of the moment.

FROM LITERALISM TO DOCTRINAL NECESSITY

This review of state-directed international terrorism suffers from a serious flaw: it has adhered to naive literalism and is thus irrelevant to contemporary debate over the plague of the modern age.

The review is, furthermore, very far from comprehensive. It barely scratches the surface even for Central America and the Middle East, and international terrorism is by no means limited to these regions. But it does suffice to raise a few questions. One stands out particularly: How is it possible for scholars and the media to maintain the thesis that the plague of the modern age is traceable to the Soviet-based "worldwide terror network aimed at the destabilization of Western democratic society"? How is it possible to identify Iran, Libya, the PLO, Cuba and other official enemies as the leading practitioners of international terrorism?

The answer, as we have seen, is very simple. We must abandon the literal approach and recognize that terrorist acts fall within the canon only when conducted by official enemies. When the U.S. and its clients are the agents of terrorist atrocities, they either disappear from the record or are transmuted to acts of retaliation and self-defense in the service of democracy and human rights. Then all becomes clear.

Turning finally to possible remedies for the plague, the standard literature offers some proposals. Walter Laqueur urges that "the obvious way to retaliate" against international terrorism "is, of course, to pay the sponsors back in their own coin," though such legitimate response may be difficult for Western societies, which fail to comprehend that others do not share their "standards of democracy, freedom and humanism." Before those afflicted with incurable literalism draw the wrong conclusions, however, it should be stressed that legitimate response does not include bombs in Washington and Tel Aviv, given the careful way in which the concept of terrorism has been crafted.

The *New York Times* called upon an expert on terrorism to offer his thoughts on how to counter the plague. His advice, based upon long experience, was straightforward: "The terrorists, and especially their commanders, must be eliminated." He gave three examples of successful counterterrorist actions: the U.S. bombing of Libya, the Israeli bombing of Tunis, and Israel's invasion of Lebanon. He recommends more of the same "if the civilized world is to prevail." The *Times* editors gave his article the title: "It's Past Time to Crush the Terrorist Monster," and they highlighted the words: "Stop the slaughter of innocents." They identify the author as "Israel's Minister of Trade and Industry."[43]

The author's name is Ariel Sharon. His terrorist career, dating back to the early 1950s, includes the slaughter of 69 villagers in Qibya and 20 at the al-Bureig refugee camp in 1953; terrorist operations in Gaza and northeastern Sinai in the early 1970s including the expulsion of some 10,000 farmers into the desert, their homes bulldozed and farm lands destroyed in preparation for Jewish settlement; the invasion of Lebanon undertaken in an effort – as now widely conceded – to overcome the threat of PLO diplomacy; the subsequent massacre at Sabra and Shatila; and others.

Some might feel that the choice of Sharon to provide "the civilized world" with lessons on how to "stop the slaughter of innocents" may be a little odd, perhaps perverse, possibly even hypocritical. But that is not so clear. The choice is not inconsistent with the values expressed in action, and in the intellectual culture expressed in words, or in silence.

In support of this conclusion, we may observe that the remedy for international terrorism – at least, a substantial component of it – lies within our grasp, and is extremely simple: stop participating in it. But no action is taken to this end, and indeed the matter is scarcely even discussed. Rather, one finds accolades to our benevolent intentions and nobility of purpose, our elevated "standards of democracy, freedom and humanism," sometimes flawed in performance. Elementary facts cannot be perceived and obvious thoughts are unthinkable. Simple truths, when expressed, elicit disbelief, horror and outrage – at the fact that they are voiced.

In a moral and intellectual climate such as this, it may well be appropriate for the world's greatest newspaper to select Ariel Sharon as our tutor on the evils of terrorism and how to combat it.

6 The World after September 11 (2001)

I am sure I am not the only one to have been reminded in the past months of some wise and prescient words of one of the most impressive figures of twentieth-century America, the radical pacifist A.J. Muste. As the U.S. entered World War II 60 years ago, he predicted with considerable accuracy the contours of the world that would emerge after the U.S. victory, and a little later, observed that "the problem after a war is with the victor. He thinks he has just proved that war and violence pay. Who will now teach him a lesson?"

Far too many people around the world were to learn the bitter meaning of these words. It is only in folk-tales, children's stories, and the journals of intellectual opinion that power is used wisely and well to destroy evil. The real world teaches very different lessons, and it takes willful ignorance to fail to perceive them.

These are, unfortunately, leading themes of history. In his major study of European state-formation, Charles Tilly observed, accurately enough, that over the last millennium, "war has been the dominant activity of European states," for an unfortunate reason: "The central tragic fact is simple: coercion *works*; those who apply substantial force to their fellows get compliance, and from that compliance draw the multiple advantages of money, goods, deference, access to pleasures denied to less powerful people."[1] These are close to historical truisms, which most of the people of the world have learned the hard way. The deference commonly includes the acclaim of the educated classes. Resort to overwhelming means of violence to destroy defenseless enemies with impunity tends to win particular admiration, and also to become natural, a demonstration of one's virtue; again, close to historical-cultural universals.

One normal concomitant of easy victories over defenseless enemies is the entrenchment of the habit of preferring force over the pursuit of peaceful means. Another is the high priority of acting without authority. The incarnation of the god who comes to Earth as the "perfect man" with the mission of eradicating evil from the world needs no higher authority. What is true of the most ancient Indian epics from millennia ago holds as well for the plagiarists of today. The preference for force, and rejection of authorization, have been notable features of the past decade of overwhelming and unchallenged power and crushing of much weaker adversaries, in accord with policy recommendations. As the first Bush Administration came into office, it undertook a National Security Policy Review dealing with "Third World threats." Parts were leaked to the press during the Gulf war. The Review concluded that "In cases where the U.S. confronts much weaker enemies" – that is, the only kind one chooses to fight – "our challenge will be not simply to defeat them, but to defeat them decisively and rapidly." Any other outcome would be "embarrassing" and might "undercut political support," understood to be thin.[2] With the collapse of the sole deterrent a few months later, the conclusions became even more firmly established, not surprisingly. These are, I think, some of the considerations that should be at the back of our minds when we contemplate the world after September 11.

Whatever one's judgment about the events of the past weeks, if we want to reach a reasonable assessment of what may lie ahead, we should attend carefully to several crucial factors. Among them are:

1. The premises on which policy decisions have been based.
2. Their roots in stable institutions and doctrines in very recent history, to a large extent involving the same decision-makers.
3. The ways these have been translated to specific actions.

I would like to say a few words about each of these topics.

The new millennium quickly produced two terrible new crimes, added to the gloomy record of persisting ones. The first was the terrorist attacks of September 11; the second, the response to them, surely taking a far greater toll of innocent lives, Afghan civilians who were themselves victims of the suspected perpetrators of the crimes of September 11. I will assume these to be Osama bin Laden and his al-Qaeda network. There has been a prima facie case from the outset, though little credible evidence has been produced despite what must be the most intensive investigations ever by the coordinated intelligence services of the major powers.[3] Such "leaderless resistance" networks, as they are called, are not easy nuts to crack.

An inauspicious sign is that in both cases the crimes are considered right and just, even noble, within the doctrinal framework of the perpetrators; and in fact are justified in almost the same words. Bin Laden proclaims that violence is justified in self-defense against the infidels who invade and occupy Muslim lands and against the brutal and corrupt governments they sustain there – words that have considerable resonance in the region even among those who despise and fear him. Bush and Blair proclaim, in almost identical words, that violence is justified to drive evil from our lands. The proclamations of the antagonists are not entirely identical. When bin Laden speaks of "our lands," he is referring to Muslim lands: Saudi Arabia, Egypt, Chechnya, Bosnia, Kashmir, and others; the radical Islamists who were mobilized and nurtured by the CIA and its associates through the 1980s despise Russia, but ceased their terrorist operations in Russia from Afghan bases after the Russians withdrew. When Bush and Blair speak of "our lands" they are, in contrast, referring to the world. The distinction reflects the power that the adversaries command. That either side can speak without shame of eradicating evil in the light of their records – that should leave us open-mouthed in astonishment, unless we adopt the easy course of effacing even very recent history.

Another fact with grim portent is that, in both cases, the perpetrators insist on underscoring the criminality of their acts. In the case of bin Laden, no discussion is needed. The U.S. pointedly rejected the framework of legitimacy that resides in the UN Charter. There has been much debate over whether the ambiguous Security Council declarations, or Article 51 of the UN Charter, provide authorization for the resort to force. It is, in my opinion, beside the point.

To resolve the debate would have been simple enough, had there been any wish to do so. There is scarcely any doubt that Washington could have obtained entirely unambiguous Security Council authorization, even if not for attractive reasons. Russia is eager to join the "coalition against terror" to gain U.S. support for its own massive terrorist crimes. China hopes to be admitted to the coalition of the just for the same reasons, and in fact, states throughout the world recognized at once that they could now enlist the support of the global superpower for their own violence and repression, a lesson not lost on the global managers either. British support is reflexive; France would have raised no objections. There would, in brief, have been no veto.

But Washington preferred to reject Security Council authorization and to insist on its unique right to act unilaterally in violation of international law and solemn treaty obligations, a right proclaimed by the Clinton Administration and its predecessors in clear and explicit words – warnings that we and others may choose to ignore, but at our peril. Similarly, Washington contemptuously dismissed the tentative offers to consider extradition of bin Laden and his associates; how real such possibilities were we cannot know, because of the righteous refusal even to consider them. This stand adheres to a leading principle of statecraft, called "establishing credibility" in the rhetoric of diplomacy and scholarship. And it is understandable. If a Mafia Don plans to collect protection money, he does not first ask for a Court order, even if he could obtain it. Much the same is true of international affairs. Subjects must understand their place, and must recognize that the powerful need no higher authority.

Thucydides remarked that "large nations do what they wish, while small nations accept what they must." The world has changed a great deal over several thousand years, but some things stay much the same.

The atrocities of September 11 are regarded as a historic event, which is true, though not, regrettably, because of their scale. In its civilian toll, the crime is not unusual in the annals of violence short of war. To mention only one example, so minor in context as to be a mere footnote, a Panamanian journalist, condemning the crimes of September 11, observed that for Panamanians the "sinister times" are not unfamiliar, recalling the U.S. bombing of the *barrio* Chorrillo during "Operation Just Cause" with perhaps thousands killed; our crimes, so there is no serious accounting.[4] The atrocities of September 11 are indeed a historic event, but because of their target. For the U.S., it is the first time since the British burned down Washington in 1814 that the national territory has been under serious attack, even threatened. There is no need to review what has been done to others in the two centuries since. For Europe, the reversal is even more dramatic. While conquering much of the world, leaving a trail of terror and devastation, Europeans were safe from attack by their victims, with rare and limited exceptions. It is not surprising, then, that Europe and its offshoots should be shocked by the crimes of September 11, a dramatic breach of the norms of acceptable behavior for hundreds of years.

It is also not surprising that they should remain complacent, perhaps mildly regretful, about the even more terrible suffering that followed. The victims, after all, are miserable Afghans – "uncivilized tribes," as Winston Churchill described them with contempt when he ordered the use of poison gas to "spread a lively terror" among them 80 years ago, denouncing the "squeamishness" of the soft-hearted ninnies who failed to understand that chemical weapons were just "the application of modern science to modern warfare" and must be used "to procure a speedy termination of the disorder which prevails on the frontier."[5]

Similar thoughts are heard today. The editors of the *New Republic*, who not long ago were calling for more military aid for "Latin-style fascists . . . regardless of how many are murdered" because "there are higher American priorities than Salvadoran human rights," now explain that "Operation Enduring Freedom is not a humanitarian intervention." From that accurate observation they conclude that "If we leave behind a country in chaos that can no longer serve as a base of operations against us, then we will have accomplished a necessary objective," and should "lose the obsession with nation-building" to try to repair what we have done to Afghanistan for 20 years, which is no concern of ours.[6]

While few are willing to sink to that level, it remains true that atrocities committed against Afghans carry little moral stigma, for one reason, because such practices have been so familiar throughout history even when there has been no pretext other than greed and domination. And retribution knows no bounds. For that there is ample historical precedent, not to speak of authority in the holiest texts we are taught to revere.

Another aspect of the complacent acceptance of atrocities was described by Alexis de Tocqueville in his report of one of the great crimes of ethnic cleansing of the continent, the expulsion of the Cherokees. He was particularly intrigued to see how Americans were able not only "to exterminate the Indian race" after "wholly depriving it of its rights," but to do so "with singular felicity, tranquilly, legally, philanthropically, without shedding blood, and without violating a single great principle of morality in the eyes of the world." "It is impossible to destroy people with more respect for the laws of humanity," he observed with wonder.[7]

That is a fair enough description of what has been unfolding before our eyes. For example, in the refugee camp of Maslakh near Herat, where hundreds of thousands of people are reported to be starving, dozens dying every night from cold and starvation. They were living on the edge of survival even before the bombing, which deprived them of desperately needed aid. It remains a "forgotten camp" as we meet, three months after September 11. Veteran correspondent Christina Lamb reports scenes more "harrowing" than anything in her memory, after having "seen death and misery in refugee camps in many parts of Asia and Africa." A month later, the reported death toll had doubled to 100 a day and aid officials warned that the camp is "on the brink of an Ethiopian-style humanitarian disaster" as the flight of refugees to the camp continued to increase, an estimated three-quarters of its population since September.[8]

The destruction of lives is silent and mostly invisible, and can easily remain forgotten, by choice. An even sorrier sight is denial – or worse, even ridicule – of the efforts to bring these tragedies to light so that pressures can be mounted to relieve them. The easy tolerance of the "vivid awfulness" that Lamb recounts merely reflects the fact that this is how the powerful deal with the weak and defenseless, hence in no way remarkable.

We have no right to harbor any illusions about the premises of the planning for the war in Afghanistan, and of the accompanying commentary. These were based on the unchallenged assumption that the threat of bombing, then its realization, would considerably increase the number of Afghans at risk of death from starvation, disease, and exposure. The press blandly reported that the numbers were expected to increase by 50 percent, to about 7.5 million: an additional 2.5 million people.[9] No comment was elicited by the report that Washington had "demanded [from Pakistan] the elimination of truck convoys that provide much of the food and other supplies to Afghanistan's civilian population,"[10] millions of them already on the brink of starvation. Pleas to stop the bombing to allow delivery of food and other aid were rebuffed without comment, mostly without even report. These came from high UN officials, major relief and aid agencies, and others in a good position to know. Afghan specialists concurred, warning that the withdrawal of aid workers and severe reduction in food supplies left "millions of Afghans . . . at grave risk of starvation." By late September, the Food and Agricultural Organization (FAO) had warned that more than seven million people would face starvation if the threatened military action were undertaken, and after the bombing began, advised that the threat of "humanitarian catastrophe" was "grave," and that the bombing had disrupted the planting of 80 percent of the grain supplies, so that the effects next year could be even more severe.[11]

What will happen we cannot know. But we know well enough the assumptions on which plans were based and executed, and commentary produced. As a simple matter of logic, it is these assumptions that inform us about the shape of the world that lies ahead, whatever the outcomes might be in the present case. The basic facts have been casually reported, including the fact that little is being done to bring food and other aid to many of those dying in refugee camps and the countryside, though supplies have long been available and the primary factor hampering delivery is lack of interest and will.

Furthermore, the longer-term effects will remain unknown, if history is any guide. Reporting is scanty today, and the consequences will not be investigated tomorrow. It is acceptable to report the "collateral damage" by bombing error, the inadvertent and inevitable cost of war, but not the conscious and deliberate destruction of Afghans who will die in silence, invisibly – not by design, but because it doesn't matter, a deeper level of moral depravity; if we step on an ant while walking, we have not purposely killed it.

People do not die of starvation instantly. They can survive on roots and grass, and if malnourished children die of disease, who will seek to determine what factors lie in the background? In the future, the topic is off the agenda by virtue of a crucial principle: We must devote enormous energy to meticulous accounting of crimes of official enemies, quite properly including not only those literally killed, but also those who die as a consequence of their policies; and we must take equally scrupulous care to avoid this practice in the case of our own crimes, adopting the stance that so impressed de Tocqueville. There are hundreds of pages of detailed documentation of the application of these principles. It will be a welcome surprise if the current case turns out differently.

And we should remember that we are not observing all of this from Mars, or describing the crimes of Attila the Hun. There is a great deal that we can do right now, if we choose.

To explore what is likely to lie ahead from a different perspective, let's ask whether there were alternatives to the resort to devastating force at a distance, a device that comes naturally to those with overwhelming might at their command, no external deterrent, and confidence in the obedience of articulate opinion.

Alternatives were prominently suggested. By the Vatican, for example, which called for reliance on the measures appropriate to crimes, whatever their scale: if someone robs my house and I think I know who did it, I am not entitled to go after him with an assault rifle, meanwhile killing people randomly in his neighborhood. Or by the eminent military historian Michael Howard, who delivered a "scathing attack" on the bombardment of Afghanistan on October 30, not on grounds of success or failure, but its design: what is needed is "patient operations of police and intelligence forces," "a police operation conducted under the auspices of the UN on behalf of the international community as a whole, against a criminal conspiracy, whose members should be hunted down and brought before an international court."[12] There certainly are precedents, including acts of international terrorism even more extreme than those of September 11: the U.S. terrorist war against Nicaragua, to take an uncontroversial example – uncontroversial, because of the judgment of the highest international authorities, the International Court of Justice and the Security Council. Nicaragua's efforts to pursue lawful means failed, in a world ruled by force; but no one would impede the U.S. if it chose to follow a lawful course.

Could the goals of apprehending and punishing the perpetrators have been attained without violence? Perhaps. We have no way of knowing whether the Taliban offers to discuss extradition were serious, since they were dismissed for the reasons already mentioned. The same is true of the war aim added as an afterthought well after the bombing began: overthrowing the Taliban regime.[13] That would doubtless have been a high priority for many Afghans, just as the same is true for innumerable others throughout the world who suffer under brutal regimes and miserable oppression. Keeping just to questions of tactics and efficacy, were there preferable ways to achieve this later goal?

Evidently, the inquiry should begin with the people of Afghanistan: what are their attitudes and opinions? To determine their views is a difficult task, no doubt, but not entirely impossible. There are some reasonable ways to proceed.

We might begin with the gathering of 1,000 Afghan leaders in Peshawar at the end of October, some of them exiles, some who trekked across the border from within Afghanistan, all committed to overthrowing the Taliban regime. It was "a rare display of unity among tribal elders, Islamic scholars, fractious politicians, and former guerrilla commanders," the *New York Times* reported. They unanimously "urged the U.S. to stop the air raids," appealed to the international media to call for an end to the "bombing of innocent people," and "demanded an end to the U.S. bombing of Afghanistan." They urged that other means be adopted to overthrow the hated Taliban regime, a goal they believed could be achieved without slaughter and destruction.[14]

A similar message was conveyed by Afghan opposition leader Abdul Haq, who was highly regarded in Washington. Just before he entered Afghanistan, apparently without U.S. support, and was then captured and killed, he condemned the bombing and criticized the U.S. for refusing to support his efforts and those of others "to create a revolt within the Taliban." The bombing was "a big setback for these efforts," he said. He reported contacts with second-level Taliban commanders and ex-Mujahiddin tribal elders, and discussed how such efforts could proceed, calling on Washington to assist them with funding and other support instead of undermining them with bombs.

The U.S., Abdul Haq said,

> is trying to show its muscle, score a victory and scare everyone in the world. They don't care about the suffering of the Afghans or how many people we will lose. And we don't like that. Because Afghans are now being made to suffer for these Arab fanatics, but we all know who brought these Arabs to Afghanistan in the 1980s, armed them and gave them a base. It was the Americans and the CIA. And the Americans who did this all got medals and good careers, while all these years Afghans suffered from these Arabs and their allies. Now, when America is attacked, instead of punishing the Americans who did this, it punishes the Afghans.[15]

For what it's worth, I think there is considerable merit in his remarks.

We can also look elsewhere for enlightenment about Afghan opinions. There has, at last, been some belated concern about the fate of women in Afghanistan. It even reached the First Lady. Maybe it will be followed some day by concern for the plight of women elsewhere in Central and South Asia, which, unfortunately, is not all that different in many places from life under the Taliban, including the most vibrant democracies. There are plenty of highly reliable and expert sources on these matters, if we choose to look. And such a radical departure from past practice would lend at least some credibility to the professed outrage over Taliban practices just at the moment when it served U.S. propaganda purposes. Of course, no sane person advocates foreign military intervention by the U.S. or other states to rectify these and other terrible crimes in countries that are U.S. allies and clients. The problems are severe, but should be dealt with from within, with assistance from outsiders if it is constructive and honest, not merely hypocritical and self-serving.

But since the harsh treatment of women in Afghanistan has at last gained some well-deserved attention, it would seem that attitudes of Afghan women towards policy options should be a primary concern. These no doubt vary considerably, and are not easy to investigate. Nevertheless, it should not be impossible to determine whether mothers in Maslakh praise the bombing, or might, rather, agree with those who fled from their homes to miserable refugee camps under the threat of bombing and expressed the bitter hope that "even the cruel Americans must feel some pity for our ruined country" and refrain from the threatened bombing that was already bringing death and disaster.[16] And Afghan women are by no means voiceless everywhere. There is an organization of courageous women who have been in the forefront of the struggle to defend women's rights for 25 years, RAWA (Revolutionary Association of the Women of Afghanistan), doing remarkable work. Their leader was assassinated by Afghan collaborators with the Russians in 1987, but they continued their work within Afghanistan at risk of death, and in exile nearby. They have been quite outspoken. A week after the bombing began, for example, they issued a public statement that would have been front-page news wherever concern for Afghan women was real, not a matter of mere expediency.

The RAWA statement of October 11 was entitled: "Taliban should be overthrown by the uprising of Afghan nation," and continued as follows:

> Again, due to the treason of fundamentalist hangmen, our people have been caught in the claws of the monster of a vast war and destruction. America, by forming an international coalition against Osama and his Taliban-collaborators and in retaliation for the 11th September terrorist attacks, has launched a vast aggression on our country . . . [What] we have witnessed for the past seven days leaves no doubt that this invasion will shed the blood of numerous women, men, children, young and old of our country.

The statement went on to call for "the eradication of the plague of Taliban and Al Qieda" by "an overall uprising" of the Afghan people themselves, which alone "can prevent the repetition and recurrence of the catastrophe that has befallen our country . . ."

In another declaration on November 25, at a demonstration of women's organizations in Islamabad on the International Day for the Elimination of Violence against Women, RAWA condemned the U.S./Russian-backed Northern Alliance for a "record of human rights violations as bad as that of the Taliban," and called on the UN to "help Afghanistan, not the Northern Alliance," warnings reiterated at the national conference of the All India Democratic Women's Association on the same days.[17]

Perhaps Afghans who have been struggling for freedom and women's rights for many years don't understand much about their country, and should cede responsibility for its future to foreigners who couldn't have placed the country on a map a few months ago, along with others who had helped destroy it in the past. Maybe, but it is not obvious.

The situation is reminiscent of the Iraq war, when the Iraqi opposition was barred from media and journals of opinion, apart from dissident journals at the margins. They forcefully opposed the U.S. bombing campaign against Iraq and accused the U.S. of preferring a military dictatorship to overthrow of Saddam by internal revolt – as was conceded publicly, when Bush (No. 1) returned to collaboration with his former friend and ally Saddam Hussein in carrying out major atrocities, as Saddam brutally crushed a southern Shi'ite revolt that might well have overthrown the murderous dictator, under the watchful eyes of the U.S. military that had total control over the region, while Washington refused even to allow rebelling Iraqi generals access to captured Iraqi arms. The Bush Administration confirmed that it would have no dealings with Iraqi opposition leaders: "We felt that political meetings with them . . . would not be appropriate for our policy at this time," State Department spokesman Richard Boucher announced on March 14, 1991, while Saddam was massacring southern rebels.[18] That had been long-standing government policy. The same is true of preference for force over pursuit of possibly feasible diplomatic options, policies that continued in the decade that followed, until today, and are quite natural, for basically the reasons that Abdul Haq enunciated.

Another sensible way to assess the prospects for the future would be to review the actions of today's commanders when they launched the first war on terrorism 20 years ago: there is ample evidence of what they achieved in Central America, Southern Africa, the Middle East and Southeast Asia, all accompanied by much the same lofty rhetoric and passion that we hear today. There should be no need to review that shameful record. Evidently, it carries important lessons about the likely future, as does the fact that the topic is scrupulously ignored in the laudatory chorus for the current and future projects, although – or perhaps because – that record is so obviously relevant.

At the end of the terrible decade of the 1980s, the external deterrent to the use of force disappeared. For its victims, the collapse of Soviet tyranny was a remarkable triumph and liberation, though the victory was soon tainted by new horrors. For others, the consequences were more complex. The basic character of the post-Cold War era was revealed very quickly: more of the same, with revised pretexts and tactics. A few weeks after the fall of the Berlin Wall, the U.S. invaded Panama, killing hundreds or even thousands of people, vetoing two Security Council resolutions, and kidnapping a thug who was jailed in the U.S. for crimes that he had mostly committed while on the CIA payroll before committing the only one that mattered: disobedience. The pattern of events was familiar enough, but there were some differences. One was pointed out by Elliott Abrams, who pleaded guilty to crimes committed when he was a State Department official during the Reagan years, and has now been appointed Human Rights specialist at the National Security Council. At the time of the invasion, he commented that for the first time in many years the U.S. could resort to force with no concern about Russian reactions. There were also new pretexts: the intervention was in defense against Hispanic narcotraffickers, not the Russians who were mobilizing in Managua, two days march from Harlingen, Texas.

A few months later, the Bush Administration presented its new Pentagon budget, an event of particular significance because this was the first submission that could not rely on the plea that the Russians are coming.[19] The Administration requested a huge military budget, as before, and in part for the same reasons. Thus it would be necessary to bolster "the defense industrial base" (aka high-tech industry), and to maintain the intervention forces that are aimed primarily at the Middle East because of "the free world's reliance on energy supplies from this pivotal region." But there was a change: in that pivotal region the "threats to our interests" that had required direct military engagement "could not be laid at the Kremlin's door," contrary to decades of propaganda. Nor could the threats be laid at Saddam's door: the Butcher of Baghdad was still a valued friend and ally, not yet having committed *his* crime of disobedience. Rather, the threat was indigenous nationalism, as it had always been.

The clouds lifted on the larger threat as well. It is not the Russians, but rather the "growing technological sophistication" of third world powers that requires that we maintain complete military dominance worldwide, even without "the backdrop of superpower competition." The Cold War confrontation was always in the background no doubt, but served more as a pretext than a reason, just as the Russians appealed to the U.S. threat to justify their crimes within their own domains. The real enemy is independent (called "radical") nationalism in the South, as now tacitly acknowledged, the traditional pretexts having lost their utility. The documentary and historical record provides ample evidence to support that conclusion.

Another consequence of the collapse of the junior partner in world control was the elimination of any space for non-alignment, and the limited measure of independence it allowed. One indication is the immediate sharp reduction in foreign aid, most radically in the U.S., where the category virtually disappeared, even if we count the largest component, which goes to a rich country for strategic reasons, and to Egypt because of its collaboration in the same enterprise. The decline of options was fully recognized. President Mahathir of Malaysia spoke for many when he said that:

> Paradoxically, the greatest catastrophe for us, who had always been anti-communist, is the defeat of communism. The end of the Cold War has deprived us of the only leverage we had – the option to defect. Now we can turn to no one.[20]

Not really a paradox, but the natural course of real-world history.

Similar fears were widely expressed. The Gulf war was bitterly condemned throughout the South as a needless show of force, evading diplomatic options; there was considerable evidence for such an interpretation at the time, more since. Many perceived what Abdul Haq describes today: the U.S. "is trying to show its muscle, score a victory and scare everyone in the world," establishing "credibility." The resort to overwhelming military force is designed to demonstrate that "What We Say Goes," in George Bush's proud words as bombs and missiles rained on Iraq. Those who did not grasp the message then should have had no problem in doing so when he instantly returned to support for Saddam's murderous violence in order to ensure "stability," a code word for subordination to U.S. power interests. The general mood in the South was captured by Cardinal Paulo Evarista Arns of Sao Paulo: In the Arab countries, he said, "the rich sided with the U.S. government while the *millions* of poor condemned this military aggression." Throughout the Third World, he continued, "there is hatred and fear: When will they decide to invade us," and on what pretext?[21]

The general reaction to the bombing of Serbia was similar, and again, there is considerable evidence that peaceful options might have been pursued, avoiding much misery. In this case, it was officially and repeatedly proclaimed that the motives were to establish "credibility" and ensure "stability." It is difficult to take seriously the claim that a subsidiary goal was to prevent the ethnic cleansing and atrocities that followed the withdrawal of monitors (over unreported Serbian objections) and the bombing immediately afterwards – a "predictable" consequence, as the commanding general informed the press as the bombing began, later reiterating that he knew of no such war aims. The rich documentary record from the State Department, OSCE, the British government, and other Western sources substantially reinforces these conclusions. Perhaps that is why the illuminating record is so consistently ignored in the extensive literature on the topic. Even in the most loyal client-states the bombing was condemned as a reversion to traditional gunboat diplomacy "cloaked in moralistic righteousness" in the traditional fashion (the respected Israeli military analyst Amos Gilboa, by no means an isolated voice).[22]

Americans are carefully protected from world opinion and critical discussion of such matters, but we do ourselves no favors by keeping to these restrictions.

We also do ourselves no favors by ignoring public documents that lucidly explain the thinking of planners. They understand very well that the world may be tripolar in economic terms – with roughly comparable economic power in North America, Europe and Asia – but that it is radically unipolar in the capacity to resort to violence and to destroy. And it should be no surprise to discover that these facts of life enter crucially into planning.

Even before September 11, the U.S. outspent the next 15 countries for "defense"[23] – which, as usual, means "offense." And it is far ahead in sophisticated military technology. The military budget was increased sharply after September 11, as the Administration exploited the fear and anguish of the population to ram through a wide array of measures that they knew would arouse popular opposition without the appeal to "patriotism" – which the powerful are free to ignore; it is the rest who must be passive and submissive. These included a variety of means to strengthen the authority of the very powerful state to which "conservatives" are deeply committed, among them, sharp increases in military spending designed to enhance the enormous disparity between the U.S. and the rest of the world. Included are the plans to extend the "arms race" into space – a "race" with one competitor only – undermining the Outer Space Treaty of 1967 and other international obligations. Ballistic Missile Defense (BMD) is only a small component, and even that is understood to be an offensive weapon: "not simply a *shield* but an *enabler* of action," the RAND corporation explained, echoing not only the thoughts but even the words of Chinese authorities, who, realistically, regard it as a weapon directed against them. Strategic analysts realistically describe the program as a means to establish U.S. global "hegemony," which is what the world needs, they explain, echoing many distinguished predecessors.

The far broader programs of militarization of space are explained in high level public documents as the natural next step in expanding state power. Armies and navies were created to protect commercial interests and investment, Clinton's Space Command observed, and the logical next frontier is space, in pursuit of the same goals. But this time there will be a difference. The British Navy could be countered by Germany, with consequences we need not discuss. But the U.S. will be so awesomely powerful that there will be no counterforce, so it is claimed.

Overwhelming dominance is necessary for well-known technical reasons. Even BMD requires nullification of the anti-satellite weapons of a potential adversary. The U.S. must therefore achieve "full spectrum dominance," ensuring that even this much simpler technology will not be available. An iron fist is needed for other reasons. U.S. military planners share the assessment of the intelligence community and outside experts that what is misleadingly called "globalization" will lead to a widening divide between the "haves" and the "have-nots" – contrary to doctrine, but in accord with reality. And it will be necessary to control unruly elements: by inspiring fear, or perhaps by actual use of highly destructive killing machines launched from space, probably nuclear-powered and on hair-trigger alert with automated control systems, thus increasing the likelihood of what in the trade are called "normal accidents": the unpredictable errors to which all complex systems are subject.

It is recognized that these programs significantly increase the danger of uncontrollable catastrophe, but that too is entirely rational within the framework of prevailing institutions and ideology, which ranks hegemony well above survival. Again, there are ample precedents throughout the history of the Cold War, and long before.

The difference today is that the stakes are much higher. It is no exaggeration to say that the survival of the species is at risk.

These seem to me some of the realistic prospects if current tendencies persist. But there is no reason for that to happen. The good news is that the reigning systems of authority are fragile, and they know it. There is a major effort to exploit the current window of opportunity to institute harsh and regressive programs and to neutralize the mass popular movements that have been forming throughout the world in unprecedented and highly encouraging ways. There is no reason to succumb to such efforts, and every reason not to. Plenty of choices and options are available. What is needed, as always, is the will and dedication to pursue them.

7 U.S./Israel–Palestine (May 2001)

The latest phase of the Israel–Palestine conflict opened on September 29, 2000, the Muslim day of prayer, when Prime Minister Ehud Barak dispatched a massive and intimidating police and military presence to the Al-Aqsa compound. Predictably, that led to clashes as thousands of people streamed out of the mosque, leaving several Palestinians dead and 200 wounded.[1] Whatever Barak may have intended, there could hardly have been a more effective way to set the stage for the shocking sequel, particularly after the visit of Ariel Sharon and his military entourage to the compound the day before, which might have passed without such serious consequences.

The opening events established the pattern for what followed. "During these crucial days there was no evidence of Palestinian gunfire," an important UN inquiry found.[2] In the following months, as far as the investigators could determine, "the IDF [Israeli Army], operating behind fortifications with superior weaponry, endured not a single serious casualty as a result of Palestinian demonstrations and, further, their soldiers seemed to be in no life-threatening danger during the course of these events," as they killed hundreds of Palestinians and imposed an even more brutal regime than before, subjecting the population to harsh collective punishment and humiliation, the hallmark of the occupation for many years.[3] The UN report found that

> the majority of Israeli casualties resulted from incidents on settlements roads and at relatively isolated checkpoints . . . as a consequence of the settlements, and irritations resulting indirectly therefrom. In this regard, account must be taken of settler violence against Palestinian civilians in areas adjoining settlements, and of IDF complicity in such violence.

The current practices, along with earlier ones, have been reviewed in extensive detail and bitterly condemned by international Human Rights organizations. Like the report of the UN inquiry, these studies have been virtually ignored in the United States.

Reports of Human Rights organizations receive wide attention when they are doctrinally useful, not otherwise; the Al-Aqsa *Intifada* breaks no new ground in that regard. To cite only the most recent illustration as I write, in April 2001 Human Rights Watch published a detailed study devoted primarily to Israeli atrocities in the Hebron district, where tens of thousands of Palestinians have been virtually imprisoned for months while a few hundred settlers are free to abuse and humiliate them and destroy their property under military protection, the pattern for many years. The study was immediately reported on wire services. The first (and perhaps only) mention in the U.S. was in paragraph 15 of a *Washington Post* article five days later.[4]

The pattern of events underscores a fact of crucial importance. It is highly misleading to use the phrase "Israel–Palestine conflict," as I did at the outset: it should be termed the "U.S./Israel–Palestine" conflict. For similar reasons, it is misleading – and particularly in the U.S., improper – to condemn "Israeli atrocities," just as such practice would have been inappropriate in the case of Russian-backed crimes in Eastern Europe, U.S.-backed crimes in Central America (where it was the practice), and innumerable other such examples.

These conclusions are illustrated graphically by the events in the first days of the Al-Aqsa *Intifada*. On September 30, the IDF killed twelve-year-old Muhammad Al-Dirra in response to rock throwing (in which he was not involved) near the small Israeli settlement at Netzarim, which is hardly more than an excuse for a major military base and road system that cut the Gaza Strip in two, one of several barriers separating Gaza City from the south (and Egypt). "IDF soldiers in a heavily protected bunker fired repeatedly upon Palestinian Red Crescent Society (PRCS) ambulances attempting to evacuate" the severely wounded boy and other casualties, Human Rights Watch reported. "The firing from the IDF outpost continued for at least forty-five minutes, although during this time there was no apparent return fire from Palestinian demonstrators or police." Ambulances sought in vain to "evacuate large numbers of Palestinians wounded by heavy IDF fire from the bunker and possibly from sniper towers in the Netzarim settlement"; earthern berms were constructed "to provide people with some protection from sniper fire from the Netzarim settlement." Amnesty International found that the IDF "apparently even targeted people helping to remove the wounded," reporting that a PRCS ambulance driver "died after Israeli troops shot him in the chest" as he sought to evacuate casualties.[5]

All of this proceeds thanks to direct U.S. support, tolerance and evasion.

The next day, October 1, "Israeli special forces firing from and around a well-protected rooftop position" killed two Palestinians, facing no apparent threat themselves. On the same day, Israel escalated the level of violence when "an IDF helicopter gunship fired recklessly and repeatedly on areas immediately adjacent to the [PRCS] field hospital at Netzarim, disrupting operations there," at least 400 meters from any clashes; and on the Egypt–Gaza border, helicopters fired missiles that killed two Palestinians and wounded dozens. The next day, October 2, helicopters firing missiles at buildings and cars in the Netzarim area killed ten Palestinians and wounded 35.[6]

IDF helicopters are U.S. helicopters with Israeli pilots. U.S. supply is critical because "it is impractical to think that we can manufacture helicopters or major weapons systems of this type in Israel," the Ministry of Defense reported.[7]

On October 3, the defense correspondent of Israel's most prestigious newspaper reported the signing of an agreement with the Clinton Administration for "the largest purchase of military helicopters by the Israeli Air Force in a decade," along with spare parts for Apache attack helicopters for which an agreement had been signed in mid-September. Also in mid-September, the Israeli press reported, U.S. Marines carried out a joint exercise with the IDF in the Negev aimed at reconquest of the territories that had been transferred to the Palestinian Authority. The Marines provided training with weapons that the IDF still lacked, and in "American fighting techniques."[8]

On October 4, the world's leading military journal reported that Washington had approved a request for Apache helicopters along with more advanced attack equipment. The same day, the U.S. press reported that Apaches were attacking apartment complexes with rockets at Netzarim. In response to queries from European journalists, U.S. officials said that "U.S. weapons sales do not carry a stipulation that the weapons can't be used against civilians. We cannot second-guess an Israeli commander who calls in helicopter gunships." White House national security spokesman P.J. Crowley added that "We are not in a position to pass judgement on decisions made on either side," calling on both sides to exercise restraint. A few weeks later, the local Palestinian leader Hussein Abayat was killed by a missile launched from an Apache helicopter (along with two women standing nearby), as the assassination campaign against the indigenous leadership was initiated.[9]

Rushing new military helicopters to Israel under these circumstances and with such authorization for use is surely newsworthy. There was no news report or editorial comment. The sole mention in the U.S. was in an opinion piece in Raleigh, North Carolina.[10] An Amnesty International condemnation of the sale of U.S. helicopters also passed in silence. That remained true in the months that followed, including a shipment in February 2001, a $.5 billion deal for Boeing Apache Longbow helicopters, the most advanced in the U.S. arsenal, noted marginally in the U.S. as business news. In a similar style, a major news story (May 17) reports the reluctance of President Bush to become more "directly involved" in the Israel–Palestine conflict, and his Administration's inability to support the Mitchell committee report by asking Israel for a settlement freeze because Prime Minister Sharon is "philosophically opposed to such a proposal." On the same day, under "World Briefing" a few lines report that the U.S. Army Corps of Engineers began construction of a $266 million Israeli military base (paid for by the U.S.) in the Negev, a symbol "of America's continuing commitment to Israel's security," Ambassador Martin Indyk declared.[11]

Well reported, however, are stern U.S. admonitions to Palestinians to end their terror, because "we do not believe in rewarding violence" (Ambassador Indyk);[12] and regular official statements deploring violence and expressing tempered disapproval of Israel's assassination program. Washington's actual attitudes are revealed by its actions; the coverage speaks for itself.

None of this is unusual. With regard to Israel–Palestine specifically, the pattern has been routine for over 30 years, ever since the U.S. separated itself from the international consensus on the conflict. Though the most significant facts are missing from mainstream commentary, and often ignored or misrepresented even in scholarly work, they are not controversial. They provide the indispensable background for any serious understanding of what is happening now.

U.S.–Israel relations improved dramatically after Israel's military victory in 1967. In the background, as always with regard to this region, lie its incomparable energy resources. Emerging from World War II as the overwhelmingly dominant global power, the U.S. undertook careful and sophisticated planning to organize the world system in its interests. That included effective control over the region's oil, previously shared with France and Britain. France was removed, and the British gradually declined to the status of a "junior partner," in the rueful words of a British Foreign Office official. Though there was much talk about the Russians, and there is no doubt that the possibility of global war was the major element in strategic planning, the immediate problem throughout was the threat of independent nationalism – a fact now largely conceded, even in official documents.[13]

In essentials, the U.S. took over the framework of control of the Middle East established by Britain after World War I. The states of the region were to be administered by what Britain called an "Arab Façade," weak and pliable; Britain's "absorption" of the colonies would be "veiled by constitutional fictions as a protectorate, a sphere of influence, a buffer State, and so on," a device more cost-effective than direct rule. When needed, British muscle would be available. The U.S. modified the system by incorporating a second tier of "local cops on the beat," as the Nixon Administration called them: local gendarmes to ensure order, preferably non-Arab, with police HQ in Washington, and U.S.–UK force in reserve.

Throughout this period, Turkey has been considered a base for U.S. power in the region. Iran was another, after the effort by its conservative nationalist government to gain control over Iran's resources was thwarted by a UK–U.S. military coup in 1953. By 1948, the U.S. Joint Chief of Staffs were already impressed with Israel's military prowess, describing the new state as the major regional military power after Turkey. Israel could offer the U.S. means to "gain strategic advantage in the Middle East that would offset the effects of the decline of British power in that area," the JCS concluded.

In 1958, the CIA advised that "a logical corollary" of opposition to Arab nationalism "would be to support Israel as the only reliable pro-Western power left in the Middle East." The reasoning was implemented only after 1967, when Israel performed a highly valued service to the U.S. by destroying Nasser, the symbol of Arab nationalism, feared and detested as a "virus" who might "infect others," a "rotten apple" who might "spoil the barrel," in the conventional terminology of planners, commonly reshaped for public purposes as the "domino theory."

By the early 1970s, a tacit tripartite alliance of "local cops" had taken shape under the U.S. aegis: Iran, Saudi Arabia, Israel (Turkey is taken for granted; Pakistan was an associate for a time). With by far the largest petroleum reserves, Saudi Arabia is the central component of the Façade; any serious departure from obedience would doubtless bring harsh penalties. The arrangements were publicly explained by U.S. intelligence specialists, and also by political figures, notably Henry Jackson, the Senate's leading specialist on the Middle East and oil. He observed that thanks to the "strength and Western orientation" of Israel and Iran, these two "reliable friends of the United States," along with Saudi Arabia, "have served to inhibit and contain those irresponsible and radical elements in certain Arab States . . . who, were they free to do so, would pose a grave threat indeed to our principal sources of petroleum in the Persian Gulf" (meaning primarily profit flow and a lever of world control; the U.S. was not dependent on Middle East oil for its own use).

U.S. domination of the Gulf region had already come under threat in 1958, when the Iraqi military overthrew the main British client regime. Internal U.S.–UK records provide a revealing account of their concerns and plans, essential background for understanding the Gulf War in 1991.[14] Nasser's Egypt, as noted, was considered the major threat until Israel's 1967 victory; U.S. aid to Israel increased rapidly, even more so in 1970 when Israel performed another important service, blocking potential Syrian support for Palestinians being massacred in Jordan. The fall of the Shah in 1979 was a serious blow. President Carter at once sent a NATO general to try to instigate a military coup. When this failed, the two remaining pillars – Saudi Arabia and Israel – joined the U.S. in an effort to overthrow the regime by providing military aid; that is the conventional device to overthrow a civilian government, employed with great success in Indonesia and Chile not long before. Exploiting its intimate relations with the Shah's regime, Israel reestablished military contacts and sent U.S. arms, funded by Saudi Arabia. The goals of the operation were explained clearly and publicly at once,[15] but largely ignored in the U.S.; later, they were reframed in the more acceptable terms of an "arms for hostage" deal, though that could not have been the initial motivation, since there were no hostages. The U.S.–Israeli–Saudi project was an entirely natural reaction to the downfall of the Shah, given the basic structure of the system of control. When Washington's friend and ally Saddam Hussein fell out of favor for disobeying orders (his huge crimes and programs to develop weapons of mass destruction were of little consequence, as the record of U.S.–UK support for him demonstrates), the U.S. turned to the "dual containment policy," aimed at Iran and Iraq.

It is within this general context that U.S.–Israel relations have evolved over the years, though Israel also became a valued contributor to Washington's operations in Latin America and elsewhere.[16] The Cold War was always in the background, primarily because of the ever-present threat of major war. But as has been true rather generally, it was a secondary factor, so the historical and documentary record reveal. The disappearance of the Russian deterrent led to important tactical modifications, but no essential change in basic policies, or the U.S.–Israel relationship. An assessment that seems to me realistic was given in April 1992 by General (ret.) Shlomo Gazit, former head of Israeli military intelligence, later a high official of the Jewish Agency and president of Ben-Gurion University, and a highly respected strategic analyst and planner. With the collapse of the Soviet Union, he wrote,

> Israel's main task has not changed at all, and it remains of crucial importance. Its location at the center of the Arab Muslim Middle East predestines Israel to be a devoted guardian of stability in all the countries surrounding it. Its [role] is to protect the existing regimes: to prevent or halt the processes of radicalization and to block the expansion of fundamentalist religious zealotry.[17]

Though welcomed in Washington as a major victory, Israel's military success in 1967 posed serious threats. Then-Defense Secretary Robert McNamara later reported that "we damn near had war" when the U.S. fleet "turned around a [Soviet] carrier in the Mediterranean"; he gave no details, but it may have been when Israel conquered the Golan Heights after the cease-fire, eliciting severe warnings from the USSR, including ominous hot-line communications. Recognizing that military confrontation is too dangerous, the great powers proposed a diplomatic settlement, formalized as UN Security Council resolution 242, November 1967. The resolution called for Israeli withdrawal from the territories it had conquered and for a full peace treaty that would recognize every state's right to live in peace and security within recognized boundaries: in brief, full peace in return for full withdrawal, with at most marginal and mutual adjustments, straightening a crooked border, perhaps.[18] It is important to bear in mind that UN 242 was strictly rejectionist – using the term here in a neutral sense to refer to rejection of the national rights of *one or the other* of the contending national groups in the former Palestine, not just rejection of the rights of Jews, as in the conventional racist usage. UN 242 called for a settlement among existing *states*: Palestinians were unmentioned, apart from oblique reference to "a just settlement of the refugee problem."

UN 242 remains a cornerstone of international diplomacy on the Israel–Arab conflict, but with two major changes. The first was a crucial shift in the international consensus, which, by the mid-1970s, had abandoned the rejectionist principles of the resolution and called for a Palestinian state in the occupied territories; the U.S. retained its rejectionist stand, but now in international isolation. The second change had to do with the U.S. interpretation of UN 242. That change dates from February 1971, when newly-elected President Sadat of Egypt accepted Washington's official policy, in fact went beyond it by offering a full peace treaty in return for Israeli withdrawal only from Egyptian territory. Israel officially welcomed this as a genuine peace offer; it was a "famous . . . milestone" on the path to peace, Yitzhak Rabin, then Ambassador to Washington, recounts in his memoirs. But while officially welcoming Egypt's expression "of its readiness to enter into a peace agreement with Israel," Israel rejected the offer, stating that it "will not withdraw to the pre-June 5, 1967 lines," a position that it maintains to the present.

The United States faced a dilemma: Should it maintain its official position, thus joining Egypt in a confrontation with Israel? Or should it change the interpretation of 242, opting for Kissinger's call for "stalemate": no negotiations, only force? Kissinger prevailed. Since then the United States has interpreted 242 to mean withdrawal only insofar as the United States and Israel determine. The earlier interpretation continued to be reiterated officially until the Clinton Administration, which argued at the December 1993 UN session that past UN resolutions are "obsolete and anachronistic" in the light of the September 1993 Israel–PLO agreement, to which we return.[19]

The official endorsement of 242 was meaningless, however, because Washington continued to provide military, diplomatic, and financial support for Israel's gradual integration of the territories. President Carter, for example, forcefully reiterated the official position,[20] while increasing U.S. aid to Israel to about half of total U.S. foreign aid, as part of the Camp David settlement. The events of 1971 have been excised from general commentary and review.[21]

After the 1971 rebuff, Sadat warned that if his efforts to reach peace continued to be rejected he would have to go to war. He was dismissed with contempt; recall that this was a period of triumphalist and racist arrogance in both Israel and the U.S., later bitterly denounced in Israel. The Labor government proceeded with its programs to settle northeastern Sinai, including the all-Jewish city of Yamit established after some 10,000 farmers and Bedouins were expelled with extreme brutality by forces commanded by General Ariel Sharon (who was reprimanded by a military commission of inquiry). Sadat warned that "Yamit means war," but was ignored.[22]

The 1973 war turned out to be a near-disaster for Israel – and the world; there was again a threat of nuclear confrontation. Even Kissinger understood that force alone is not enough. He turned to the natural back-up strategy: since Egypt could not be ignored, the major Arab deterrent must be removed from the conflict. The result, achieved by Carter at Camp David, freed Israel "to sustain military operations against the PLO in Lebanon as well as settlement activity on the West Bank" (Israeli strategic analyst Avner Yaniv),[23] as Israel proceeded to do at once with massive support from the Carter Administration and its successors.

Sadat became a greatly admired "man of peace" in 1977, though his heroic stance was far less forthcoming than in 1971; by 1977 he had joined the international consensus calling for Palestinian rights. The crucial difference is that by 1977 the U.S. had reluctantly adopted Sadat's 1971 proposal, in the wake of the 1973 war ("Kissinger's war," it might be called). All of this too has been excised from sanitized history.

U.S. isolation became still more extreme as the international consensus abandoned its rejectionism. Matters came to a head in January 1976, when the Security Council debated a resolution, supported by the Arab "confrontation states" (Egypt, Jordan, Syria) and publicly backed by the PLO, calling for a two-state settlement incorporating UN 242 but now supplemented with a Palestinian state in the occupied territories. Israel refused to attend the session, instead bombing Lebanon, killing 50 civilians, with no pretext other than retaliation against the UN. The resolution was supported by Europe, Russia (which was in the mainstream of diplomacy throughout the period), the non-aligned countries, in fact near-unanimously. The U.S. vetoed the resolution, again in 1980.[24] At the General Assembly, the U.S. regularly voted alone (with Israel, occasionally some other client-state) against resolutions with a similar thrust. Technically, there are no vetoes at the General Assembly, but a U.S. vote against, even in isolation (as is common, on a wide range of issues), is effectively a veto. In fact, a double veto, since such occasions are typically vetoed from commentary and even from history, as the events just reviewed have been. The U.S. also blocked a series of other diplomatic initiatives: from Europe, the Arab states and the PLO. The press commonly did not even mention them.

The record is instructive. To select one example among many, on December 10, 1986, *New York Times* Israel correspondent Thomas Friedman wrote that the Israeli group Peace Now has "never been more distressed" because of "the absence of any Arab negotiating partner." A few months later, he quoted Shimon Peres as deploring the lack of a "peace movement among the Arab people [such as] we have among the Jewish people," and saying that there can be no PLO participation in negotiations "as long as it is remaining a shooting organization and refuses to negotiate." He was speaking almost three years after Israel had rejected another one of Arafat's offers for negotiations leading to mutual recognition, which the *Times* had refused to report. Note: *refused.* Six days before Friedman's article on the distress of Peace Now, a headline in the mass-circulation Israeli journal *Ma'ariv* read: "Arafat indicates to Israel that he is ready to enter into direct negotiations." The offer was made during Peres's tenure as prime minister. Peres's press advisor confirmed the report, commenting that "there is a principled objection to any contact with the PLO, which flows from the doctrine that the PLO cannot be a partner to negotiations." Yossi Beilin, at the dovish extreme of Peres's Labor coalition, observed that "the proposal . . . was dismissed because it appeared to be a tricky attempt to establish direct contacts when we are not prepared for any negotiations with any PLO factor." Other high officials took a much harsher stance. None of this was reported in the mainstream U.S. media, though Friedman was alone in using the occasion to issue one of his periodic laments over the bitter fate of the only peace forces in the Middle East, which lack any Arab negotiating partner. Soon after, he received a Pulitzer Prize for "balanced and informed coverage" of the Middle East, of which this is a representative sample, and was appointed *Times* chief diplomatic correspondent.[25]

There is a conventional term for Washington's success in blocking diplomatic settlement, in international isolation: it is "the peace process," a choice of terminology that would not have surprised Orwell. The peace process in this sense has been bipartisan. There is an illusion that the (first) Bush Administration took a harsh line towards Israel.[26] The truth is closer to the opposite. An illustration is the official Administration position of December 1989 (the Baker Plan), which endorsed without reservations the May 1989 plan of Israel's Peres–Shamir coalition government. That plan in turn declared that there can be no "additional Palestinian state . . . " (Jordan already being a "Palestinian state"), and that "There will be no change in the status of Judea, Samaria and Gaza [the occupied territories] other than in accordance with the basic guidelines of the [Israeli] Government." Israel would conduct no negotiations with the PLO. But Israel would permit "free elections," to be conducted under Israeli military rule, with much of the Palestinian leadership in prison without charge or expelled. The plan was unreported in the U.S. apart from the last provision, praised as a positive and forthcoming offer. What one does read is that Baker strongly reiterated U.S. support for "total withdrawal from territory in exchange for peaceful relations" – while he was quietly lending decisive support to programs to ensure that nothing of the sort would happen.[27]

Through the first months (1988) of the first *Intifada*, Washington's increasingly desperate efforts to pretend that Arafat was not willing to consider a diplomatic settlement were beginning to elicit international ridicule. The Reagan Administration therefore agreed to accept Arafat's long-standing offers and to enter into negotiations; the standard interpretation was that Arafat had at last capitulated to Washington's steadfast advocacy of peace and diplomacy. Washington's actual reaction, unreported in the U.S., was made explicit in the first session of the negotiations: U.S. Ambassador Robert Pelletreau informed Arafat that he must abandon any thought of an international conference – unacceptable, because of the international consensus – and call off the "riots" in the occupied territories (the *Intifada*), "which we view as terrorist acts against Israel." In short, the PLO must ensure a return to the pre-*Intifada* status quo, so that Israel would be able to continue its expansion and repression in the territories with U.S. support. That was well understood in Israel. In February 1989, Prime Minister Rabin assured a Peace Now delegation that the negotiations are only "low-level discussions" that avoid any serious issue and grant Israel "at least a year" to resolve the problem by force. "The inhabitants of the territories are subject to harsh military and economic pressure," Rabin explained, and "in the end, they will be broken," and will accept Israel's terms. The version for the U.S. public was quite different.[28]

The last of the regular UN General Assembly resolutions supplementing UN 242 with an affirmation of Palestinian national rights was in December 1990, 144–2. A few weeks later, the U.S. went to war with Iraq, and George Bush triumphantly announced the New World Order in four simple words: "What We Say Goes," surely in the Middle East. The world understood, and withdrew. The U.S. was finally in a position to impose its own unilateral rejectionist stand, and did so, first at Madrid in late 1991, then in the successive Israel–PLO agreements from 1993. With these measures, the "peace process" has advanced towards the Bantustan-style arrangements that the U.S. and Israel intended, as is clear in the documentary record and, more important, the record on the ground.

Surely it was clear on September 13, 1993, when Rabin and Arafat formally accepted the Declaration of Principles (DOP) in Washington with much fanfare. The DOP outlines what was to come with little ambiguity.[29] There have been few surprises since.

The DOP states that the "permanent status," the ultimate settlement down the road, is to be based on UN 242 alone. The suppressed historical record makes it very clear what that means. First, the operative meaning of UN 242 is the U.S. version: partial withdrawal, as the U.S. and Israel determine. Second, the primary issue of diplomacy since the mid-1970s had been whether a diplomatic settlement should be based on UN 242 alone, as the U.S. insisted, or UN 242 supplemented with the resolutions that the U.S. had blocked calling for recognition of Palestinian national rights, the position of the rest of the world. The DOP kept explicitly to Washington's unilateral rejectionism. One could choose to be deluded – many did so. But that was a choice, and an unwise one, particularly for the victims.

Arafat was compelled to "renounce terror," once again. The sole purpose was humiliation – not of Arafat personally, but of the Palestinian people, for whom he is a symbol of nationalism.[30]

As Secretary of State George Shultz informed Reagan in December 1988, Arafat had said "Unc, unc, unc" and "cle, cle, cle," but he had not yet said "Uncle" in properly servile tones. The importance of this further renunciation of the right to resist was unnoticed, because no such right exists in the U.S. doctrinal framework. That was made clear in the (unreported) U.S.–PLO negotiations of 1989, as just reviewed; and before that, in December 1987, when the UN General Assembly debated its major resolution condemning international terrorism, opposed by the U.S. and Israel alone because the resolution supports "the right to self-determination, freedom and independence, as derived from the Charter of the United Nations, of peoples forcibly deprived of that right . . . , particularly peoples under colonial and racist regimes [meaning South Africa] and foreign occupation or other forms of colonial domination [meaning the

Israeli-occupied territories]."[31] Washington's success in effectively vetoing the resolution, from reporting and history as well, had significant effects for Lebanon and the occupied territories, though the U.S. did belatedly abandon its support for the Apartheid regime.

In return for Arafat's capitulation, the U.S. and Israel conceded nothing.

The DOP incorporates the U.S. version of the peace process in all essential respects. One cannot really accuse Israel of violating the Oslo agreements, except in detail.[32] Without violating the wording of the DOP (or the carefully constructed subsequent resolutions), Israel continued to settle and integrate the occupied territories with U.S. support and assistance. Intentions were not concealed. They were announced openly by Rabin and Peres and implemented by them and their successors.[33]

The exact scale of the U.S.–Israel settlement programs is not entirely clear because of the devices that are used to conceal them. Settler leaders allege that the settler population doubled to 210,000 since Oslo (not counting 180,000 in Arab East Jerusalem, effectively annexed in violation of Security Council orders, but with tacit U.S. support). They report further that 10 percent of the settlers keep addresses within Israel, hence are not counted. Construction in the settlements for the year 2000 was reported to be more than three times as high as in Tel Aviv, more than ten times as high as in Jerusalem, and in general far higher relative to population than within the Green Line (Israel proper). Population growth and public expenditures have also been much higher: 60 percent of the construction in the territories is state-funded, compared to 25 percent within Israel, and all the governments have employed a variety of inducements to encourage settlement.[34]

The Rabin–Peres formula, adopted by their successors and Washington, has been that settlement will be limited to "natural growth," under a policy of "freezing settlements." But "there is freezing and there is reality," the Israeli press reports, adding that the far right is "happy to adopt the Rabin formula," grateful for the "massive increase in building authorization" under Barak, initiated under Rabin shortly after he had accepted the DOP. Israel's most prominent diplomatic correspondent, Akiva Eldar, writes that "According to official statistics, full compliance with the [Israel–U.S.] formula would mean that Israel announces a total freeze – plus demolishes 500 apartments. Right now, there are 9,844 new (and empty) apartments either finished, or under construction . . . Thus the Israelis made a mockery of the American deal, and the Americans stayed silent" – and forked up the cash. He adds that plans of religious extremists (mostly American) for Hebron include construction on valuable archaeological sites, over the strong protest of the Archaeological Council. Thirty-eight senior Israeli archaeologists called on Barak to cancel the construction plans (which proceed). The Council chairman condemned the plans as "in grave violation of the law and custom that enables archaeological digging and research to be conducted in the ancient sites in our land," destroying "the Hebron of our forefathers and King David, and the historical and archaeological infrastructure of the Land of Israel and the People of Israel's past in our land." And, of course, continuing the dispossession and torture of the Palestinians, the vast majority.[35]

In late 2000, as Barak's term was drawing to a close, his Ministry of Construction announced that 10,000 units were under construction in the occupied territories, two-thirds in urban settlements; the Ministry of Housing announced $25 million to subsidize construction and infrastructure for 2001, in addition to the similar sum announced in April for 25 "bypass roads" – an extensive highway system designed to integrate the settler population within Israel, while leaving the Palestinian population invisible and isolated. "The Barak government is leaving Sharon's government a surprising legacy," the press reported as the transition took place a few months later: "the highest number of housing starts in the territories since the time when Ariel Sharon was Minister of Construction and Settlement in 1992 before the Oslo agreements." Figures of the Barak Ministry reveal that the rate of new construction increased steadily from 1993 to 2000, when it reached five times the level of 1993, 3½ times 1994, to be increased further under the Sharon–Peres government.[36] In July 2000, contracts were awarded for 522 new dwellings in Israel's Har Homa, a project on land expropriated from an Arab enclave in southeast Jerusalem that has lost 90 percent of its land since Israel's takeover in 1967 through "town planning" (a euphemism for replacing Arabs by Jews, reminiscent of some uses of "urban planning" in the U.S.).

The Har Homa project, on Jabal Abu Ghneim, completes Israel's encirclement of the vastly expanded "Jerusalem" region. The project was initiated in the last months of Shimon Peres's Labor government, put on hold after strong domestic and international protest during Benjamin Netanyahu's Likud Administration, resumed energetically (and without protest) under Barak. For the

Israeli far right, however, Labor's Har Homa project was much less significant than its E-1 program, which received much less publicity. This involved new housing and road construction to extend Greater Jerusalem to the city of Ma'aleh Adumim to the east, virtually splitting the West Bank in two. Knesset member Michael Kleiner, the head of the expansionist "Land of Israel Front" ("Hazit Eretz Yisrael"), greeted the announcement of the project with much appreciation, observing that this plan, which "was the initiative of the former [Peres] Housing Minister Benjamin Ben-Eliezer [now Minister of Defense in the Sharon–Peres government] with the authorization of Yitzhak Rabin," is "the most important" of the Front's demands, more so than Har Homa.[37]

In the Sharon–Peres government, the task of concealing the ongoing programs and rejecting international protests is assigned to Foreign Minister Peres. A report on the government programs for more extensive settlement is headlined "Peres rejects international objections to settlements." Peres repeated the "natural growth" formula designed to quiet protest, a traditional contribution of the doves.[38]

The basic principle was described in 1996, during the last months of Peres's Administration, by Housing Minister Ben-Eliezer, as he announced the plans for Har Homa and for carrying further the Rabin–Peres programs to expand Greater Jerusalem in all directions, to include Ma'aleh Adumim (east), Givat Ze'ev (north), Beitar (south), and beyond. Labor "does everything quietly," Ben-Eliezer explained, with "the complete protection of the Prime Minister [Peres]," using such terms as "natural growth" instead of "new settlements." Labor dove Yossi Beilin censured the incoming Netanyahu government for its inflammatory rhetoric. The Rabin government, he wrote, "increased settlements by 50 percent" in "Judea and Samaria" (the West Bank) after Oslo, but "we did it quietly and with wisdom," whereas you foolishly "proclaim your intentions every morning, frighten the Palestinians and transform the topic of Jerusalem as the unified capital of Israel – a matter which all Israelis agree upon – into a subject of world-wide debate."

Beilin's statement is only partially accurate; the "quiet wisdom" extends well beyond Jerusalem.[39] The differences of style can presumably be traced to the constituencies of the two political groupings. Labor, the party of educated professionals and westernized elites, is more attuned to Western norms and understands that the sponsors prefer "not to see" what they are doing. Likud's crude methods of achieving basically the same results are an embarrassment to Western humanists, and sometimes lead to conflict and annoyance (see note 26).

Ma'aleh Adumim is described as one of the "neighborhoods of Jerusalem" in U.S. reporting. Accordingly, Clinton's final offer could not have been more reasonable and generous when he said that "what is Jewish should be Israeli" – "failing to mention," the foreign press observed, "that this would entail Israel annexing settlements it built in occupied east Jerusalem," in fact far beyond in all directions. But that is an irrelevance. The great virtue of Clinton's "creative compromise . . . is that at least we now know what the only realistic final deal looks like," Thomas Friedman explained. The President has spoken. What more can there be to say?[40]

Those who stubbornly remain unsatisfied will discover that Ma'aleh Adumim uses 1/16 of the 50,000 dunams allotted to it in Israeli planning, a standard percentage, designed to permit "natural growth." The story of Ma'aleh Adumim is recounted by B'Tselem (see note 38).[41] The town was established under the Labor government in the mid-1970s, and grew rapidly "with the help of a massive flow of resources from the government," the town website reports. The official Metropolitan Jerusalem Plan anticipates expansion by 285 percent from 1994 to 2010, to 60,000 residents. Its lands too were expropriated from several Palestinian villages, including Abu Dis, which according to the plans of the doves, is to become the Palestinian Al-Quds (that is, Jerusalem) by linguistic sleight-of-hand; but deprived of its lands, in contrast to Israeli "Jerusalem," which will occupy a fair chunk of the West Bank. The state authorities found that there had been "widespread illegal building" by Jewish settlers. The "solution" was simple, as in other settlements: "to provide retroactive permits rather than to demolish the structures." The solution is demolition, often brutal, when Arabs build illegally, as they must to survive because of the stringent conditions imposed on Arab construction.

The expulsion of the Jahalin Bedouin from 1993 to allow further expansion of Ma'aleh Adumim was carried out in a particularly cruel fashion. They sought "to avert their terrible fate" – and terrible it was, very visibly so – "by petitioning the High Court of Justice," which lived up to its tradition of meekly obeying state authorities, though it did express the hope that the IDF would ease the expulsion "as an act of grace." In November 1999, the High Court rejected another Palestinian petition opposing further expansion of Ma'aleh

Adumim, suggesting that "some good for the residents of neighboring [Palestinian villages] might spring from the economic and cultural development" of the all-Jewish city.

The end result, B'Tselem concludes, is that here as throughout the territories, "the helpless local population is totally subject to regulations set by the military force of the occupation in order to promote its political interests," increasingly so during the Oslo peace process.

The Ma'aleh Adumim Municipality explains that "The political objective in establishing the town was settlement of the area east of Israel's capital along the Jerusalem–Jericho route," thus separating Ramallah and the northern Palestinian enclave from Bethlehem and the southern one. Every U.S.–Israeli peace plan includes some version of this condition, along with expansion of "Jerusalem" to the north and south. As before, the final Clinton–Barak proposals of January 2001 include another salient to the north, effectively partitioning the northern sector. The three enclaves are separated from the former Jerusalem, the traditional center of Palestinian life.[42] They are hemmed in by extensive infrastructure construction, including "a vast road system, running for some 400 km which bypasses Palestinian population centres and enables settlers and military forces protecting them to move speedily and safely through the West Bank."[43] Constructed on 160,000 dunams of expropriated land, the bypass road system also prevents expansion and development of Palestinian villages and impedes flow of commerce and people, though Arabs can travel on what are officially called "Palestinian roads," many quite hazardous; the Bethlehem–Ramallah road, for example (perhaps to be closed entirely if the Clinton–Barak formula, or something like it, is implemented). In addition, "access roads" lead to Jewish settlements, with their swimming pools and well-watered gardens (Palestinian villages and towns have little water, often none during the dry season). If a single settler passes on an access road, all Palestinian traffic is stopped, "causing long delays and much resentment." Regular Israeli closures imprison the population further, "often preventing or greatly detaining even emergency traffic, such as ambulances."[44] The Israeli press has reported many examples of the kind of brutality and purposeful humiliation one expects of an occupying army that can act without restraint.

Every step of the way, this proceeds with U.S. authorization and subsidy, funneled through various channels, along with critical military and diplomatic support. The U.S. has also taken pains to ensure that the escalating state terror during the current confrontations will be free even from observation, with its inhibiting effect. On March 27, 2001, the U.S. vetoed a Security Council resolution calling for international observers. According to European sources cited in the Israeli press, the proposal was "scuttled" by Washington's "four no's," which "shocked the representatives of the four European countries that put together the resolution – Ireland, Britain, Norway and France." The U.S. rejected any mention of the word "siege" or the principle of land-for-peace, of settlements, or of international law and the Geneva Convention. Arabs and their allies had already abandoned their own resolution, hoping that Europe could "negotiate with the Americans over the formula." A U.S. diplomat explained that "the United States believes the UN should stay out of the settlement debate" and that "the Geneva Convention issue" should be resolved between Israel and the Palestinians, without "prejudgment" through UN involvement.[45]

The matter of the Geneva Conventions is particularly significant.[46] These were adopted in the aftermath of World War II to bar the practices of the Nazis, including transfer of population of the conqueror to occupied territory or any actions that harm the civilian population.[47] Responsibility for monitoring observance of the Conventions was assigned to the International Red Cross, which has determined that Israel's settlement programs violate the Fourth Convention. The ICRC position has been endorsed by numerous resolutions of the UN Security Council and General Assembly. Applicability of the Convention to the Israeli-occupied territories has been affirmed by the U.S. as well: by UN Ambassador George Bush (September 1971), and by joining in unanimous adoption of Security Council resolution 465 (1980), which condemned Israeli settlements as "flagrant violations" of the Convention. Even Clinton was unwilling to take a public stand in blatant violation of a central part of international humanitarian law; the U.S. therefore abstained when the Security Council in October 2000 called on Israel "to abide scrupulously by its responsibilities under the Fourth Geneva Convention," which it was again violating flagrantly (resolution 1323, passed 14–0).

Under the Conventions, it is the responsibility of the High Contracting Parties, including the European powers and the U.S., "to respect and to ensure respect" for the Conventions "in all circumstances." They "should do everything in their power to ensure that the humanitarian principles underlying the Conventions are applied universally," the ICRC has determined. It is therefore Washington's responsibility to prevent settlement and expropriation, along with collective punishment and all other measures of intimidation, repression, and violence. The ICRC has also determined (February 2001) that Israel's closures and blockades are in violation of its Convention obligations, not to speak of the excessive and unlawful use of force repeatedly condemned by every significant human rights organization in Israel, the U.S., and elsewhere, and again the UN, in an EU-sponsored resolution, passed unanimously apart from the U.S.[48]

It follows that the U.S. is in express violation of its obligations as a High Contracting Party. Not only is it not acting to ensure respect for the Conventions, as it is obligated to do, but it has been actively engaged in violating them. All significant U.S.–Israel activities in the territory are in flat violation of international law. The concessions offered by Clinton and Barak, which are defined as the only "realistic" plan and have gained such acclaim for their magnanimity and generous spirit, do not exist, any more than Russia could make "generous concessions" when it withdrew from Afghanistan, or Germany when it was driven from occupied France. It is hardly necessary even to discuss the specific arrangements, repugnant as they are on elementary moral grounds.

There is a good reason why Washington wants any reference to the Geneva Conventions suppressed, and why the media cooperate so fully – even to the extent of informing readers that the "disputed territories" are considered to be occupied territories by the Palestinians, which is true enough: the Palestinians and everyone else apart from Israel and its superpower patron.

There are substantial forces in Israel that have long been in favor of some kind of Palestinian state in the occupied territories. Prominent among them are Israeli industrialists, who were calling for a Palestinian state even before the Oslo agreements. The president of the Israeli Industrialists' Association, Dov Lautman, recommended the NAFTA model that was then under negotiation – "a transition from colonialism to neo-colonialism," the labor correspondent of the journal of the Labor Party commented, "a situation similar to the relations between France and many of its former colonies in Africa." The Israeli coordinator of operations in the territories explained that the goal of his work is to "integrate the economy of the territories into the Israeli economy."[49] A Bantustan-style statelet would allow Israeli firms to place assembly plants on the Palestinian side of the border, providing cheap labor with no need for concern about environmental or other constraints on profit making, also relieving concerns that some of those derided as "beautiful souls" might see the way workers are treated and call for minimally decent conditions and wages.

Again on the NAFTA model, a separate state would provide a useful weapon against the Israeli working class, offering ways to limit their wages and benefits, and to undermine unions; much as in the U.S., where manufacturers develop excess capacity abroad that can be used to break strikes, and threaten "transfer" to Mexico to disrupt union organizing, a significant consequence of NAFTA that has probably impressed Israeli manufacturers.[50] Poor Israeli workers in "development towns" and the Arab sector would be particularly affected, as has already happened. During the neoliberal onslaught of the 1990s, Israeli port workers struggled against privatization of the ports and dismantling of collective-bargaining agreements endorsing rights they had won. Employer associations tried to break strikes by diverting cargo ships to Egypt and Cyprus, but that carries heavy transportation costs. A port in Gaza would be ideal. With the collaboration of local authorities in the standard neocolonial fashion, port operations could be transferred there, strikes broken, and Israeli ports transferred to unaccountable private hands.[51]

It is not surprising that Israel is coming to resemble the U.S., with very high inequality and levels of poverty, stagnating wages and deteriorating working conditions, and erosion of its formerly well-functioning social systems. As in the U.S., the economy is based heavily on the dynamic state sector, sometimes concealed under the rubric of military industry. It is also not surprising that the U.S. should favor arrangements that make its outpost look pretty much like the sponsor itself.

There are also nationalist reasons to oppose territorial expansion. One growing concern is the "demographic crisis" resulting from the differential Jewish and Arab birth rates (and among the Jewish population, the difference between the secular and religious populations). Demographic projections indicate that before too long Israeli Arabs and ultra-religious Jews, many non-Zionist, will become a major part of the population. A conference of prominent figures on the problem in March 2001 received considerable media attention, as did a call from the respected analyst Shlomo Gazit for establishment of a temporary dictatorship to implement stern internal measures to deal with "the demographic danger," which he regards as "the most serious threat that Israel faces." For the same reason, he issued a strong call for total withdrawal from the occupied territories, unlike the Clinton–Barak or other plans.[52]

The essential meaning of the Oslo peace process is well understood by prominent Israeli doves. Just before he joined the Barak government as Minister of Internal Security, historian Shlomo Ben-Ami observed in an academic study that "in practice, the Oslo agreements were founded on a neocolonialist basis, on a life of dependence of one on the other forever." With these goals, the Clinton–Rabin–Peres agreements were designed to impose on the Palestinians "almost total dependence on Israel," creating "an extended colonial situation," which is expected to be the "permanent basis" for "a situation of dependence." Ben-Ami went on to become the chief negotiator and architect of the Barak proposals.[53]

Step by step, the U.S. and Israel have labored for 30 years to construct a system of permanent neocolonial dependency. The project took new forms as the "Oslo peace process" was put in place, along lines projected in the DOP and spelled out in close detail in the interim agreements. The plans have been implemented in the settlement and construction programs carried out regardless of who is in office, often most effectively under the Labor doves, who tend to be more immune from criticism. Throughout, the plans and implementation have relied crucially on the military, diplomatic and financial support of the U.S., and not least, the ideological support of articulate educated opinion.

Notes

PREFACE

1. "Origins and Fundamental Causes of International Terrorism," UN Secretariat, reprinted in M. Cherif Bassiouni, ed., *International Terrorism and Political Crimes* (Charles Thomas, 1975).
2. Claire Sterling, Walter Laqueur; see chapter 5. For references and discussion, see my *Towards a New Cold War* (*TNCW*) (Pantheon, 1982), 47f., and my chapter in Chomsky, Jonathan Steele and John Gittings, *Superpowers in Collision* (Penguin, 1982, revised edition, 1984). For extensive discussion and documentation on the topic, see Edward S. Herman, *The Real Terror Network* (South End Press, 1982).
3. A distinct category is the much more severe crime of aggression, as in the case of the U.S. attack against South Vietnam, then all of Indochina; the Soviet invasion of Afghanistan; the U.S.-backed invasions of Timor and Lebanon by its Indonesian and Israeli clients, etc. Sometimes the categories are blurred; we return to some cases.
4. *Washington Post*, June 30, 1985; *Time*, October 11, 1982; Goodman, *New York Times*, February 7, 1984.
5. See references of note 3, and chapter 5, pp. 130–2.
6. *Economist*, June 14; Victoria Brittain, *Guardian*, June 6; Anthony Robinson, *Financial Times*, June 7, 1986, from Johannesburg. The report was also carried by BBC World Service. The ship that was sunk may have been a Cuban food ship. See also *Israeli Foreign Affairs*, July 1986.
7. There was no mention at all in the *New York Times*, *Wall Street Journal*, *Christian Science Monitor*, the news weeklies and other journals listed in the magazine index. The *Washington Post* ran a 120-word item from Moscow on p. 17, June 8, reporting Soviet condemnation of the South African attack.
8. For background, in October 1976 a Cubana airliner was destroyed by a bomb in flight with 73 killed including the entire Cuban Olympic gold medal fencing team (compare the actual events of the "Munich massacre," one of the peak moments of Palestinian terrorism). The terrorist action was traced to Orlando Bosch, probably the leading figure of international terrorism, who had been trained by the CIA along with his close associates in connection with the terrorist war against Cuba and "had close relations with (and has been on the payroll of) the secret police of Chile and Venezuela," who, in turn, "were tutored by the CIA and maintain close relations with it today" (Herman, *Real Terror Network*, 63). What would the U.S. response have been? The question is academic, since the first sign of a Cuban soldier near Venezuela would probably have evoked a major attack against Havana. On the Israeli invasion of Lebanon, see chapter 2 and references cited. The figure of about 200 Russians killed "operating in

the area of Syrian air defense forces" during the (unprovoked and unexpected) Israeli attack on Syrian forces in Lebanon is given by *Aviation Week & Space Technology*, December 12, 1983. Syrian forces had entered Lebanon with the agreement of the U.S. and Israel, and were scheduled to complete a six-year stay later in the summer of 1986. On these events, see my *Fateful Triangle* (South End Press, 1983).

9. On the real world, see Gabriel Kolko, *Politics of War* (Random House, 1968), the classic and still unsurpassed account, despite much valuable subsequent scholarship; *TNCW*; and my *Turning the Tide* (*TTT*) (South End Press, 1985), and sources cited. On more recent material, see my *Deterring Democracy* (Verso, 1991; Hill & Wang, 1992), chapter 11, and sources cited. Melvyn Leffler, "Adherence to Agreements: Yalta and the Experiences of the Early Cold War," *International Security*, Summer, 1986; Leffler's conclusion is that "In fact, the Soviet pattern of adherence [to Yalta, Potsdam, and other wartime agreements] was not qualitatively different from the American pattern." It should be noted that in Greece and South Korea in the late 1940s the U.S. organized mass slaughter operations as part of the worldwide program of destroying the anti-fascist resistance, often in favor of Nazi and Japanese collaborators.
10. Released Soviet archives reveal that "U.S. and British intelligence were supporting Ukrainian and Polish underground rebel actions against Soviet forces long before victory over Germany," tying down several hundred thousand Soviet troops and killing thousands of officers, thus retarding significantly the liberation of Europe from Nazi rule, with grim consequences too obvious to be discussed. That continued without substantial change after the war. Jeffrey Burds, "The Early Cold War in Soviet West Ukraine, 1944–1948," *The Carl Beck Papers* No. 1505, January 2001, Center for Russian and East European Studies, University of Pittsburgh. These may be the most significant of the revelations so far from released Russian archives, and among the least known.
11. See *TNCW*, chapter 3, and my introduction to Morris Morley and James Petras, *The Reagan Administration and Nicaragua* (Monograph Series No. 1, Institute for Media Analysis, New York, 1987).
12. The groundwork had already been laid in the United States and in a series of conferences for future terrorologists organized by Israel, which has an obvious interest in this propaganda operation. Commenting on the second Israeli-organized conference on terrorism, held in Washington, Wolf Blitzer observes that the focus on Arab terrorism and the enthusiasm expressed by many notable speakers for Israeli terrorism and aggression (particularly, its 1982 invasion of Lebanon), provided "clearly a major boost for Israel's own *Hasbara* campaign in the United States, as recognized by everyone involved" (Blitzer, *Jerusalem Post*, June 29, 1984); the word "hasbara," literally "explanation," is the term for Israeli propaganda, expressing the thesis that since Israel's position is so plainly correct on every issue, it is only necessary to explain; propaganda is for those with something to

conceal. For more on the judgments expressed in the conference, see chapter 3, note 20.

13. Kennedy's program was limited to the second and third plank of the Reagan agenda; the first, enacted with the support of Congressional Democrats in direct violation of the will of the public, reflects the decline in relative U.S. power in the intervening years. It is no longer feasible to pursue "great societies at home and grand designs abroad," in the words of Kennedy advisor Walter Heller, so the former must be abandoned. On public attitudes, see *TTT*, chapter 5, and Thomas Ferguson and Joel Rogers, *Atlantic Monthly*, May 1986. On the relation of Reagan's programs to those of the latter phases of the Carter Administration, which the Reaganites extended, see *TNCW*, chapter 7, and *TTT*, chapters 4 and 5. See also Joshua Cohen and Joel Rogers, *Inequity and Intervention* (South End Press, 1986).
14. On these matters, see *TNCW*, particularly chapters 1 and 2. The human rights program, largely a Congressional initiative reflecting the change in public consciousness, was not without significance, despite its exploitation for propaganda purposes and the hypocritical application, which consistently evaded atrocities by client-states, exactly the opposite of the standard charge. See Chomsky and Herman, *Political Economy of Human Rights*, particularly vol. I.
15. *World Press Review*, February 1986.

INTRODUCTION

1. Technical study cited by Charles Glaser and Steve Fetter, "National Missile Defense and the Future of U.S. Nuclear Weapons Policy," *International Security* 26.1, Summer 2001.
2. See Strobe Talbott and Nayan Chanda, *The Age of Terror* (Basic Books and Yale University Center for the Study of Globalization, 2001).
3. See below, for identification. For more detail and sources not cited here, see the chapters that follow. On international terrorism in the earlier period, see Chomsky and Edward Herman, *The Political Economy of Human Rights* (South End Press, 1979, two volumes). For general review of the first phase of the "war on terror," see Alexander George, ed., *Western State Terrorism* (Polity/Blackwell 1991).
4. Andrew Bounds, "How the Land of Maize [Guatemala] became a Land of Starvation," *Financial Times*, June 11, 2002.
5. Carothers, "The Reagan Years," in Abraham Lowenthal, ed., *Exporting Democracy* (Johns Hopkins University Press, 1991); *In the Name of Democracy* (University of California Press, 1991); *New York Times Book Review*, November 15, 1998.
6. In May 2002, I listened to hours of personal testimonials by *campesinos* and indigenous people about their traumatic experiences as they were driven off the land by fumigation that destroyed their rich and diversified crops, poisoned their children and their land, and killed their animals, leaving the lands free for resource extraction by multinationals, and eventually, perhaps, agro-export with seeds provided by

Monsanto after the biological diversity and the age-old traditions of successful peasant agriculture have been destroyed. This was in Cauca, where poor people had succeeded in electing their own Governor, a proud and impressive indigenous leader, perhaps the first in the hemisphere. The successes of the social bloc led to a sharp increase in paramilitary terror and guerrilla repression, and fumigation of areas that had not even been inspected to see if coca or poppies are grown among the coffee bushes and other varied crops, all destroyed. Cauca gained first place for human rights violations in 2001, no small achievement in this terrorist state. The very idea that the U.S. has the right to destroy crops it doesn't like in some other country is taken for granted in the terrorist superpower, but is so outlandish that comment is barely possible – no one, of course, has the right to destroy far more lethal substances produced in North Carolina and Kentucky.

7. I had a chance to witness some of the effects first-hand in Diyarbakir, the semi-official Kurdish capital, in February 2002. As in Colombia, it is inspiring to see the courage of the victims, and of the urban intellectuals who support them and persistently confront the draconian laws and practices, facing penalties that can be extremely harsh.
8. For a review, see my *New Military Humanism* (Common Courage, 1999), *A New Generation Draws the Line* (Verso, 2000), and *Rogue States* (South End Press, 2000). See Human Rights Watch (HRW), *The Sixth Division: Military-paramilitary Ties and U.S. Policy in Colombia* (September 2001). Also *Crisis in Colombia* (February 2002), prepared by HRW, Amnesty International, and the Washington Office on Latin America for congressional certification hearings, an unusually detailed review of crimes and impunity of the Colombian military. The record was once again ignored by the State Department, which certified Colombia on the basis of the "improvement" in human rights that is routinely visible to the government, though no one else, in client-states. In this case the service was performed by Secretary of State Colin Powell, *Memorandum*, (May 1, 2002).
9. Judith Miller, *New York Times*, April 30, 2000, p. 1 article reporting without comment the latest State Department report on terror, which also singles out two other leading terrorist states (Algeria and Spain) for their achievements in combating terror. Steven Cook, "U.S.–Turkey Relations and the War on Terrorism," Analysis Paper No. 9, *America's Response to Terrorism*, November 6, 2001, Brookings.
10. See references of note 8. For more extensive comment on the current phase of the "war on terror," see my *9–11* (Seven Stories, 2001) and my essays in Ken Booth and Tim Dunne, eds, *Worlds in Collision* (Palgrave, 2002) and James Sterba, ed., *Terrorism and International Justice* (Oxford, 2002).
11. Yossi Beilin, *Mehiro shel Ihud* (Revivim, 1985), 42; an important review of cabinet records under the Labor Party. For more detail on what follows, see my *Fateful Triangle* (*FT*) (South End Press, 1983; updated edition 1999), chapters 4, 5.1, 3, 5.
12. Justin Huggler and Phil Reeves, *Independent*, April 25, 2002.
13. Beilin, *Mehiro shel Ihud*, 147.

14. For reports of shocking atrocities on orders of the high command and with virtual impunity, drawn from the Hebrew press in Israel, see my *Necessary Illusions* (South End Press, 1989), Appendix 4.1. Also *FT*, chapter 8, including some personal observations, published in the Hebrew press. See Boaz Evron, *Yediot Ahronot*, August 26, 1988, for a reaction, beginning with some disbelief until he found even more awful confirming evidence in a Kibbutz journal. For extensive discussion and analysis, see Zachary Lockman and Joel Beinin, eds, *Intifada* (South End Press, 1989); Joost Hiltermann, *Behind the Intifada* (Princeton, 1991); Patricia Strum, *The Women are Marching* (Lawrence Hill, 1992).
15. See essays by Mouin Rabbani, Sara Roy, and others in Roane Carey, ed., *The New Intifada* (Verso, 2001); and Roy, *Current History*, January 2001.
16. Brian Whitaker, *Guardian*, May 22, 2002.
17. Armey, CNBC, "Hardball," May 1, 2002. Lewis, "Solving the Insoluble," *New York Times*, April 13, 1998. Rabin rejected the possibility of a Palestinian state, as did Shimon Peres while in office.
18. Clive Ponting, *Churchill* (Sinclair-Stevenson 1994), 132; Churchill, *The Second World War*, vol. 5 (Houghton Mifflin, 1951), 382.
19. Piero Gleijeses, *Conflicting Missions* (University of North Carolina, 2002), 16, 22, 26, citing JFK, the CIA, and State, from released secret documents; *Foreign Relations of the United States*, 1961–63, vol. XII, American Republics, 13ff.
20. Patrick Tyler, *New York Times*, April 25; John Donnelly, *Boston Globe*, April 28, 2002.
21. David Johnston, Don Van Natta Jr. and Judith Miller, "Qaeda's New Links Increase Threats From Far-Flung Sites," *New York Times*, June 16, 2002. Chapter 6, note 3, below.

CHAPTER 1

1. On the matters discussed here, see *TNCW*, particularly chapters 1 and 2.
2. Cited by Richard Fox, *Reinhold Niebuhr* (Pantheon, 1985), 138.
3. John Dillin, *Christian Science Monitor*, April 22, 1986.
4. "A majority of Americans across the board favors the Saudi peace plan" (Mark Sappenfield, *Christian Science Monitor*, April 15, 2002, reporting poll results). The plan, adopted by the Arab states in March 2002, reiterates the call for a two-state political settlement in terms of the international consensus that has prevailed since 1976 (see below), which Washington continued to oppose.
5. *New York Times*, June 2, 1985.
6. *New York Times*, March 17, 1985.
7. See *TNCW*, 267, 300, 461; *FT*, 67, 189.
8. Rabin, *The Rabin Memoirs* (Little, Brown, 1979, 332). In keeping with his moderate stance, Rabin believes that the "refugees from the Gaza Strip and the West Bank" should be removed to East of the Jordan; see

TNCW, 234, for representative quotes. See *FT* on the long-standing conception of "transfer" of the indigenous population as a solution to the problem, and its current variants; for example, by the racist Rabbi Kahane, or democratic socialist Michael Walzer, who suggests that those who are "marginal to the nation" – that is, Arab citizens of Israel – be "helped" to leave. The phrase "marginal to the nation" lifts the curtain on the contradiction between standard democratic principle and mainstream Zionism, and its realization in Israel. See *TNCW* and *FT* for discussion of this matter, which is close to unmentionable in the United States.

9. Friedman provided serious and professional reporting from Lebanon during the 1982 war, and sometimes does from Israel as well; see for example his report on the Gaza Strip, April 5, 1986.
10. Friedman, *New York Times Magazine*, October 7, 1984, *New York Times*, March 17, 1985; editorial, *New York Times*, March 21, 1985; and much other commentary and news reporting.
11. See chapter 2, note 58 and text, for details. For more extensive discussion of the "peace process" and "rejectionism" in the non-Orwellian senses of these terms – that is, in the real world – and of the successful efforts of the indoctrination system to eliminate the facts from history, see *FT*.
12. For more extensive discussion, see my review of Kissinger's memoirs, reprinted in *TNCW*.
13. Sadat's offer was in response to the proposal by UN Mediator Gunnar Jarring, which Sadat accepted. Israel officially recognized this to be a serious peace offer, but preferred territorial expansion to peace. When Jarring died on May 29, 2002, there were obituaries in major U.S. newspapers, but the most important event in his political career was omitted, with one exception: the *Los Angeles Times*, which stated falsely that both sides refused to accept Jarring's proposal (Dennis McLellan, June 1, 2002, reprinted in the *Boston Globe*).
14. Eric Pace, *New York Times*, October 7, 1981.
15. For discussion, see *TTT* and my essays in *U.S. International and Security Policy: The New Right in Historical Perspective*, *Psychohistory Review* 15.2, Winter 1987 (Lawrence Friedman, ed.), and in Thomas Walker, ed., *Reagan vs. The Sandinistas* (Westview, 1987). Also my introduction to Morley and Petras, *The Reagan Administration*. The record of deceit on these matters is impressive.
16. On these matters, including the origins of the "strategic asset" concept, the post-1973 negotiations leading to the 1979 Camp David agreement, and the immediate U.S. actions to undermine the September 1982 "Reagan Plan" as well as the "Shultz Plan" for Lebanon a few months later, see *FT*. The reality, sufficiently clear at the time, is very different from versions repeated by the media and most of scholarship, though sometimes partially acknowledged years later; see, e.g., chapter 2, note 47 and text.
17. Rubinstein, *Davar*, official journal of the Labor Party, August 5, 1983.
18. General (ret.) Mattityahu Peled, "American Jewry: 'More Israeli than Israelis'," *New Outlook*, May–June 1975.

19. Pail, "Zionism in Danger of Cancer," *New Outlook*, October–December1983, January 1984.
20. See *TNCW*, 247f., for details. On the new legislation, see Aryeh Rubinstein, *Jerusalem Post*, November 14, 1985. For some Israeli commentary, comparing Israeli laws and South African Apartheid, see Ori Shohet, "No One Shall Grow Tomatoes . . . ," *Ha'aretz* Supplement (September 27, 1985, translated in *News from Within* (Jerusalem), June 23, 1986), discussing the devices that ensure discrimination against Arab citizens of Israel and Arabs in the occupied territories with regard to land and other rights. The title refers to military regulations that require West Bank Arabs to obtain a license to plant a fruit tree or vegetables, one of the devices used to enable Israel to take over lands in the occupied territories on grounds of inadequate title.
21. Paul Berman, "The Anti-Imperialism of Fools," *Village Voice*, April 22, 1986, citing "an inspired essay" by Bernard Lewis in the *New York Review* expounding this convenient doctrine. For some other ingenious applications of the concept of anti-Semitism, see *FT*, 14f. On the Doueimah massacre, see *TTT*, 76.
22. Analyst, *Pentagon Papers*, Gravel edition, Beacon Press 1971, II.22. The U.S. military threat, as acknowledged, was essential to enable the U.S. creation to prevent the political settlement prepared at the 1954 Geneva conference.
23. For discussion, see *TNCW* and my *For Reasons of State* (Pantheon, 1973).
24. Julia Preston, *Boston Globe*, February 9, 1986.
25. For discussion of these matters, see references of note 15. The point at issue is the permitted range of expression in the national forum, not the individual contributions, which are to be judged on their own merits.
26. See, e.g., Timothy Garton Ash, "New Orthodoxies: I," *Spectator* (London), July 19, 1986. The comical "debate over 'moral equivalence' in the U.S." (in which only one side receives public expression despite elaborate pretense to the contrary) merits a separate discussion.
27. Shaul Bakhash, *New York Review of Books*, August 14, 1986.
28. "Non-Orwellian Propaganda Systems," *Thoreau Quarterly*, Winter/Spring 1984. See my talk to a group of journalists reprinted here, and the ensuing discussion, for more on these topics.
29. Reich, *New York Times*, July 24; Heller, *New York Times*, June 10, 1986.
30. *New York Times*, April 21, 1986.

CHAPTER 2

1. *New York Times*, October 17, 18, 1985.
2. *Ha'aretz*, March 22, 1985; for other sources, see *FT*, 54, 75, 202
3. Herzog, Yossi Beilin, *Mechiro shel Ihud* (Tel Aviv, 1985), 147. Gazit, *Hamakel Vehagezer* (Tel Aviv, 1985), quoted in *Al Hamishmar*, November 7, 1985. Rabin, *Washington Post*, December 6; *Newsweek*, December 15, 1975; *TNCW*, 267–8. When I refer to Reagan, I am

speaking not of the symbolic figure but of the policy-makers and PR specialists of the Administration.

4. *Yediot Ahronot*, November 15, 1985.
5. Ze'ev Schiff, *Ha'aretz*, February 8, 1985; see *FT* for testimony from participants, not reported in the U.S., and for denial of the facts by apologists for Israeli terror, on the grounds that the media are anti-Semitic and "pro-PLO" while "Arabs exaggerate" and "no onus falls on lying" in "Arab culture" (Martin Peretz; the latter insight in *New Republic*, August 29, 1983).
6. See note 48, below.
7. Godfrey Jansen, *Middle East International*, October 11, 1985, citing *LAT*, October 3.
8. It appears in *Against the Current*, January 1986.
9. Cf. *FT*, 127, 176.
10. Bernard Gwertzman, *New York Times*, October 2, 7, 1985.
11. Beverly Beyette, *Los Angeles Times*, report on International Conference on Terrorism, *Los Angeles Times*, April 9, 1986.
12. Edward Schumacher, *New York Times*, October 22, 1985.
13. *New Republic*, October 21, 1985, January 20, 1986; Associated Press, April 4, 1986.
14. Robert McFadden, "Terror in 1985: Brutal Attacks, Tough Response," *New York Times*, December 30, 1985.
15. UPI, *Los Angeles Times*, December 28, 1985; McFadden, "Terror in 1985"; Dershowitz, *New York Times*, October 17, 1985. Alexander Cockburn, *Nation*, November 2, 1985, the sole notice of the shameful hypocrisy, to my knowledge.
16. Ross Gelbspan, *Boston Globe*, December 16, 1985. On Contra atrocities, see the regular reports of Americas Watch and numerous other careful and detailed inquiries, among them, *Report of Donald T. Fox, Esq. and Prof. Michael J. Glennon to the International Human Rights Law Group and the Washington Office on Latin America*, April 1985. They cite a high-ranking State Department official who described the U.S. stance as one of "intentional ignorance." The extensive and horrifying record is also generally disregarded by the media and others, and even flatly denied (without a pretense of evidence) by apologists for Western atrocities, e.g., Robert Conquest, "Laying Propaganda on Thick," *Daily Telegraph* (London), April 19, 1986, who assures us that the charges by Oxfam and others are not only false but "silly." Conquest is noted for his exposure of Communist crimes and bitter denunciations of apologists who deny them. See also Gary Moore, *National Interest*, Summer 1986, with a similar message; or Jeane Kirkpatrick (*Boston Globe*, March 16, 1986), who tells us that "the Contras have a record of working hard to avoid harming civilians. They have done nothing that compares with the systematic brutality the Sandinista government visits on dissenters and opponents"; comparable lies and apologetics for Soviet atrocities would not be tolerated for a moment in the media. See also note 44, and chapter 3, note 14. The usual procedure is not to deny but simply to ignore atrocities committed by Western proxies or clients. For comic relief, one may turn to the productions of a con-

siderable industry devoted to fabricating claims that critics of U.S. violence reject or ignore reports of atrocities by official enemies. For some examples, including quite spectacular lies, see *Political Economy of Human Rights*, vol. II; my "Decade of Genocide in Review," *Inside Asia* (London), February–March 1985 (reprinted in James Peck, ed., *The Chomsky Reader* (Pantheon, 1987), and "Visions of Righteousness," *Cultural Critique*, Spring 1986; Christopher Hitchens, "The Chorus and Cassandra," *Grand Street*, Autumn 1985.

17. *New York Times*, June 29, 1985.
18. And in Israel. After his accession to power, there was an increase in the use of torture in prisons, administrative detention, expulsion in violation of international law, and sealing of houses, practices that were common under the previous Labor government much lauded by left-liberal American opinion, but reduced or suspended under Menachem Begin. Danny Rubinstein, *Davar*, February 4, 1986; Eti Ronel, *Al Hamishmar*, June 11, 1986. On torture, see *Ha'aretz*, February 24, 1986; and Ghadda Abu Jaber, *1985 Policy of Torture Renewed*, Alternative Information Center, Jerusalem, February 1986; *Koteret Rashit*, May 7, 1986. See also Amnesty International, "Town Arrest Orders in Israel and the Occupied Territories," October 2, 1984.
19. Curtis Wilkie, *Boston Globe*, March 10; Julie Flint, *Guardian* (London), March 13; Jim Muir, *Middle East International*, March 22; Breindel, *New York Times* Op-Ed, March 28; Nora Boustany, *Washington Post*, March 12, 1985. A photo of the wall graffiti appears in Joseph Schechia, *The Iron Fist* (ADC, Washington, 1985).
20. *Guardian* (London), March 2, 6, 1985.
21. Ilya, *Jerusalem Post*, February 27, 1985; Magnus Linklater, Isabel Hilton and Neal Ascherson, *The Fourth Reich* (Hodder & Stoughton, London, 1984, 111); *Der Spiegel*, April 21, 1986 (see chapter 3); *New York Times*, March 13, 1985.
22. Ihsan Hijazi, *New York Times*, January 1, 1986; Hijazi notes that the reports from Israel differed.
23. *Christian Science Monitor*, January 30, 1986.
24. For detailed examination, see *FT*. Or compare, for example, what appeared in *Newsweek* with what bureau chief Tony Clifton describes in his book *God Cried* (Clifton and Catherine Leroy, Quartet, 1983), published in London. Or consider *My War Diary* by Col. Dov Yermiya, one of the founders of the Israeli army, published in violation of censorship in Israel (see *FT* for many quotes) and later in English translation (South End Press, 1983), but entirely ignored in the media, though it is obviously a work of considerable importance. There are numerous other examples.
25. Landrum Bolling, ed., *Reporters Under Fire* (Westview, 1985). Included, for example, is a critique of the media by the Anti-Defamation League of B'nai Brith and other accusations which barely rise to the level of absurdity (see *FT* for analysis of these documents), but not a study by the American-Arab Anti-Discrimination Committee that presents evidence of "a consistent pro-Israeli bias" in press coverage of the war.

26. Kifner, *New York Times*, March 10; Muir, *Middle East International*, February 22, 1985; Mary Curtius, *Christian Science Monitor*, March 22; Jim Yamin, *Christian Science Monitor*, April 25; Yamin, interview, *MERIP Reports*, June 1985; David Hirst, *Guardian* (London), April 2; Robert Fisk, *Times* (London), April 26, 27; *Philadelphia Inquirer*, April 28, 1985. On Israeli efforts to fuel hostilities in the Chouf region from mid-1982, see *FT*, 418f.
27. *Middle East International*, March 22, 1985.
28. UPI, *Boston Globe*, September 22, 1984; Olmert, interview, *Al Hamishmar*, January 27, 1984; Hirsh Goodman, *Jerusalem Post*, February 10, 1984; Wieseltier, *New Republic*, April 8, 1985; on Hasbara, see preface, note 15.
29. Don Oberdorfer, "The Mind of George Shultz," *Washington Post Weekly*, February 17, 1986; Rubin, *New Republic*, June 2, 1986; Friedman, *New York Times*, February 16, 1986, among many other reports. Like Wieseltier, Rubin asserts that this Syrian-sponsored "terrorism . . . is not a cry of outrage against a Western failure to pursue peace but an attempt to block diplomacy altogether," since "almost any conceivable solution is anathema to the Syrian government." Rubin knows that Syria has supported diplomatic solutions close to the international consensus, but since they are remote from U.S. rejectionism, these solutions are not "conceivable" and do not count as "diplomatic options"; see chapter 1. On Lebanese perceptions, see chapter 5, note 22.
30. *Los Angeles Times*, October 18, 1985.
31. *New York Times*, October 18, 1985.
32. Ze'ev Schiff, "The Terror of Rabin and Berri," *Ha'aretz*, March 8, 1985; also General Ori Or, commander of the IDF northern command, IDF radio; FBIS, 15 April, 1985.
33. Gershom Schocken, editor of *Ha'aretz*, *Foreign Affairs*, Fall, 1984.
34. Shimon Peres, *New York Times*, July 8, 1983. On the atrocities in Khiam, see *TNCW*, 396–7; *FT*, 191; Yoram Hamizrahi, *Davar*, June 7, 1984; press reports cited in the Israeli Democratic Front publication *Nisayon Leretsach-Am Bilvanon: 1982* (Tel Aviv, 1983).
35. Jim Muir, *Sunday Times* (London), April 14, 1985; *Christian Science Monitor*, April 15, 1985; Joel Greenberg, *Christian Science Monitor*, January 30, 1986; Sonia Dayan, Paul Kessler and Géraud de la Pradelle, *Le Monde diplomatique*, April 1986; Menachem Horowitz, *Ha'aretz*, June 30, 1986.
36. *Information Bulletin 21*, 1985, International Center for Information on Palestinian and Lebanese Prisoners, Deportees, and Missing Persons, Paris. *Israel & Palestine* (Paris), July 1986). On IDF-run prisons in Lebanon, see *FT*, 23ff.
37. Benny Morris and David Bernstein, *JP*, July 23, 1982; for comparison by Israeli journalists of life under the PLO and under Israel's Christian allies in Lebanon, a picture considerably at variance with the standard U.S. picture, see *FT*, 186f. Particularly significant is the report from Lebanon by Israeli journalist Attallah Mansour, of Maronite origin. For more on Nabatiya, see *FT*, 70, 187.

38. *Economist*, November 19, 1977.
39. John Cooley, in Edward Haley and Lewis Snider, eds, *Lebanon in Crisis* (Syracuse, 1979). See *TNCW*, 321; *FT*, 70, 84.
40. Edward Haley, *Qaddafi and the United States since 1969* (Praeger, 1984), 74.
41. James Markham, *New York Times*, December 4, 1975.
42. AP, *New York Times*, February 21; Julie Flint, *Guardian* (London), February 24; Ihsan Hijazi, *New York Times*, February 28; AP, February 20, 1986. The only detailed account in the U.S., to my knowledge, was by Nora Boustany, *Washington Post*, March 1, though with the IDF role largely excised, possibly by the editors, since reporters on the scene knew well what was happening – including murder of fleeing villagers by Israeli helicopter gunships, beating and torture in the presence of Israeli officers, etc., as some have privately indicated.
43. Ihsan Hijazi, *New York Times*, March 25; Dan Fisher, *Los Angeles Times*, March 28; Associated Press, April 7; Hijazi, *New York Times*, April 8, 1986.
44. See, for example, Robert Leiken, "Who Says the Contras Cannot Succeed?," *Washington Post*, July 27, 1986 – dismissing without argument the extensive record of atrocities by the terrorists he supports in the usual style of apologists (see note 17), and with the Maoist prattle familiar from his writings. See my introduction to Morley and Petras, *The Reagan Administration*, and chapter 3, note 3; and my *Culture of Terrorism* (South End Press, 1988), 205–6, 213.
45. Peres, *New York Times*, July 8, 1983; Breindel, *New York Times*, Op-Ed, March 28; *New York Times*, September 16, 1983, June 3, 1985; Kamm, *New York Times*, April 26, 1985; Friedman, *New York Times*, January 9, February 20, February 18, 1985; Brzezinski, *New York Times*, October 9, 1983; Reagan, press conferences, *New York Times*, March 29, 1984, October 28, 1983. See also the remarks by Rabbi Alexander Schindler, President of the Union of American Hebrew Congregations (Reform): the PLO "threatened to destroy what was left of Beirut rather than surrender"; sending the Marines to oversee their departure instead of permitting Israel to finish the job was "surely the most ignominious" assignment the Marines were ever given (UPI, *Boston Globe*, October 28, 1984). These intriguing illustrations of religion in the service of state violence are omitted from the *Times* account the same day.
46. *New York Times*, June 7, 1983.
47. Quandt, *American-Arab Affairs*, Fall, 1985; Hillel Schenker, Interview with David Shipler, *New Outlook* (Tel Aviv), May 1984.
48. The opposition Labor Party backed the war, partly because poll results indicated that 98 percent of Likud and 91 percent of Labor supporters regarded it as justified. As the war ended with the horrendous bombing of Beirut in mid-August, support for Begin and Sharon reached its peak of 82 percent and 78 percent, respectively, dropping to 72 percent and 64 percent, respectively, after the Sabra-Shatila massacres. See *FT*, 251–62, 394; 378f.
49. Philip Weiss, *New Republic*, February 10, 1986.

50. Schiff and Ya'ari, *Israel's Lebanon War* (Simon & Schuster, 1984), 35; John Kifner, *New York Times*, July 25, 1981. Schiff and Ya'ari claim that "despite the great pains taken to pinpoint the targets and achieve direct hits, over 100 people were killed," including 30 "terrorists." The Schiff-Ya'ari book is a translation of parts of the Hebrew original; about 20 percent of the original was excised by the Israeli censor according to Ya'ari (*Kol Hair*, February 2, 1984), about 50 percent according to the American scholar Augustus Norton, citing a "respected correspondent – unconnected to the authors" (*Middle East Journal*, Summer, 1985). Censorship in Nicaragua, under attack by a U.S. proxy army, arouses great indignation in the U.S. The most extreme censorship in Israel, of course, is directed against Arabs, including Israeli citizens. See *FT*, 139f., and *TTT*, 73f., for a small sample. For a more detailed comparison of Israeli and Nicaraguan censorship, and the much worse U.S. record under lesser threat (as noted by Supreme Court Justice Brennan), see my *Necessary Illusions* (South End Press, 1989), chapter 5 and appendices; also appendix II.2.
51. Walsh, *Washington Post Weekly*, March 4, 1985; Wilkie, *Boston Globe*, February 18, 1985.
52. *FT*, 448, 440, citing Israeli press; *News from Within* (Tel Aviv), October 1, 1985; *Yediot Ahronot*, November 4, 1983.
53. *Ha'aretz*, June 25, 1982; see *FT*, 200f., for further quotes and similar analyses by other Israeli commentators.
54. B. Michael, *Ha'aretz*, November 13, 1983; Bachar, *Yediot Ahronot*, November 11, 1983; Morris, *JP*, June 5, 1984.
55. The *New Republic*, ever vigilant to defend Israel from the "many press people" who are "prepared to believe just about anything reflecting badly on the Jewish state (and, almost as a corollary, anything reflecting well on its enemies)," denounced the *Washington Post* for having "collaborated in one of the great calumnies" by observing that Sharon had attempted to construct what he called "a 'new order' (the Hitler phrase)" in Lebanon (Martin Peretz, *New Republic*, March 18, 1985; *New Republic*, March 19, 1984). The phrase was indeed Hitler's, and Sharon used it, as does Israeli commentary generally. One month before Peretz's condemnation of the *Post* for stating the facts accurately, a headline in the rightwing mass circulation journal *Yediot Ahronot* read: "'Sharon announced in advance his plan for "a new order"'," citing American Ambassador Morris Draper who quoted Sharon in a closed meeting of the Jewish Federation in Los Angeles (February 23, 1984). The usage is standard; see *FT* for other examples, and for other cases where the *New Republic* carefully avoids Israeli sources in its efforts to contain deviations from the party line (e.g., 215f., 258f.).
56. Olmert, *Ma'ariv*, November 22, 1983; Milson, *Koteret Rashit*, November 9, 1983; Sharon, cited by Ze'ev Schiff, *Ha'aretz*, May 23, 1982; Milshtein, *Hadashot*, September 26, 1984; Rubinstein, *Ha'olam Haze*, June 8, 1983. On Ben-Gurion's aspirations before and after the state was established, see *FT*, 51, 160f.; Shabtai Tevet, *Ben-Gurion and*

the Palestinian Arabs (Oxford, 1985) and the review by Benny Morris, *Jerusalem Post*, October 11, 1985.

57. *FT*, 199, citing an interview in *Ha'aretz*, June 4, 1982; *FT*, 117, 263.
58. *Nouvel Observateur*, May 4; *Observer* (London), April 29; *Jerusalem Post*, May 16; *San Francisco Examiner*, May 5; *Washington Post*, July 8, 1984. See my "Manufacture of Consent," December 1984, published by the Community Church, Boston, and my "United States and the Middle East," *ENDpapers* (UK), Summer 1985, for further details. On earlier Israeli determination to evade a political settlement, with regular U.S. support, see *FT* and Beilin, *Mehiro shel Ihud*.
59. *Ha'aretz*, September 29, 1985 (cited by Amnon Kapeliouk, *Le Monde diplomatique*, November 1985); *Koteret Rashit*, October 9, 1985.
60. Julie Flint, *Guardian Weekly*, January 19, 1986.
61. The *Post* does not describe this as a "terrorist act" carried out by the "terrorist commander" Menachem Begin. Haganah also apparently participated; see chapter 5, note 34.
62. Christian Williams, Bob Woodward and Richard Harwood, "Who Are They?," *Washington Post*, February 10,1984; editorial, *New York Times*, May 19, 1976. On the reality, see *TNCW*, *FT*. The behavior of certain human rights organizations in this regard is noteworthy. Thus to ensure that it would have no unpleasant information, the International League for Human Rights suspended its Israeli affiliate on the sole grounds that the governing Labor Party had attempted to destroy it by measures so crude that they were quickly blocked by the Israeli Courts; see my *Peace in the Middle East?* (Pantheon, 1974, 196–7), *FT*, 142, 178, and references cited. Such behavior with regard to any other country would be elicit outrage, but it does not affect the reputation of the International League. Similarly, the human rights information journal *Human Rights Internet*, which simply reports without comment allegations of human rights violations, permits the Anti-Defamation League to respond to charges concerning Israel, a practice excluded for any other state; thus the Communist Party, which has domestic credentials comparable to the ADL as a human rights organization, is not given space to respond to charges against the USSR, rightly of course.
63. *New Outlook*, Tel Aviv, October1985; *Davar*, July 18, 1985. Military historian Uri Milshtein writes that contrary to the standard accounts, Israel initiated the conflict that led to the "war of attrition" with tank firing against Egyptian positions, killing dozens of soldiers; *Monitin*, August 1984.
64. Thomas Friedman, *New York Times*, January 31, 1986.
65. Hirst, *Manchester Guardian Weekly*, April 20, 1986; Harkabi, quoted by Amnon Kapeliouk, *Le Monde diplomatique*, February 1986.
66. The PLO claimed that the three Israelis murdered had been involved in these operations, a highly implausible charge as Israeli journalist David Shaham comments (John Bulloch, "PLO Victims were Mossad Agents," *Daily Telegraph* (London), October 3, 1985; Shaham, *Al Fajr*, November 29, 1985).

67. *Ha'aretz*, June 12, 1986. The report gives no indication that a trial took place.
68. *FT*, 77; David Shipler, *New York Times*, November 25, 1983; *New York Times*, January 26, 1984. In 1989, the *Washington Post* ran a story on the release of Palestinian prisoners held under administrative detention, many "at the controversial Negev tent city prison of Ketziot," another torture chamber. The story mentioned incidentally that "Meanwhile, before dawn, the Israeli navy stopped a boat sailing from Lebanon to Cyprus and seized 14 people described as suspected terrorists," taking them to Israel for "interrogation." The Israeli peace organization Dai l'Kibbush reports that in 1986–87, Israeli military courts convicted dozens of people kidnapped at sea or in Lebanon of "membership in a forbidden organization" but no anti-Israel activity or plans; the Palestinians kidnapped allegedly belonged to the PLO, and the Lebanese, to Hizbullah and in at least one case to the major Shi'ite organization Amal, all legal in Lebanon. Linda Gradstein, *Washinton Post*, April 6, 1989; "Political Trials," Dai l'Kibbush, Jerusalem, August 1988, *News from Within*, December 14, 1988.
69. *New York Times*, June 30, July 1; *Boston Globe*, July 1, 4, 12; *Middle East Reporter* (Beirut), June 30; *Observer* (London), July 1; Jansen, *Middle East International*, July 13, 1984.
70. Thomas Friedman, *New York Times*, February 5; the U.S. "refrained from making a judgment on the Israeli action" (*New York Times*, February 5); also Norman Kempster, *Los Angeles Times*, February 5, 1986.
71. *News from Within* (Jerusalem), November 1, 1985.
72. *Los Angeles Times–Boston Globe*, June 29, 1984. On the severe repression in the Golan, see *FT*, 132f.
73. See Uri Milshtein, *Monitin*, August 1984, for a recent account.
74. See preface.
75. *FT*, 188f.
76. *Rabin Memoirs*, 280–1.
77. *New York Times*, October 12, 1985. Meanwhile the *Times* denounces Iran, "which has yet to extradite or punish those who hijacked a Kuwaiti airliner and killed two Americans in December, 1984," and demands that the West boycott Libya if Qaddafi continues "to shelter hijackers." Editorial, *New York Times*, May 14, 1986. It has yet to say anything similar, or anything, about those who shelter the hijacker of the Soviet airliner, or about the long record of hijacking and piracy by Washington's Israeli clients.
78. Abraham Sofaer, *Foreign Affairs*, Summer 1986.
79. Livia Rokach, *Israel's Sacred Terrorism*, a study based on Moshe Sharett's personal diary (AAUG, 1980, 20f.); "Sixty Minutes," CBS, 7 p.m., January 19, 1986.
80. Sune Persson, *Mediation and Assassination* (London, 1979); Michael Bar-Zohar, *Ben Gurion: a Biography* (Delacorte, 1978), 180–1; Stephen Green, *Taking Sides* (Morrow, 1984), 38f.; Kimche, *Seven Fallen Pillars* (Secker & Warburg, 1953), 272–3. Similarly, the assassins of Lord

Moyne, from the same terrorist group, were honored by commemorative stamps, along with other terrorists; *FT*, 166.

81. *Globe & Mail* (Toronto), October 9, 1985.
82. *New York Times*, September 27, 1985, a picture caption without a story; *Asian Wall Street Journal*, August 22, cited by Alexander Cockburn, *Nation*, September 2, 1985; Housego, *New York Times Book Review*, July 20, 1986. In France, another terrorist state, there was virtually no protest over the atrocity or the punitive acts taken by France against New Zealand in "retaliation" for the trial of the captured terrorists. Rather, a report from Paris after the settlement with New Zealand observes, "the action called forth not self-criticism but patriotism. In France's view, New Zealand and its Prime Minister, David Lange, quickly became villains for holding the two agents, unjustly detained, in the common view here, for the crime of having served the national interest. In France, little was made in the press of the death of the Greenpeace crew member, or the fact that the sovereignty of New Zealand had been violated." Despite promises of the Socialist government to take "legal action" if "criminal acts" had been committed, "the only legal action taken was against several members of the French Government for disclosing information to the press," and "there has been no public investigation" (*New York Times*, July 30, 1986). A demonstration organized in Paris after the sinking of the ship brought out 150 people and one noted intellectual: René Dumont. Though well attended by the media, the event was given no coverage by TV and the press, including the Socialist press and *Libération*. *Le Monde* withheld its four-line announcement of the rally until after it was held. French Greens and peace groups were "hesitant to challenge the mass chauvinism revealed in France by the Greenpeace affair" while the Socialist Party congress gave "a hero's welcome" to Minister Hernu, officially responsible for the atrocity (Diana Johnstone and Elizabeth Schilling, *In These Times*, October 23, 1985). French terrorism against Greenpeace began with its first protest over French nuclear testing in its Pacific colonies in 1972, when a French mine sweeper rammed and nearly sank its yacht and commandos "swarmed aboard, savagely beat and nearly blinded [Greenpeace director] David McTaggart and one other male crew member with rubber truncheons" (James Ridgeway, *Village Voice*, October 8, 1985, noting also Soviet harassment of Greenpeace).
83. See my articles "Watergate: A Skeptical View," *New York Review*, September 20, 1973; editorial, *More*, December 1975; and introduction to N. Blackstock, ed., *COINTELPRO* (Vintage, 1976). Extended version of the introduction, "Domestic Terrorism," *New Political Science* 21.3, 1999.
84. Shultz, *Boston Globe*, June 25, 1984; *New York Times*, June 25, 1984, December 30, 1983; Associated Press, *Boston Globe*, April 23, 1984, *New York Times*, April 1, 1984; *International Herald Tribune*, May 5, 1986; Colin Nickerson, *Boston Globe*, February 3, 1986, on the convention. *Africasia*, July 1985, for details on the captured South African commandos, an episode largely ignored in the U.S. On the airliners,

see *Boston Globe, New York Times, Washington Post*, November 11, 1983; *Boston Globe*, February 21, 1984. These barely noted incidents occurred in the midst of mass hysteria over the shooting down of KAL 007 by the USSR, which merited seven full pages in the densely-printed *Times* index in September 1983 alone. Subsequently, particularly after the 9–11 terrorist atrocities, there was a change in the image of the forces recruited, organized, and trained by the CIA and its associates to pursue their war against Russia (not to help the Afghans, which would have been legitimate). Bin Laden and his associates were no longer "the moral equivalent of the Founding Fathers" (Ronald Reagan; see Samina Amin, *International Security* 26.5, Winter 2001/2). Their terrorist acts inside Russia were serious enough to have brought a Russia–Pakistan war ominously close (John Cooley, *Global Dialogue* 2.4, Autumn 2000).

85. Barry Munslow and Phil O'Keefe, *Third World Quarterly*, January 1984. During the Reagan years, South African depredations in the neighboring countries left 1.5 million killed and caused over $60 billion in damage, while Washington continued to support South Africa and condemned Nelson Mandela's ANC as one of the "more notorious terrorist groups" in the world. Joseba Zulaika and William Douglass, *Terror and Taboo* (Routledge, 1996), 12. 1980–88 record, Merle Bowen, *Fletcher Forum*, Winter 1991. On expansion of U.S. trade with South Africa after Congress authorized sanctions in 1985 (overriding Reagan's veto), see Gay McDougall, Richard Knight, in Robert Edgar, ed., *Sanctioning Apartheid* (Africa World Press, 1990).
86. Dan Fisher, *Los Angeles Times*, June 21; McGrory, *Boston Globe*, June 21; David Adams, *New Statesman*, April 19; *New York Times*, June 21, 1985. On Ansar, see *FT*, 231f.; interview, *Hotam*, April 11, 1986. See also Amnesty International, "The detention of Palestinians and Lebanese in the military prison of Atlit" [in Israel], 18 April 1984, on the detention of Palestinians and Lebanese transferred from Southern Lebanon and held incommunicado without means of communication with families or the Red Cross, denied lawyers or any evidence concerning their detention and illegal removal to Israel.
87. *Los Angeles Times*, July 1, 1985.
88. David Ignatius, *Wall Street Journal*, June 18, 1985.
89. *New York Times*, June 21, June 18, July 1, 1985.
90. Bernard Lewis, *New York Review*, August 15; *New Republic*, July 8; Reagan, Address to the American Bar Association, July 8 (*Boston Globe*, July 9); Podhoretz, *Los Angeles Times*, June 26; *New York Times*, July 2, 1985.
91. Thomas Friedman, *New York Times*, June 23; *New York Times*, June 19, 1985.
92. Associated Press, *Boston Globe*, July 4; Friedman, *New York Times*, July 4; *Boston Globe*, July 4, 1985.
93. John Cooley, *Green March, Black September* (Frank Cass, London, 1973), 197; see *FT* and Beilin, Mehiro shel Ihud, for many similar statements.
94. *FT*, 181–2.

95. Rabin, speaking to the Knesset, *Hadashot*, March 27, 1985; Tamari, interview, *Monitin*, October 1985. On the perception of soldiers, see the excerpts from the Israeli press translated in *FT*, which differ from the material offered in *Hasbara* exercises here (see preface, note 15). Or the comments by paratrooper Ari Shavit on the 1978 invasion of Lebanon, presented in *Koteret Rashit* (May 13, 1986) as a counterpart to a discussion of the operation by the military command, recalling the "kind of ecstasy" with which heavily armed units poured fire into villages, or anywhere, after it had "become clear that there would be no war here" but rather something more "like a hike." No doubt the truth about other armies is similar, but their fables about "purity of arms" are not taken seriously.
96. Rokach, *Israel's Sacred Terrorism*; Uri Milshtein, *Al Hamishmar*, September 21, 1983; Kennett Love, *Suez* (McGraw-Hill, 1969), 10f., 61–2.
97. *New York Times*, December 4, 1984. On the scholarly record, see *TNCW*, 331.
98. *Los Angeles Times*, November 24; *Boston Globe*, December 19; *New York Times*, December 20; *Boston Globe*, December 20, 1983.
99. *Globe & Mail* (Toronto), July 11; *Boston Globe*, July 24; *New York Times*, July 24; *Boston Herald*, July 25, 1985; *New York Times*, January 5, 6; *Boston Globe*, January 5, 6, 1984.
100. See chapter 1. James Markham, *New York Times*, December 3, 1975, reporting 57 killed based on Palestinian and Lebanese sources; see text at note 41. *New York Times*, March 23, 1985; *New York Times*, December 4, 1975.
101. *Time*, March 5, 1973; *New York Times*, February 22, 1973, giving the figure of 15 killed.
102. There was no supporting evidence in the case of the Libyan jet, but the Soviet allegation might be correct, though it obviously provides no justification for the atrocity; see R. W. Johnson, *Shoot-Down* (Viking, 1986), a study particularly interesting for its dissection of U.S. government lies. The dismissive American reviews are revealing. Joel Brinkley writes that the book is "flawed" because of its "strident tone" of "disdain bordering on contempt" for major figures in the Reagan Administration, and states falsely that it largely derives from the American press (*New York Times Book Review*, July 20, 1986). Douglas Feaver claims that Johnson "discredits his thesis with disinformation of his own on points that are easily checked," noting that on p. 2 he quotes the International Civil Aviation Organization's report only in part (*Book World, Washington Post Weekly*, July 7, 1986). As is also easily checked, Johnson quotes the sentence Feaver cites in full on p. 234, where it is relevant, quoting on p. 2 only the parts that are relevant there.
103. *New York Times*, February 22, 23; editorial, February 23; February 25, 26, 1973. Amiram Cohen, *Hotam*, February 10, 1984. The incident was briefly recalled during the KAL 007 affair, evoking false claims that Israel "immediately accepted responsibility" and "paid reparations";

Michael Curtis, letter, *New York Times*, October 2; Martin Peretz, *New Republic*, October 24,1983.

104. For comparison of the reaction to the two events, see Robert Scheer, *Guardian Weekly*, September 25, 1983; for discussion of other similar incidents, also passed over lightly given the agent of the atrocity, see my "1984: Orwell's and Ours," *Thoreau Quarterly*, Winter/Spring 1984 and "Notes on Orwell's Problem" in *Knowledge of Language* (Praeger, 1986).

105. On the Lydda-Ramle expulsions, see Benny Morris, *Middle East Journal*, Winter 1986; on the other cases, see *FT*, *TTT*, and sources cited. Schocken, *Foreign Affairs*, Fall 1984. On efforts to assassinate the Palestinian political leadership in 1948, organized by Moshe Dayan, see Uri Milshtein, *Al Hamishmar*, September 21, 1983; *Hadashot*, January 11, 1985. A recently-discovered Israeli intelligence report of June 30, 1948 concludes that of the 391,000 Arab refugees (152,000 from outside the area assigned to Israel in the UN Partition recommendation), at least 70 percent fled as a result of Jewish military operations (primarily Haganah/IDF) including direct expulsion, an apparent underestimate, Benny Morris observes in his analysis. The report also notes that this took place in the face of intense efforts of the Arab leadership to stem the flow. He also notes that the "circumstances of the second half of the exodus," from July to October, "are a different story"; "after June '48 there were many more planned expulsions" (*Middle Eastern Studies* (London), January 1986; interview with Haim Bar'am, *Kol Ha'ir*, May 9, 1986).

106. For review of several of the Israeli versions (including the only account to have appeared in a major U.S. journal, a shameful cover-up by Ze'ev Schiff and Hirsh Goodman in the *Atlantic Monthly*), see James Ennes, "The USS Liberty: Back in the News," *American-Arab Affairs*, Winter 1985–86. Perhaps the most intriguing is that of Yitzhak Rabin, then Chief of Staff, who describes the attack on the ship as "the most alarming development in the entire campaign," during which he experienced "sheer terror." He places it on June 7 (it was June 8), an inconceivable error, which can perhaps be understood as an effort to obscure the apparent reason for the attack: to conceal from the U.S. the planned invasion of Syria after the cease-fire. Rabin, *Memoirs*, 108f. In his memoirs, the highly regarded scholar Raymond Garthoff, with close intelligence connections and personal experience, writes that "Our military and intelligence agencies were unanimous in finding it to have been a deliberate and unprovoked Israeli air and sea attack, but President Johnson was determined to accept belated Israeli apologies and claims that it had resulted from misidentification of the U.S. ship no matter how lacking in credibility these excuses were." *A Journey Through the Cold War* (Brookings Institution, 2001), 214.

107. On the southern Lebanon case, see Mark Bruzonsky, *Middle East International*, May 16, 1986; also *Boston Globe*, April 15; David Shipler, *New York Times*, April 16, 1986. See *Houston Chronicle* (AP), May 18, (UPI) May 21, 1984, on the case of New Mexico businessman Mike Mansour,

jailed for 22 days and, he alleges, tortured and forced to sign a confession, which he repudiates.

108. Robert Tucker, *Commentary*, October 1982.
109. Dario Fernandez-Morera, *History of European Ideas*, vol. 6, no. 4, 1985.

CHAPTER 3

1. *Amnesty International Report 1985* (London, 1985); *Political Killings by Governments* (AI Report, London, 1983).
2. William Beecher, *Boston Globe*, April 15, 1986.
3. The U.S. government claims that from September 1980, Nicaragua began to send arms to the guerrillas who were largely mobilized by the Carter–Duarte terrorist war against the population, a mere trickle, even if we accept the documentary evidence provided at face value. The evidence for arms flow from early 1981 is virtually nil (cf. *TTT* and the testimony of CIA analyst David MacMichael before the International Court of Justice; UN A/40/907, S/17639, 19 November 1985). It is assumed without question that to provide arms to people attempting to defend themselves against a terrorist attack backed by the United States is criminal, if not proof of an attempt to conquer the Hemisphere. The Court ruled in June 1986 that arms supply might have proceeded "up to the early months of 1981," though further allegations "are not solidly established," and ruled that as a matter of law, such arms supply, even if it existed, would not constitute "armed attack" justifying a U.S. response, as Washington claimed. It found that U.S. actions "violated the principle [of the UN Charter] prohibiting recourse to the threat or use of force" in international affairs, along with other crimes. Washington ignored the judgment of the Court, having already declared that it would not be subject to Court jurisdiction, reacting by escalation of the "unlawful use of force" for which it had just been condemned by the Court, including the first official orders to its mercenary forces to attack undefended civilian targets. Meanwhile respected advocates of world order agreed that the U.S. should not submit to Court jurisdiction because America "still needs the freedom to protect freedom," as in Nicaragua (Thomas Franck, *New York Times*, July 17, 1986). Contra supporter Robert Leiken of the Carnegie Endowment for International Peace "blamed the court, which he said suffers from the 'increasing perception' of having close ties to the Soviet Union" (Jonathan Karp, *Washington Post*, June 28, 1986) – ties that mysteriously emerged after the same court ruled in favor of the U.S. in the case of Iran.
4. Editorial, *Washington Post* (*Guardian Weekly*, February 22, 1981); Alan Riding, *New York Times*, September 27, 1981. See *TTT* for references not given here or below.
5. Ambrose Evans-Pritchard, *Spectator*, May 10, 1986; with the task of decapitation largely accomplished, he continues, the numbers of corpses "are down and the bodies are dropped discreetly at night into the middle of Lake Ilopango and only rarely wash up onto the shore

to remind bathers that the repression is still going on." Editorials, *New Republic*, April 2, 1984, April 7, 1986. On recent atrocities, see Americas Watch, *Settling into Routine* (May 1986), reporting that political killings and disappearances – 90 percent at the hands of Duarte's armed forces – continue at well over four a day, a real improvement in this leading terrorist state, along with numerous other government atrocities. In retrospect, the reality is sometimes conceded, for example by the School of the Americas, which trains Latin American officers for tasks of the kind they accomplished in El Salvador, and proudly proclaims that in the 1980s, "Liberation Theology . . . was defeated with the assistance of the U.S. Army." Cited by Adam Isacson and Joy Olson, *Just the Facts* (Washington: Latin America Working Group and Center for International Policy, 1999), ix.

6. Chris Krueger and Kjell Enge, *Security and Development Conditions in the Guatemalan Highlands* (Washington Office on Latin America, 1985); Alan Nairn, "The Guatemala Connection," *Progressive*, May 1986; Benjamin Beit-Hallahmi, *The Israeli Connection* (Pantheon, 1987).
7. Herman and Brodhead, *Demonstration Elections* (South End Press, 1984). They define the term to refer to elections "organized and staged by a foreign power primarily to pacify a restive home population," discussing several other examples as well and showing in detail that they are no less farcical than elections held under Soviet authority. Their term "demonstration elections" was borrowed and radically misused with reference to Nicaragua by Robert Leiken (*New York Review*, December 5, 1985). See Brodhead and Herman's letter along with others by British Parliamentary observers (June 26, 1986), and Leiken's response, tacitly conceding the accuracy of their critique (by evasion) while claiming that they designed their concept "as a way of focusing attention on Western imperialism while diverting it from Soviet imperialism . . . in line with their apparent belief that there is only one superpower villain"; this is the standard reflex of advocates of state terror, in this case, requiring the suppression of Brodhead and Herman's harsh critique of elections in Poland along with much else. See Alexander Cockburn (*Nation*, December 29, 1985, May 10, 1986) and Leiken's response (*New York Review of Books*, June 26); also my introduction to Morley and Petras, *The Reagan Administration*.
8. Council on Hemispheric Affairs, *Washington Report on the Hemisphere*, April 16, 1986. From President Cerezo's January inauguration through June murders are estimated at 700, a rise of 10 percent over the preceding year; how many are political, or what the actual numbers are, is unknown (Edward Cody, *Washington Post*, July 6, 1986). Alan Nairn and Jean-Marie Simon estimate political killings at over 60 a month, victims of "an efficient system of political terrorism" run by the Guatemalan military using such devices as a "computer file on journalists, students, leaders, people of the left, politicians and so on" (*New Republic*, June 30, 1986). "Guatemala's bureaucracy of death appears more comfortably entrenched than at any time since the mid-1960s," they conclude, noting that "Cerezo has yet to denounce a

single army killing" and that "his interior minister said that political murders are no longer a problem."

9. John Haiman and Anna Meigs, "Khaddafy: Man and Myth," *Africa Events*, February 1986.
10. See *TTT* for an ample selection; also chapter 2, notes 16, 44, and references of note 7 above.
11. Michael Ledeen, *National Interest*, Spring 1986. See note 4 and text.
12. Editorial, *New York Times*, April 20, 1985; *Washington Post*, January 11, 1986; Rabin, *Boston Globe*, January 25, 1986; *El Pais* (Madrid), April 25, 1986.
13. E. J. Dionne, "Syria Terror Link Cited by Italian," June 25, 1986; the *Times* editors are surely aware that the remainder of the U.S. government case that they applauded remains unsubstantiated.
14. *New York Times*, June 27, 1985; *Christian Science Monitor*, March 25, 1986. See Leslie Cockburn, *Out of Control* (Atlantic Monthly Press, 1987), 26. Cuban mercenaries fighting with the U.S. proxy army attacking Nicaragua allege that they were trained in a paramilitary base in Florida; Stephen Kinzer, *New York Times*, June 26, 1986. The U.S. government has, however, arrested plotters attempting to overthrow the dictatorship of Suriname in New Orleans (described by the U.S. attorney as "a 'jumping-off point' for mercenaries seeking to become involved in South and Central America"), charging them with violation of the U.S. Neutrality Act (*Christian Science Monitor*, July 30, 1986), just as it had previously blocked efforts to overthrow the murderous Duvalier regime it supported in Haiti. The chief of intelligence of the main Contra force, Horacio Arce, defected in 1988 to Mexico, where he described his training by U.S. instructors in El Salvador and in a base in the U.S., the arms flow from Israel, his CIA contacts in Honduras, and other details, including the goal of attacking civilian targets to undermine social programs. See chapter 5, at note 15.
15. Bob Woodward and Charles Babcock, *Washington Post*, May 12, 1985; see chapter 5, at note 28.
16. Ihsan Hijazi, *New York Times*, April 20, 1986. The careful reader of the *Times* will find, buried in a report from Athens by Henry Kamm (May 29, 1986), a denunciation of terrorism by Syrian President Assad, specifically the killing of 144 Syrians in a "major terrorist action," presumably referring to the bombs on Syrian buses.
17. Philip Shenon, *New York Times*, May 14, 1985; Lou Cannon, Bob Woodward, et al., *Washington Post*, April 28, 1986.
18. *New Republic*, January 20, 1986; Edwin Meese, Associated Press, April 4, 1986; see chapter 2.
19. Frank Greve, *Philadelphia Inquirer*, May 18, 1986.
20. Nef, *Middle East International* (London), April 4, 1986; Johnson, *Sunday Telegraph* (London), June 1, 1986. Elsewhere, in an Israeli-organized propaganda conference on terrorism in Washington (see preface, note 15), Johnson praised Israel for taking "drastic measures" to fight "the terrorist cancer," as in its 1982 invasion of Lebanon: "The truth is, by having the moral and physical courage to violate a so-called sovereign

frontier, and by placing the moral law above the formalities of state rights, Israel was able for the first time to strike at the heart of the cancer, to arrest its growth and to send it into headlong retreat" (quoted by Wolf Blitzer, *Jerusalem Post*, June 29, 1984) – the opposite of Israel's intent, as discussed in chapter 2, but intent aside, a truly impressive display of moral and physical courage, and an interesting insight into Johnson's conception of "moral law."

21. Haley, *Qaddafi and the U.S.*, 271f. For extensive details on the Reaganite obsession with Libya and plans to kill Qaddafi, see Seymour Hersh, *New York Times Magazine*, February 27, 1987. Hersh's important article appeared during the window of opportunity commonly provided by exposure of some scandal, in this case the Iran–Contra affair, which aroused much attention, but avoiding the most crucial aspects. See chapter 4, and for background and detail, Jonathan Marshall, Peter Dale Scott, and Jane Hunter, *The Iran-Contra Connection* (South End Press, 1987) and *Culture of Terrorism*.
22. Larry Speakes, national TV, 7:30 p.m., April 14; *New York Times*, April 16; Associated Press, April 14; *New York Times*, April 15; Lewis, *New York Times*, April 17; Bernard Weinraub, *New York Times*, April 15; Jeff Sallot, *Globe & Mail* (Toronto), April 24, 1986.
23. Haley, *Qaddafi and the U.S.*, 8, 264.
24. *New Statesman* August 16, 1985.
25. See *FT*, 210; Haley, *Qaddafi and the U.S.*, who makes a praiseworthy effort to take the performance seriously.
26. "The Central Intelligence Agency, barred from providing military aid to Nicaragua rebels, secretly funneled several million dollars to the rebels for political projects over the past year, U.S. government officials say," also allowing "the CIA to maintain a strong influence over the rebel movement, even though a Congressional ban existed from October 1984 through September 1985, prohibiting the agency from spending money 'which would have the effect of supporting, directly or indirectly, military or paramilitary operations in Nicaragua,' the officials said." One purpose of what U.S. officials described as "a major program" was to "create the aura that [the contras] are an actual political entity among our allies in Europe." Congressman Sam Gejdenson stated that "We suspected that the CIA had never really withdrawn from the scene, but the extent of the agency's direct involvement in the Contra war may astound even the most jaded observer." UNO (Contra) Documents obtained by Associated Press "show much of UNO's political money going to military organizations allied with the umbrella group" established by the U.S., while some of the funds were used to pay off Honduran and Costa Rican officials "to enable the rebels to operate in those countries." Much of the money was funneled through a London-based bank in the Bahamas. Associated Press, April 14; *Boston Globe*, April 14, 1986. The disclosures passed with no comment at the time, and little afterwards. Subsequently, the *Miami Herald* reported that over $2 million of the $27 million provided by Congress for "humanitarian assistance" was used to pay Honduran officers "to turn a blind eye to illegal Contra

activities on Honduran soil" (editorial, *Boston Globe*, May 13, 1986), along with much evidence of corruption that received some limited notice.

27. Hersh, *New York Times Magazine*, February 27, 1987.
28. Associated Press, March 27, 1986, citing *El Pais* (Madrid).
29. R. C. Longworth, *Chicago Tribune*, March 30, 1986.
30. Richard Higgins, *Boston Globe*, March 25, 1986.
31. Fred Kaplan, *Boston Globe*, March 26, 1986.
32. London *Sunday Times*, April 6, 1986.
33. Cockburn, *Wall Street Journal*, April 17; also *Nation*, April 26, 1986. Lelyveld, *New York Times*, April 18, 1986.
34. Another injured black GI died several months later.
35. *New York Times*, April 16, 1986.
36. *New York Times*, April 18, 1986; the *Times* report states that at 7 p.m.. F-111s bombed military targets "near Benghazi" and "near Tripoli," and that at 7:06 p.m. they bombed "the Tripoli military airport, the final target." As had already been reported, the F-111s bombed a residential neighborhood in Tripoli.
37. Associated Press, April 14, 1986.
38. James Markham, *New York Times*, April 25, 1986.
39. *Der Spiegel*, April 21, 1986; the front cover features the phrase "Terror against Terror," a well-known Gestapo slogan, presumably not selected by accident. See also Norman Birnbaum's article, same issue.
40. Text of interview provided by an American journalist with *Stars and Stripes* in Germany. See also Hersh, *New York Times*, February 27, 1987.
41. See, e.g., James Markham, *New York Times*, May 31, citing a "West Berlin police investigator" who "said he believed that the Libyan Embassy in East Berlin 'conceived' the attack" – well short of the "certainties" asserted earlier – and cites Manfred Ganschow, but not on his denial of any evidence; or Robert Suro, *New York Times*, July 3, on possible involvement of Syria and the Abu Nidal anti-Arafat terrorists in the discotheque bombing, referring to "evidence that *reportedly* showed" Libyan involvement (my emphasis); or Bernard Weinraub, *New York Times*, June 9, referring to possible Syrian involvement and what Administration officials "said" they knew about Libyan intercepts. In the years that followed a Syrian link was emphasized, attributed to U.S. and German officials, courts and intelligence, indicating again that there was no firm basis for the initial claims. See, *inter alia*, Robert McCartney, *Washington Post*, January 11, 12, 1988. See also Hersh, *New York Times*, February 27, 1987, on denials of Washington's claims by Ganschow and German officials, and on internal recognition that the evidence was flimsy at best. In later years, Libya was implicated. Evidently, whatever subsequent claims or discoveries might be, they are irrelevant to anything discussed here.
42. Shaul Bakhash, *New York Review of Books*, August 14, 1986.
43. *Christian Science Monitor*, April 22, 1986; see chapter 1, at note 3.
44. *Toronto Globe & Mail*, editorials, March 28, 18, 5, 1986, referring specifically to Nicaragua.

45. See Associated Press, *International Herald Tribune*, May 6, for extensive discussion; *New York Times*, May 6, 1986, a briefer mention, and the text of the statement against terrorism.
46. Associated Press, April 14; survey of world press reaction, Associated Press, April 15; survey of U.S. editorial reaction, April 16; editorial, *New York Times*, April 15; Peres, *New York Times*, April 16, 1986.
47. After the Libya bombing, there were numerous references to Jefferson's punitive expedition against the Barbary pirates; no one seems to have gone back a few steps in history to describe the days when "New York had become a thieve's [*sic*] market where pirates disposed of loot taken on the high seas," as piracy enriched the American colonies, like the British before them (Nathan Miller, *The Founding Finaglers* (David McKay, 1976), 25–6). Piracy was not exactly a North African invention.
48. Associated Press, April 21; *New York Times*, April 20; survey of religious reactions, Associated Press, April 17; also April 19, reporting a news conference of 14 religious and community groups in Seattle condemning the bombing in contrast to support for it by the Western Washington Rabbinic Board; Nye, *Boston Globe*, April 16; Rostow, *New York Times*, April 27, 1986.
49. Glass, *Spectator* (London), May 3; Cockburn, *In These Times*, July 23, 1986.
50. *Dissent*, Summer 1986. Observing on the scene, Ramsey Clark concluded from the pattern of bombing that the well-to-do suburb where the worst civilian casualties occurred appears to have been a specific target; *Nation*, July 5, 1986. The question is plainly irrelevant to the issue of terrorism (Clark does not suggest otherwise).
51. *New Republic*, September 6, 1982; for other samples of his interpretations of state violence as perpetrators vary, see chapters 1, 2, above, and *FT*.
52. *Washington Post* weekly edition, August 4, 1986.
53. Ignatius, *Washington Post Weekly*, July 28, 1986.
54. *Christian Science Monitor*, June 25, July 16, 1986.
55. *Economist*, July 26, 1986; *Christian Science Monitor*, July 24, 1986.
56. One must take these numbers with a grain of salt, given the ideological considerations that enter into defining an act as "terrorist." Thus bombing of abortion clinics was excluded from the category of "terrorism" at one time, and may still be. According to columnist Cal Thomas of the Moral Majority, there were 300 bombings "on property where abortions are performed" from 1982 through late 1984, which he thinks are "probably not a good idea . . . tactically, as well as politically" – though apparently just fine morally; *Boston Globe*, November 30, 1984.
57. AP, *Globe & Mail* (Toronto), July 4; Stephen Engelberg, "Official Says F.B.I. Has Suspects in Blasts Laid to Extremist Jews," *New York Times*, July 17; Peyman Pejman, *Washington Post*, July 5, 17, 1986.
58. See note 18 and chapter 2. Recall that the record of Zionist terrorism against civilians goes back many years, long before the establishment of the State of Israel; see *FT*, 164f.

59. June 7, 1982.
60. *Business Week*, August 10, 1981. Haley, *Qaddafi and the U.S.*,98.

CHAPTER 4

1. See introductory notes.
2. That includes even books and technical papers on linguistics, because of sins of the kind that so offend Abrams, though with different targets.
3. On the facts as leaked in England, see Alexander Cockburn, *Nation*, November 22, 1986. Some of those involved claim that they were not objecting to the contents of the article but only to the inappropriateness of allowing a discussion of "thought control" in a society that "is unusual if not unique in the lack of restraints on freedom of expression" (my opening words). That claim is transparently untenable, even if one accepts the remarkable principle that lies behind it. The journal has published articles of this nature without evoking a hysterical response, threats to cancel subscriptions, letters from the State Department, etc.; see, e.g., Carole and Paul Bass, "Censorship American-style," dealing with how controversial stories are killed by "market forces and weak-kneed publishers" (*Index on Censorship*, 3/85). The difference is that in the present case, the article dealt with media treatment of states that are to be worshipped, not critically discussed by standards applicable to others.
4. America and the World 1983, *Foreign Affairs*, Winter 1983. In later years, the tendencies Watts described became a matter of elite concern in the U.S. as well. The prominent political analyst Samuel Huntington warned that for much of the world – most, he suggests – the U.S. is "becoming the rogue superpower," considered "the single greatest external threat to their societies." The dominant "realist" version of international relations theory predicts that coalitions may arise to counterbalance the rogue superpower, so the stance should be reconsidered, he argues, on pragmatic grounds. He was writing before the U.S.–UK bombing of Serbia, which aroused great fear and concern in much of the world. Commenting later on the unilateralism of the Clinton and (George W.) Bush Administrations, another distinguished political scientist, Robert Jervis (President of the American Political Science Association), reiterated Huntington's conclusion, writing that "In the eyes of much of the world, in fact, the prime rogue state today is the United States." *Foreign Affairs*, March/April 1999; July/August 2001.
5. *Boston Globe*, October 28, 1986; November 4, 1986. Robert C. Johansen, "The Reagan Administration and the U.N.: The Costs of Unilateralism," *World Policy Journal*, Fall 1986.
6. Richard Bernstein, "The UN versus the United States," *New York Times Magazine*, January 22, 1984. Not "the U.S. versus the UN," on the assumptions he takes for granted.

7. Michael White, *Guardian Weekly*, November 9, 1986. This is not evidence that the world is being "Finlandized" or "taken over by Communists," as the U.S right-wing fantasizes; the same poll shows that the European population is very critical of the USSR, of course.
8. See chapter 3, note 45.
9. Jeffrey Smith, *Washington Post*, November 9, 1986.
10. The plan was apparently activated in a secret National Security directive of January 14, 1983 (No. 77, *Management of Public Diplomacy Relative to National Security*). Alfonso Chardy, "Secrets Leaked to Harm Nicaragua, Sources Say," *Miami Herald*, October 13, 1986.
11. *Newsweek*, August 3, 1981. On the disinformation program concerning Libya, see chapter 3. On other disinformation programs and media cooperation, see my *Turning the Tide*; Edward S. Herman and Frank Brodhead, *The Bulgarian Connection* (Sheridan Square, 1986).
12. Alfonso Chardy, Knight-Ridder Service, *Boston Globe*, October 28, 1986.
13. Robert Reinhold, "Ex-General Hints at Big Role as U.S. Champion of Contras," *New York Times*, October 14, 1986. Chris Horrie, *New Statesman*, October 31, 1986, reporting on the Annual Conference of the WACL, noting in particular the prominence of RENAMO (the South African-backed guerrillas terrorizing Mozambique) and their cozy relations with Singlaub, and probably the U.S. administration. Scott Anderson and John Lee Anderson, *Inside the League* (Dodd, Mead & Co., 1986); only the ADL and the U.S. government concealed documentation and refused to cooperate with their research, they report. See *Necessary Illusions*, App. V.4, for more on connections between Reagan–Bush (No. 1) and neo-Nazis and related elements, who are guilty of only "antique and anemic" anti-Semitism as compared with the real anti-Semitism of those who support the international consensus on a two-state settlement (*New Republic*).
14. On these matters, see *TTT* and sources cited. See Michael McClintock, *Instruments of Statecraft* (Pantheon, 1992), on the reliance on Nazi manuals in developing postwar U.S. counterinsurgency documents, with the assistance of Wehrmacht generals. Also Jeffrey Burds, "The Early Cold War in Soviet West Ukraine, 1944–1948," *The Carl Beck Papers* No. 1505, January 2001, Center for Russian and East European Studies, University of Pittsburgh, on Western support for Hitler's partisan armies during the war, in an effort to delay Russia's defeat of the Nazis.
15. On the ebb and flow of human rights concerns regarding Iran, closely tracking Iran's service to U.S. interests or defiance of them, see Mansour Farhang and William Dorman, *The U.S. Press and Iran* (University of California, 1987); and for further discussion, *Necessary Illusions*, chapter 5 and app. 5.2–3.
16. On these matters, see my *FT*, 457f.
17. Michael Widlanski, "The Israel/U.S.–Iran Connection," Tel Aviv, *Austin American Statesman*, May 2, 1986.
18. See William C. Rempel and Dan Fisher, "Arms Sales Case Putting Focus on Israel's Policies," *Los Angeles Times*, May 5, 1986, noting that

"veteran American investigators" say that "Israel has long been regarded as a conduit for secret arms sales," and that "there is little question that the flow to Iran of Israeli arms, at least, has continued" during the past five years, citing a West German estimate of half a billion dollars of military equipment. Douglas Frantz, "Israel Tied to Iranian Arms Plot," *Chicago Tribune*, April 24, 1986; Reuven Padhatzur, *Ha'aretz*, April 28, 1986. Much material of this nature has been circulated by Jane Hunter, editor of the excellent journal *Israeli Foreign Affairs*.

19. Leslie H. Gelb, "Iran Said to Get Large-Scale Arms from Israel, Soviet and Europeans," *New York Times*, March 8, 1982.
20. Patrick Seale, "Arms Dealers Cash in on Iran's Despair," *Observer* (London), May 4, 1986.
21. Miles Wolpin, *Military Aid and Counterrevolution in the Third World* (Lexington Books, 1972), 8, 128, citing Congressional Hearings; on Brazil, *New York Times*, November 1, 1970. For more on the euphoric public response to the Indonesian massacre, and the background, see my *Year 501* (South End Press, 1993); and on 1958, Audrey and George Kahin, *Subversion as Foreign Policy* (New Press, 1995).
22. For further discussion, see *Towards a New Cold War*; Laird cited by Thomas Ferguson and Joel Rogers, *Right Turn* (Hill & Wang, 1986), 97, an important discussion of factors in domestic affairs.
23. For more on these matters, see *Towards a New Cold War*, *Fateful Triangle*, and references of chapter 3, note 6.
24. See chapter 1.
25. See my books cited earlier; also Allan Nairn, *Progressive*, May, September 1986.
26. Haley, *Qaddafi and the U.S.*, 31.
27. See chapter 3.

CHAPTER 5

1. Among other sources, see Edward S. Herman, *The Real Terror Network* (South End Press, 1982); Herman and Frank Brodhead, *The Rise and Fall of the Bulgarian Connection* (Sheridan Square Publications, 1986); Alexander George, "The Discipline of Terrorology," in George, ed., *Western State Terrorism* (Polity/Blackwell, 1991). Also the discussion of Walter Laqueur's *The Age of Terrorism* (Little, Brown and Co., 1987), in my *Necessary Illusions*, 278ff.; see this book for references, where not cited here.
2. "States, Terrorism and State Terrorism," in Robert Slater and Michael Stohl, *Current Perspectives on International Terrorism* (Macmillan, 1988). Stohl concludes that "In terms of terrorist coercive diplomacy the USA has . . . been far more active in the Third World than has the Soviet Union." Other studies show a similar pattern. In a review of military conflicts since World War II, Ruth Sivard finds that 95 percent have been in the Third World, in most cases involving foreign forces, with "western powers accounting for 79 percent of the interventions,

communist for 6 percent"; *World Military and Social Expenditures 1981* (World Priorities, 1981), 8.

3. United States Code Congressional and Administrative News, 98th Congress, Second Session, 1984, October 19, volume 2; par. 3077, 98 STAT. 2707 (West Publishing Co., St. Paul, Minn.).
4. *US Army Operational Concept for Terrorism Counteraction* (TRADOC Pamphlet No. 525–37, 1984); Robert Kupperman Associates, *Low Intensity Conflict*, July 30, 1983. Both cited in Michael Klare and Peter Kornbluh, eds, *Low Intensity Warfare* (Pantheon, 1988), 69, 147. The actual quote from Kupperman refers specifically to "the threat of force"; its use is also plainly intended.
5. *Jerusalem Post*, August 4, 1988. See also Mark Heller, p. 36.
6. General John Galvin, commander of the Southern Command (SOUTHCOM); Fred Kaplan, *Boston Globe*, May 20, 1987. Kinsley, *Wall Street Journal*, March 26, 1987. See below, note 15. For further details, see *Culture of Terrorism*, 43, 77.
7. For details on the highly successful demolition job, see *Culture of Terrorism* and *Necessary Illusions*. On the immediate destruction of the Esquipulas IV accords of February 1989 by the White House and congressional doves with media cooperation, see my article in *Z Magazine*, May 1989, reprinted in my *Deterring Democracy* (Verso, 1991, Hill & Wang 1992, extended edition).
8. Richard Boudreaux and Marjorie Miller, *Los Angeles Times*, October 5, 1988; Associated Press, November 21, 1987; Witness for Peace, *Civilian Victims of the U.S. Contra War*, February–July 1987, p. 5. *The Civilian Toll 1986–1987*, Americas Watch, August 30, 1987; Americas Watch Petition to U.S. Trade Representative, May 29, 1987.
9. *Boston Globe*, November 9, 1984, citing also similar comments by Democratic dove Christopher Dodd.
10. A search of the liberal *Boston Globe*, perhaps the least antagonistic to the Sandinistas among major U.S. journals, revealed one editorial reference to the fact that Nicaragua needs air power "to repel attacks by the CIA-run Contras, and to stop or deter supply flights" (November 9, 1986).
11. Cited by Stohl, *Current Perspectives on International Terrorism*. Unfortunately, that was not the practice at the Tribunals, or since.
12. Kirkpatrick, *Commentary*, January 1981; Kristol, *Wall Street Journal*, April 11, 1986; December 13, 1973.
13. See *Necessary Illusions*, 60.
14. Julia Preston, *Boston Globe*, February 9, 1986; MacMichael, see *Culture of Terrorism*; Doyle McManus, *Los Angeles Times*, May 28, 1988; Vaky, see *Necessary Illusions*.
15. Ibid., 204–5. When the tactics finally succeeded, they were described quite frankly in the mainstream press, and lauded as a "Victory for U.S. Fair Play" that leaves Americans "United in Joy" (*New York Times* headlines), showing that "we live in a romantic age" (Anthony Lewis). For quotes and background, see *Deterring Democracy*, chapter 10.
16. For documentation on these matters, see *Necessary Illusions*.

17. *Torture in Latin America*, LADOC (Latin American Documentation), Lima, 1987, the report of the First International Seminar on Torture in Latin America (Buenos Aires, December 1985), devoted to "the repressive system" that "has at its disposal knowledge and a multinational technology of terror, developed in specialized centers whose purpose is to perfect methods of exploitation, oppression and dependence of individuals and entire peoples" by the use of "state terrorism inspired by the Doctrine of National Security." This doctrine can be traced to the historic decision of the Kennedy Administration to shift the mission of the Latin American military to "internal security," with far-reaching consequences.
18. Raymond Garthoff, *Reflections on the Cuban Missile Crisis* (Brookings Institution, 1987), 17.
19. Ibid., 16f., 78f., 89f., 98. See the references of note 1. Also Bradley Earl Ayers, *The War that Never Was* (Bobbs-Merrill, 1976); Warren Hinckle and William Turner, *The Fish is Red* (Harper & Row, 1981); William Blum, *The CIA* (Zed, 1986); Morris Morley, *Imperial State and Revolution* (Cambridge, 1987); Taylor Branch and George Crile, "The Kennedy Vendetta: Our Secret War on Cuba," *Harper's*, August 1975.
20. See *Towards a New Cold War*, 48–9; *Culture of Terrorism*, 40; Stohl, *Current Perspectives on International Terrorism.*
21. *Jerusalem Post*, August 16, 1981; see *FT*, chapter 5, sections 1, 3.4, for further quotes, background, and description. See chapter 2, at note 92.
22. Glass, *Index on Censorship* (London), January 1989.
23. See *FT*, 184f., and sources cited.
24. Ehud Ya'ari, *Egypt and the Fedayeen* (Hebrew) (Givat Haviva, 1975), 27f.; a valuable study based on captured Egyptian and Jordanian documents. At the same time, Salah Mustapha, Egyptian military attaché in Jordan, was severely injured by a letter bomb sent from East Jerusalem, presumably from the same source; ibid.
25. Israeli military historian Uri Milshtein, *Hadashot*, December 31, 1987, referring to Eliav's 1983 book *Hamevukash.*
26. See chapter 2. *Ha'aretz*, April 5, 1989.
27. See chapter 3, at note14.
28. Boustany, *Washington Post Weekly*, March 14, 1988; Woodward, *Veil* (Simon & Schuster, 1987), 396f.
29. On the Iron Fist operations and the Tunis bombing, see chapter 2.
30. See chapter 3.
31. See Edward Herman, *The Terrorism Industry* (Pantheon, 1990); Herman and Gerry O'Sullivan, "'Terrorism' as Ideology and Cultural Industry," George, ed., *Western State Terrorism.*
32. Lawrence Harke, *University of Miami Law Review*, vol. 43, 1989, 667f.
33. Bernadotte, see chapter 2, at note 80. Shamir, "Terror," *Hazit*, August 1943; parts reprinted in *Al Hamishmar*, December 24, 1987. Berlin, *Personal Impressions* (Viking, 1981), 50.
34. See *FT*, 164–5n.; Gafi Amir, *Yediot Ahronot Supplement*, August 14, 1988. De Haan, see *Towards a New Cold War*, 461–2.
35. Israel Shahak, "Distortion of the Holocaust," *Kol Ha'ir*, May 19, 1989. Enbal, *Yediot Ahronot*, August 3, 1990. See now Zuckerman, *A Surplus*

of Memory (University of California, translation of 1990 Hebrew original).

36. GA resolution 42/159 (December 7, 1987), apparently unreported in the U.S. text appears as Appendix III, *State Terrorism at Sea*, EAFORD Paper No. 44, Chicago, 1988.
37. See chapter 2, note 85.
38. For details, see *Necessary Illusions*. Also my articles in *Z Magazine*, March, September 1989, parts reprinted in the 1999 updated edition of *FT*.
39. Emphasis in *JP*. See references of preceding note. The unacceptability of an international conference not controlled by Washington follows from its opposition to a political settlement in accord with the near-universal international consensus.
40. See chapter 2.
41. See chapter 2, note 29. *New York Times*, November 28, 1988.
42. See chapter 2.
43. *New York Times*, September 30, 1986.

CHAPTER 6

1. Charles Tilly, *Coercion, Capital, and European States* (Blackwell, 1990).
2. Maureen Dowd, *New York Times*, February 23, 1991.
3. Eight months later, the FBI can say only that "investigators believe the idea of the September 11 attacks on the World Trade Center and Pentagon came from al Qaeda leaders in Afghanistan," though the plotting and financing, they believe, trace to Germany and the United Arab Emirates. "'We think the masterminds of it were in Afghanistan, high in the al Qaeda leadership,'" FBI director Robert Mueller said in some of "his most detailed public comments on the origins of the attacks" of September 11. Walter Pincus, *Washington Post*, June 6, 2002. If the source is only surmised eight months later, it could not have been known at the time. On October 5, Britain had released what it claimed to be definitive evidence, leaving "absolutely no doubt" of the guilt of bin Laden and the Taliban, Prime Minister Blair proclaimed. The evidence was remarkably thin, considering the plausibility of the case and intensity of the investigation. The more serious press treated it dismissively. The *Wall Street Journal* described the documents as "more like a charge sheet than detailed evidence" (Mark Champion, *Wall Street Journal*, October 5, p. 12). But it makes no difference, an accompanying story points out, quoting a senior U.S. official, who explains: "The criminal case is irrelevant. The plan is to wipe out Mr. Bin Laden and his organization" – and whoever may be in the way. It is of some interest that by the norms of the intellectual culture, none of this has any bearing on the perfect justice of the actions undertaken.
4. Ricardo Stevens, NACLA *Report on the Americas*, November/December 2001. He remarks "how much alike these victims are to the boys and girls, to those who are unable to be born that December 20 [1989] that

they imposed on us in Chorrillo; how much alike they seem to the mothers, the grandfathers and the little old grandmothers, all of them also innocent and anonymous deaths, whose terror was called Just Cause and the terrorist called liberator." The barrio Chorrillo "bore the brunt" of the U.S. invasion, the editors comment, adding that "the number of civilian casualties from the brief U.S. invasion is unknown; but credible estimates run as high as several thousand."

5. Andy Thomas, *Effects of Chemical Warfare: A Selective Review and Bibliography of British State Papers* (Stockholm International Peace Research Institute (SIPRI), Taylor & Francis, 1985), chapter 2. The targets were to be "uncivilised tribes" (Afghans), but also Russians, during the 1919 invasion, considered highly successful by the military command. See *Turning the Tide*, 126; *Deterring Democracy*, 181f. See also Thomas Whiteside, *New Yorker*, February 11, 1991. Also Robin Young, *The Times* (London), January 3, 1997, describing these as "newly released documents." The consequences of Churchill's advice are not likely to be known, however. In 1992, Prime Minister John Major announced an "open government" initiative. Its first act was to remove documents on these matters from the Public Records Office. George Robertson, *Freedom, the Individual, and the Law* (Penguin, seventh edition, 1993), 198.
6. *New Republic*, 2, 1984; November 5, 2001.
7. Alexis de Tocqueville, *Democracy in America* (Everyman's Library, 1994), Vol. I, 355.
8. Christina Lamb, London *Daily Telegraph*, December 9, 2001. Doug McKinlay, *Guardian*, January 3; Kim Sengupta, *Independent*, January 4, 2002.
9. Elisabeth Bumiller and Elizabeth Becker, *New York Times*, October 17, 2001. By March 2002, the World Food Program reported that the number of people needing food aid had risen to nine million. Barbara Crossette, *New York Times*, March 26; Ahmed Rashid, *Wall Street Journal*, June 26, 2002.
10. John Burns, *New York Times*, September 16, 2001.
11. Samina Amin, *International Security* 26.3, Winter 2001–2. "UN Food Agency Warns of Mass Starvation in Afghanistan," AFP, September 28; Edith Lederer, "U.S. Bombing Disrupting Planting which Provides 80 percent of Annual Grain Harvest," Associated Press, October 18, 2001. Eight months later, the World Food Program reported that "wheat stocks are exhausted, and there is no funding to replenish them"; Rashid, *Wall Street Journal*. On the day of the AFSC meeting where this talk was given, international food agencies were meeting in Vienna to assess the situation at the war's end, concluding that over a million people are "beyond their reach" because of the disruption of the war and "face death from starvation and disease" (Imre Karacs, *Independent on Sunday*, December 9, 2001).
12. Tania Branigan, *Guardian*, October 30, 2001. Howard, *Foreign Affairs*, January/February 2002. Carla Del Ponte, chief UN war crimes prosecutor, urged that an international tribunal would be the best way to prosecute Osama bin Laden (AP, *Boston Globe*, December 20, 2001).

13. As the bombing began, Bush warned Afghans that they would be bombed until the authorities turned over bin Laden and his associates. Several weeks later, British Defence Chief Admiral Sir Michael Boyce announced that the bombing would continue "until the people of the country themselves recognize that this is going to go on until they get the leadership changed," apparently the first announcement of the new war aims. Patrick Tyler and Elisabeth Bumiller, October 12, quoting Bush; Michael Gordon, *New York Times*, October 28, 2001, quoting Boyce.
14. Barry Bearak, *New York Times*, October 25; John Thornhill and Farhan Bokhari, *Financial Times*, October 25, October 26; John Burns, *New York Times*, October 26; Indira Laskhmanan, *Boston Globe*, October 25, 26, 2001.
15. Anatol Lieven, *Guardian*, November 2, 2001.
16. Colin Nickerson and Indira Lakshmanan, *Boston Globe*, September 27, 2001.
17. *News*, Islamabad, November 27; *Times of India*, November 26, 2001.
18. Boucher, *Mideast Mirror* (London), March 15, 1991. For more on the topic, see my essay in Cynthia Peters, ed., *Collateral Damage* (South End Press, 1992), and "Afterword," in *Deterring Democracy* (1992 extended edition).
19. National Security Strategy of the United States (White House, March 1990). For excerpts see *Deterring Democracy*, chapter 1.
20. At G-15 Summit in Jamaica, February 1999, an important meeting virtually ignored in the U.S. Dina Izzat, *Al-Ahram Weekly*, February 11–17, 1999. See my *New Military Humanism* (Common Courage, 1999), chapter 6, for some discussion.
21. Quoted by Thomas Fox, *Iraq* (Sheed & Ward, 1991), ix; see my article in Peters, ed., *Collateral Damage*, for this and many other examples.
22. *New Military Humanism*. For more on official war aims, and a review of the rich pre-bombing documentary record from official Western sources, see also my *A New Generation Draws the Line* (Verso, 2000).
23. Christopher Hellman, *Defense Monitor* (Washington), August 2001. For more extensive discussion and sources on what follows, see my *Peering into the Abyss of the Future* (Lakdawala Memorial Lecture, New Delhi, November 3, 2001; Institute for Social Sciences, New Delhi.

CHAPTER 7

1. Graham Usher, "The al-Aqsa Intifada," *Middle East International*, 13 October 2000.
2. John Dugard (South Africa), Kamal Hossain (Bangladesh), and Richard Falk (USA), *Question of the Violation of Human Rights in the Occupied Arab Territories, including Palestine*, UN Economic and Social Council, Commission on Human Rights, E/CN.4/2001/121, 16 March 2001. Israel refused to cooperate, but a wide range of Israeli sources were consulted. For some early reports on the Al-Aqsa *Intifada*, see Human Rights Watch, *Israel, the Occupied West Bank and Gaza Strip, and the*

Palestinian Authority Territories, vol. 1.3 (E), October 2000; Amnesty International, "Israel and the Occupied Territories: Excessive Use of Lethal Force," October 19, 2000. See Adam Leigh, "Human Rights Groups Condemn the Use of 'Excessive and Deadly Force'," *Independent* (London), 18 October 2000.

3. For many examples, see *Fateful Triangle* (*FT*; particularly chapter 4, section 5), *World Orders, Old and New* (1996, Epilogue). Also introductory notes.
4. HRW, *Center of the Storm*, April 11, 2001. Daniel Williams, *Washington Post*, April 16, 2001. For earlier examples at Hebron, see references of preceding note. Even brief personal experience is shocking.
5. HRW, *Center of the Storm*. In an eyewitness report from Netzarim, the outstanding Israeli journalist Amira Hass describes the failure to report gunfire from the settlement and IDF submachinegun fire from "distant surveillance towers . . . against thousands of unarmed demonstrators" to prevent them from approaching fortified positions where soldiers were not in danger. Hass, "Media Omissions, Army Lies," *Le Monde Diplomatique*, November 2000.
6. HRW, *Center of the Storm. Report on Israeli Settlement* (Washington DC), November–December 2000, noting the confirmation by IDF deputy chief of staff Moshe Ya'alon.
7. General Amos Yaron, deputy director, *Globes* (journal of Israel's Business Arena), December 21, 2000. If a Serbian General had Yaron's record, he would be on trial at the Hague, as is evident even from the muted Kahan Commission report on the Sabra-Shatila massacre. See *FT*.
8. Amnon Barzilai, *Ha'aretz*, October 3, 2000; also Avi Hoffmann, *Jerusalem Post*, September 8. Uri Blau, *Kol Ha'ir*, 26 January 2001, with a photograph of "Marine forces in an exercise in the Negev."
9. Robin Hughes, *Jane's Defence Weekly*, October 4; Charles Sennott, *Boston Globe*, October 4; Dave McIntyre (Washington), Deutsche Presse-Agentur, October 3, 2000. Gideon Levy, *Ha'aretz*, December 24, and Graham Usher, *Middle East Report*, Winter 2000, on the murders in Beit Sahur on November 9. By February 2002, the Israeli press reported 48 assassinations, with 26 victims of "collateral damage." The IDF claimed 21, with 18 accidental victims. In many cases, including some that sharply escalated the cycle of violence, U.S. helicopters and missiles were used. The High Court rejected an appeal for a ban on deliberate murder without charges. Gideon Levy, *Ha'aretz*, February 3; Report of the mission of the Human Rights Committee of England and Wales, April 2002, concluding that "There could not be a more fundamental apparent violation of basic human rights and humanitarian norms, than a calculated and cold-blooded killing, planned and acknowledged by the state."
10. Ann Thompson Cary, "Arming Israel . . . ," *News and Observer* (Raleigh NC), October 12, 2000. Data-base searches here and below by David Peterson.
11. "Amnesty International USA Calls for Cessation of All Attack Helicopter Transfers to Israel," AI release, October 19, 2000. *Aviation*

Week & Space Technology, February 26, *Jane's Defence Weekly*, February 28, 2001, and other military journals. *International Defense Review*, April 1, 2001. Reuters, AFP, February 19; Associated Press, February 20, financial pages; *Wall Street Journal*, February 20, 2001, a sentence in section B, p. 10, in business announcements. *America*, March 5, 2001. See also Robert Fisk, "Death in Bethlehem, Made in America," *Sunday Independent*, April 15, 2001. Jane Perlez, "U.S. Gingerly Discusses Taking More Active Role, *New York Times*, May 17; William Orme, World Briefing, May 17, 2001.

12. Laurie Copans, *Boston Globe*, March 3, 2001.
13. See chapter 6, note19; *Deterring Democracy*, chapter 1. For sources not given below, see *World Orders*.
14. For a review of these records, see *Deterring Democracy*, chapter 6.
15. See chapter 4.
16. See Israel Shahak, *Israel's Global Role* (Association of Arab-American University Graduates (AAUG), 1982); Benjamin Beit-Hallahmi, *The Israeli Connection* (Pantheon 1987); Jane Hunter, *Israel's Foreign Policy* (South End Press, 1987). More generally, Jonathan Marshall, Peter Dale Scott, and Jane Hunter, *The Iran-Contra Connection: Secret Teams and Covert Operations in the Reagan Era* (South End Press, 1987).
17. *Yediot Ahronot*, April 1992, cited by Israel Shahak, *Middle East International*, March 19, 1993.
18. The wording of 242 was left deliberately imprecise in the hope of securing at least formal agreement by Israel and the Arab states. "Withdrawal" was generally understood (by the U.S. as well) to mean to the pre-June 1967 borders, with minor and mutual adjustments. That remained official U.S. policy, though by 1971, not operative policy. See below.
19. The Clinton Administration also called for abolition of the special committee on Palestinian rights, which it termed "biased, superfluous and unnecessary," and refused to condemn Israel's settlement activity because it is "unproductive to debate the legalities of the issue." Clinton also reversed longstanding official U.S. support for UN Resolution 194 of December 11, 1948, which affirms the right of return for Palestinian refugees. Jules Kagian, *Middle East International*, December 17, 1993; Middle East Justice Network, February–March 1994. See *World Orders*, chapter 3.
20. See Jimmy Carter, reviewing official declarations through 1991, *Washington Post*, November 26, 2000.
21. See chapter 1.
22. See *FT*, 105f.
23. Yaniv, *Dilemmas of Security* (Oxford 1987), 70.
24. See chapter 1 on Israel's interpretation and reactions.
25. For extensive review, see *Necessary Illusions*, Appendix 5.2.
26. The basis is U.S. annoyance at the brazen manner of settlement under Yitzhak Shamir. When the style returned to the norm, with no significant change in substance, cordiality returned.
27. Baker cited by Carter, *Washington Post*, November 26, 2000. Note Baker's use of the word "territory," not "the territory" or "the territ-

ories." In U.S. diplomacy since 1971, omission of the definite article in the English version of UN 242 (but not the equally authoritative French version) has been the device for claiming that UN 242 meant only partial withdrawal, contrary to the international interpretation, including the U.S. until 1971. There has been much legalistic debate over the matter; pointless, because the meaning of a declaration is determined by the decisions of the most powerful actors, which are accepted in the doctrinal system, even if they are sharply contrary to the actual wording. There are many illustrations. For review of several involving peace treaties, see *New Military Humanism*, 114–28.

28. See chapter 5.
29. For what it is worth, I don't say this in retrospect. See my article in *Z Magazine*, October 1993 (dated September 2), discussing the draft of the DOP. See *World Orders*, chapter 3 on the document.
30. The masters apparently find the game amusing. They replayed it, for example, when Arafat was confined to his compound in Ramallah in April 2002, surrounded by Israeli tanks, and sternly admonished to renounce terrorism, a meaningless gesture as everyone understood, but useful for the purposes of humiliation of Palestinians. In contrast, Sharon was designated a "man of peace" by President Bush, who was hailed for arranging the release of Arafat from his dungeon in return for U.S.–UK supervision of the accused assassins of Israeli cabinet minister Rehavam Ze'evi. Ze'evi was killed in the anticipated reaction to Israel's escalation of the cycle of violence by the first assassination of a political leader, Abu Ali Mustafa, in a missile attack with a U.S. helicopter; there were no charges against him. The Mustafa assassination passed in silence (apart from some comment about the presence of American citizens in the apartment house attacked by the IDF assassins), but the reaction was quite different when Ze'evi was killed in retaliation. It is inconceivable that there should be any effort to punish those responsible for killing Mustafa. For close examination of the two cases, see Mouin Rabbani, Znet (<www.zmag.org>), June 19, 2002.
31. See chapter 5.
32. The agreements were carefully crafted by Israeli negotiators (with U.S. backing) with unclear and sometimes conflicting provisions, escape hatches, vague reciprocity conditions, etc., in such a way as to make it possible for supporters of the occupation to argue that Israel is not violating the agreements. In contrast, the concessions by the Palestinians are far-reaching, and given the relations of power, are in effect. For review of the crucial Oslo II Interim agreement, see *World Orders* (1996 edition, Epilogue).
33. Ibid.
34. Shlomo Tsezna, "the building in the territories was frozen, and continues at full speed," *Ma'ariv*, August 18, 2000; Akiva Eldar, *Ha'aretz*, May 1, 2001. See also *Economist*, April 26, 2001, and innumerable reports in the foreign and particularly the mainstream Israeli press, many reviewed in *World Orders* and the updated 1999 edition of *FT*.
35. Tsezna, *Ma'ariv*, August 18, 2000; Eldar, *Ha'aretz*, May 1 2001.

36. *Report on Israeli Settlement*, November–December 2000. Shlomo Tsezna, *Ma'ariv*, February 27, 2001. Sharon is often condemned as a war criminal; Peres is one as well. Among his accomplishments are the murderous Iron Fist operations in Lebanon in the mid-1980s and the 1996 invasion of Lebanon, supported by Clinton until international protest over the bombardment of the UN refugee camp at Qana, killing over 100 civilians who had fled there, became so strong that Clinton had to withdraw support and instruct Israel to terminate the aggression, as it did.
37. Baruch Kra, *Ha'aretz*, February 6, 2000, translated in *Report on Israeli Settlement*, March–April 2000. On all of these matters, see again *World Orders*. On Har Homa, see my article in Haim Gordon, ed., *Looking Back at the June 1967 War* (Praeger, 1999), papers from a 1997 conference at Ben Gurion university, Beersheva; excerpts in the extended 1999 edition of *FT*.
38. Ziv Maor and Aluf Benn, *Ha'aretz*, April 10, 2001.
39. The Israeli Human Rights organization B'Tselem reported in May, 2002, that settlers control 42 percent of the West Bank. Nagav Shragai, *Ha'aretz*, May 13; Dan Izenberg, *Jerusalem Post*, May 14, 2002; not reported in the national U.S. press. Citing B'Tselem and other sources, the *Economist* (June 22, 2002) estimates that Israel controls over 80 percent of the West Bank, counting 20 percent "illegally declared" to be "state land," which is also barred to Palestinians, and another 20 percent controlled by the IDF. These land acquisition policies leave Palestinian villages "scattered and isolated, between the [Jewish] settlements," which were dispersed in order to achieve this outcome, B'Tselem alleges. "Palestinian communities have become settlements in an Israeli West Bank," a Palestinian analyst observes. The programs are expanding under the Sharon government. All of this proceeds with tacit U.S. support and indirect funding.
40. Jane Perlez, *New York Times*, December 26, 2000. Perlez, *New York Times*, January 8; Judy Dempsey, *Financial Times*, January 9; Friedman, January 2, 2001.
41. Nadav Shragai, *Ha'aretz*, February 16, 2000. Yuval Ginbar, *On the Way to Annexation: Human Rights Violations Resulting from the Establishment and Expansion of the Ma'aleh Adumim Settlement* (B'Tselem, July 1999). *Report on Israeli Settlement*, January–February 2000.
42. For further details on the cantonization policies, and how they were implemented by the U.S. and Israel, see Sara Roy, in Roane Carey, ed., *The New Intifada*, and *Current History*, January 2002. There was considerable progress in informal negotations at Taba in January 2001. Details are available in a document prepared by the EU's special envoy, Miguel Moratinos, accepted as valid by both sides, and reviewed extensively by Israel's leading diplomatic correspondent, Akiva Eldar (*Ha'aretz*, February 15, 18, 2002). The negotations were called off by Prime Minister Barak, who also "instructed his chief negotiator, Gilad Sher, to tell the Palestinians that the map presented by then foreign minister Shlomo Ben-Ami, which reduced the area of the settlement bloc (including the Ma'aleh Adumim-Givat Ze'ev tract) to only 5

percent of the West Bank, had no validity." The status of that tract, which effectively bisects the West Bank, remained a major point of dispute, as at Camp David. The Palestinians proposed an explicit map (contrary to much propaganda), with Israel retaining 3 percent of the West Bank and "a land swap that would be equitable in size and value and in areas adjacent to the border with Palestine, and in the same vicinity as those annexed by Israel." Israel refused, offering only a much smaller disconnected area on the Sinai border. There were other disagreements, but it is conceivable that the negotiations might have reached agreement had they not been cancelled.

43. Dugard et al., *Questions of the Violation of Human Rights*.
44. Ibid.
45. Amira Hass, "Four U.S. rejections scuttled Security Council resolution," *Ha'aretz*, April 13, 2001. Washington's frequent opposition to Human Rights (its enemies aside) may have been a factor in the selection of Sweden, France and Austria rather than the U.S. for the three Western seats at the UN Human Rights Commission shortly after. Many other hypotheses were entertained; Barbara Crossette, Christopher Marquis, *New York Times*, May 4, 2001. Secretary of State Colin Powell is quoted as saying that the vote on the Palestinians angered countries that sought to retaliate; David Sanger, *New York Times*, May 9, 2001. Powell may have been referring to the Security Council veto, or perhaps to the EU-sponsored resolution of April 18; see note 47, below. On December 14, 2001, the U.S. again vetoed a Security Council resolution calling for dispatch of monitors to oversee reduction of violence. Ten days before, the U.S. boycotted – thus undermined – an international conference in Geneva that reaffirmed the applicability of the Fourth Geneva Convention to the occupied terrorities, so that most U.S.–Israeli actions there are war crimes – and when "grave breaches," as many are, serious war crimes. These include settlements and the practice of "wilful killing, torture, unlawful deportation, wilful depriving of the rights of fair and regular trial, extensive destruction and appropriation of property . . . carried out unlawfully and wantonly." Conference of High Contracting Parties, *Report on Israeli Settlement*, January–February 2002.
46. For review, see Human Rights Watch, *Center of the Storm*. Also Francis Boyle, "Law and Disorder in the Middle East," *The Link* 35.1, January–March 2002, and Allegra Pacheco's article in Carey, ed., *The New Intifada*.
47. There are reservations concerning military necessity that are inapplicable in the present case.
48. Agence France Presse, "UN Human Rights Commission Condemns Israel on Three Counts," April 18, 2001. The vote was 50–1; Costa Rica abstained and one country was absent. There were a few scattered mentions in the U.S. press (April 19), none in the national press.
49. Asher Davidi, *Davar*, February 17, 1993; translated by Zachary Lockman in *Middle East Report* (MERIP), September–October 1993.
50. See Kate Bronfenbrenner, *Uneasy Terrain: The Impact of Capital Mobility on Workers, Wages, and Union Organizing* (Cornell, September 6, 2000),

under contract with the U.S. Trade Deficit Review Commission, updating a 1997 study, also undertaken under NAFTA rules. Such studies are routinely ignored in public commentary, but not by workers (or, presumably, employers).

51. See economic correspondent Efraim Davidi, "Globalization and Economy in the Middle East," *Palestine-Israel Journal* VII.1 and 2, 2000.
52. Ya'ir Sheleg, *Ha'aretz*, March 24, 2001, on the conference and reactions. Shlomo Gazit, Amir Rappoport, *Yediot Ahronot*, March 26, 2001; also Reuven Weiss, reviewing Gazit's distinguished background.
53. Ben-Ami, *A Place for All* (Hebrew) (Hakibbutz Hameuchad, 1998). Cited by Efraim Davidi, "Globalization and Economy".

Index

Compiled by Sue Carlton